You and Your Action Research Project

What are the most effective ways of planning and doing action research projects?

This book gives practical guidance on doing an action research project. Written for practitioners across professions, who are studying on work-based learning programmes and award-bearing courses, this book is packed full of useful advice and takes the reader through the various stages of a project, including:

- starting your action research project;
- monitoring and documenting the action;
- techniques for dealing with the data;
- making claims to knowledge and validating them;
- legitimising your research;
- making your research public: creating your living educational theory.

The book's practical approach will appeal to practitioners and will encourage them to try out new strategies for improving their work. It will also be essential reading for those resource managers who are responsible for providing courses and support in schools, colleges and higher education institutions.

This third edition of a best-selling book has been thoroughly updated and improved by a number of features, with new case studies from a wide range of disciplines, extracts from validated dissertations and theses (with information on how to access more examples via the internet), points for reflection, checklists of reflective questions, and up-to-the-minute information on current debates and ideas.

Jean McNiff is an independent researcher and writer, Professor of Educational Research at York St John University, and Adjunct Professor at the University of Limerick.

Jack Whitehead is Lecturer in Education at the University of Bath, and former President of the British Educational Research Association.

You and Your Action Research Project

Third edition

Jean McNiff and Jack Whitehead

Routledge
Taylor & Francis Group

LONDON AND NEW YORK

First published 2010
by Routledge
2 Park Square, Milton Park, Abingdon, Oxon, OX14 4RN

Simultaneously published in the USA and Canada
by Routledge
711 Third Avenue, New York, NY 10017

Routledge is an imprint of the Taylor & Francis Group, an informa business

© 2010 Jean McNiff and Jack Whitehead
Typeset in Palatino by Prepress Projects Ltd, Perth, UK
Printed and bound in Great Britain by
CPI Antony Rowe, Chippenham, Wiltshire

British Library Cataloguing in Publication Data
A catalogue record for this book is available from the British Library

Library of Congress Cataloging-in-Publication Data
McNiff, Jean.
You and your action research project / Jean McNiff and Jack Whitehead.
– 3rd ed.
p. cm.
Includes bibliographical references.
1. Action research in education—Methodology. I. Whitehead, Jack. II.
Title.
LB1028.24.M46 2009
370.7'2–dc22   2009008762

ISBN10: 0–415–48708–0 (hbk)
ISBN10: 0–415–48709–9 (pbk)
ISBN10: 0–203–87155–3 (ebk)

ISBN13: 978–0–415–48708–5 (hbk)
ISBN13: 978–0–415–48709–2 (pbk)
ISBN13: 978–0–203–87155–3 (ebk)

Contents

Introduction

This book is a comprehensive guide to how and why you can and should do action research. For practitioners across the professions who are doing, or are about to embark on, an action research project, the book is written in a way that recognises your capacities and will help you refine them.

Refining your capacities so that you do a really good project is important, because action research has become a recognised practice internationally, which is a move forward even from the second edition of this book, which appeared in 2003. Interest has exploded around the world in the idea of practitioners studying their practices and offering explanations for what they are doing. There is a range of possible reasons for this, one of which is the current global economic situation. Work-based learning, and therefore action research, is seen by many governments as a potential response towards economic recovery and social sustainability through the improved professionalisation of workforces. Another possible reason is world political instability. Countries everywhere seem to be expressing a deep need to re-establish their identity, while recognising a new imperative of sharing their singularities in a common effort to secure world sustainability. Action research is seen as offering a way forward, by emphasising the need for the lifelong learning of citizens to realise their potential contributions to emergent cultures of solidarity.

We authors, Jack and Jean, are delighted at the situation, given that we have both been practising and advocating action research approaches separately and together for the last thirty years or so. We are concerned, however, at some aspects. We are concerned that action research is too often seen as an answer to all social and economic problems, and we are resistant to the idea that it should be used only as a means of securing a competitive edge and political superiority. We are especially concerned when action research is cast only in the mould of professional development and not theory generation, so that practitioners are seen as workers whose job is to implement the theories of academics and so protect their interests, rather than as practitioners who are competent to offer their own cogent explanations for practice. We are concerned about the situation that encourages these kinds of positionings and discourses in the first place. Therefore, although we strongly advocate that practitioners should commit seriously to improving practice as an ongoing feature of that practice, we also emphasise that they need to give explanations for their practices, which is a process of theorising, and show how they hold themselves accountable for what they are doing. This moves action research beyond a focus on serving existing economic and political self-interests into a new focus on the development of an economic and political sphere, in which people share their stories of practice as the main currency of learning how to live together successfully. It moves action research beyond the domain of professional development and into the domain of knowledge creation.

Our aims, at a practical level, are to encourage practitioners to engage with the responsibility of offering explanations for what they are doing, and to generate their living educational theories of practice. We believe that the world would be a better place if everyone committed to showing how they hold themselves accountable for what they are doing in terms of the values and understandings they use to give meaning and purpose to their lives. Action research is, for us, a methodology based on philosophy and practice that enables people to do this. At a theoretical level, our enduring aim is to reconceptualise educational theory, so that it is no longer seen as the domain only of academics, whose job is to produce theory, to be applied by practitioners to their practices; nor is education seen only as the domain of teachers. Theory should also be seen as the domain of street vendors and physicians, whose job is to offer their explanations for what they are doing in order to show how theory is embodied in the way they live; education should also be seen as their domain, as they contribute to their own and other people's learning. There is nothing unusual in this stance. We all potentially do and live theory in our moment-to-moment practices with one another; and we all help ourselves and one another to learn. The difference is that our everyday explanations for why we do what we do are not often articulated as knowledge creation and theory generation, and our dealings with one another are not often called education. This needs to change and a new language needs to develop.

Action research is commonly hailed as a methodology for social and cultural change. We agree, but we think that social and cultural change is the responsibility of individuals working collectively. We believe that change happens first in individuals' minds, so that they bring their new learning to an improved understanding of practice and the practice itself improves. We do not believe that social and cultural change happens because people 'change' one another. Change comes from people themselves and is a feature of daily living. Furthermore, people need to offer reasons for why they are changing, and such insights are developed through focusing first on their learning. For us, therefore, action research is about improving practice through improving learning, and articulating the reasons and potential significance of the research, in the interests of helping us all to find better ways of living together successfully.

This book represents our present best thinking. It is considerably different from previous editions. We have expanded themes and ideas, and have brought our learning over the past six years to the job. We have included many examples from the now considerable knowledge base, much of it located in our own and other people's books and websites, that shows how practitioners, working individually and together, are recreating their world as the place where they enjoy living. You can access these websites at www.actionresearch.net and www.jeanmcniff.com. We urge you to contribute to and expand the knowledge base by offering your living theory of practice, so that people can learn with and from you. We hope this book will offer some pointers about how you can do so.

Jean McNiff and Jack Whitehead

(contact Jack at jack@actionresearch.net)
(contact Jean at jeanmcniff@mac.com)

Part I

First principles

Action research is about two things: action (what you do) and research (how you learn about and explain what you do). The action aspect of action research is about improving practice. The research aspect is about creating knowledge about practice. The knowledge created is your knowledge of your practice.

The three chapters in Part I deal with these issues. The question that informs this part is 'What do I need to know in order to do a high-quality action research project?' The chapters supply this information.

- Chapter 1 outlines some key ideas about action research and research in general. These ideas should inform your wider thinking.
- Chapter 2 makes a case for why you should do action research. These ideas help you to think about why it is important to do an action research project.
- Chapter 3 explains some of the significant features of action research that you need to bear in mind when designing and doing your action research project.

Chapter 1

Action research: what it is and what it is not

Action research is about finding ways to improve your practice, so it is about creating knowledge. The knowledge you create is knowledge of practice. These questions therefore arise: What do I need to know about action research? Why do I need to know it? What else do I need to know to help me do a good project?

This chapter engages with the first question. Chapters 2 and 3 deal with the second and third.

The chapter sets out what you need to know about action research in order to conduct a successful project. It outlines the basic principles of action research so that you can see what you need to do to improve your practice.

The chapter addresses these questions, which form section headings:

- What is action research? What it is not?
- What are the main characteristics of action research? How is it different from traditional research?

However, engaging with questions about action research means first appreciating what is involved in all kinds of research, not only action research. It means appreciating the different stances, aims and purposes that are involved in different research perspectives. The aims and purposes of action research are about improving learning for improving practice, which are different from the aims and purposes of traditional forms of research. It also means being clear about why you should do action research and the possible contributions you can make. These issues are developed in Chapter 2.

continued on next page

To begin, let's look at what action research is and what it is not. The theme is developed in Chapter 3, which discusses some of the main characteristics of action research.

Note: this chapter sets out basic issues that you may wish to return to again and again. No examples are given here, although many examples appear throughout the book to illustrate specific points.

What is action research? What it is not?

We do research when we want to find out something that we did not already know. We then say what we have come to know, and explain how we have come to know it. This is the case for all research, including action research. So, to appreciate what is special about action research, consider first what is involved in all kinds of research.

What is involved in all kinds of research

All research involves explaining (1) the reasons and purposes of the research; (2) the means of achieving the purposes; and (3) the significance of what has been achieved, as follows.

Reasons and purposes of research

As noted, doing research is about finding things out that you did not already know, and also creating new knowledge that no one knew before. You can therefore contribute to the body of existing knowledge, perhaps of a specific field. There are many ways of finding out and creating knowledge, so there are many ways of doing research. You use different forms of research for different purposes. No one form is better or worse; each form is different and serves a different purpose.

To clarify: Think of the different vehicles that you use for your work. You keep a Porsche at the front of your house to get from one place to another quickly. You keep a sit-on lawn mower at the back of your house to cut the grass. You would not use the lawn mower to get to different places quickly, and you would not use the Porsche to cut the grass. Each is a vehicle, with its own purposes. It is the same with research; each form of research has its own purposes. You choose the form of research depending on what you wish to achieve.

All research has three main purposes:

1 creating new knowledge and making claims to knowledge;
2 testing the validity of knowledge claims;
3 generating new theory.

Purpose 1: creating new knowledge and making claims to knowledge

All research aims to find out something that is not already known, whether it is a discovery, such as penicillin, or a new creation, such as a new manufacturing process. The new knowledge can be objective, such as knowledge of facts and figures, and also subjective, when a person develops new understandings.

Coming to know something for the first time means you can say, 'I have found out how to do this' or 'I understand this better'. You make a claim to new, or original, knowledge; you say, 'I know this now'.

Original knowledge claims are special and stand out from existing knowledge claims. Here are some examples of claims about existing knowledge:

- I can run fast.
- John is my good friend.
- It is raining.

Here are some examples of claims about new knowledge:

- I now know how to do this.
- I appreciate more fully how and why I am good at my job.
- I understand this better.

The highest aim of all research, including action research, is to create new, original knowledge.

Purpose 2: testing the validity of knowledge claims

However, making claims to knowledge, especially original claims, can be problematic because saying that you know something is equivalent to saying that you are holding something as true. A knowledge claim therefore comes to stand as a truth claim, so you can expect people to say, 'Why should I believe you? Show me that what you are saying is true.' It then becomes your responsibility to produce authenticated evidence to back up your claim and test its validity or truthfulness. If you are not able or prepared to do this, you should not expect people to believe you, and your knowledge claim is in danger of losing its credibility. You therefore need to show how and why your knowledge claim may be believed; this is the basis of and reason for doing research.

Purpose 3: generating new theory

This process of showing how and why a knowledge claim may be believed means offering an explanation. You say, 'I can explain what I know and how I have come to know it.' Another word for 'explanation' is 'theory'.

You say, 'I have a theory about what I know and how I have come to know it.' We have millions of theories. When we turn the key in the lock we do so according to a theory about how keys and locks work. When we see people opening their umbrellas we assume that it has started raining because we have theories about the relationships between rain and umbrellas. When you make a claim that you can explain something, you are claiming that you have a theory about that thing; you can say how and why it works as it does.

Now let's look at how these purposes are achieved. This brings us to ideas about methodologies.

Methodologies in research

Methodology can be understood as how to generate new theory. The processes involved usually take the form of steps along a pathway. This pathway may be linear and can also be branching. Sometimes you create the pathway by walking it (Horton and Freire 1990).

The key steps in most kinds of research are:

*   Identify a research issue.
*   Identify research aims and formulate a research question.
*   Set out a research design.
*   Take action.
*   Gather data.
*   Identify criteria and standards by which to make judgements about the quality of the research.
*   Generate evidence from the data in relation to the criteria and standards of judgement.
*   Make a claim to knowledge.
*   Link the claim with existing knowledge.
*   Test the validity of the claim.
*   Submit the claim to critique.
*   Explain the potential significance of the research and claim.
*   Generate theory from the research.
*   Modify practice in light of the evaluation.
*   Write a report and disseminate findings.

Here are the points in detail. They are developed in specific chapters, as noted.

Identify a research issue

All research begins by identifying a research issue, which can be set out in a tightly formulated way, such as a hypothesis to be tested, or in a looser way, such as an idea to be explored. Examples of research issues would be:

- 'The need to investigate the relationship between inspirational films on television and socially acceptable behaviour'. This kind of issue is dealt with in traditional social science research.
- 'How can I improve the quality of my work?' This kind of issue is dealt with in action research.

Identify research aims and formulate a research question

All researchers state the aims and purposes of their research, i.e. that they hope to make claims to new knowledge, test the validity of the claims and generate new theory. Research aims are often set out as research questions: the form of question varies according to the form of research. Questions of the kind, 'What is happening here?' or 'What are they doing?', which tend to be asked in traditional social science research, are different from questions of the kind, 'What am I doing? How do I improve my work?' (Whitehead 1989), which is the kind of questions asked in action research. In traditional social science research, the researcher stands outside the research situation and observes what other people are doing. They therefore adopt an outsider or spectator perspective. In action research, the researcher becomes the centre of the research. The focus is on the improvement of personal learning, so they adopt an insider, self-study perspective (see Chapter 3).

Set out a research design

The research design may be understood as the overall plan. It explains why the research should be conducted (the rationale for the research) and how it will be conducted. Will it proceed as a fixed set of action steps through which everything works towards finding an answer and leads to closure? In this case, you walk along a linear path to an end-point (Figure 1.1).

Or will it proceed in a developmental transformational way, in which new questions are addressed as they emerge through the process? In this case you stand on the edge, prepared to step into the void of unknowing and prepared to take the risk (Figure 1.2).

The design outlines how the validity of any claims to knowledge will be tested, so that the steps show what is involved in moving from the initial identification of a research issue to the successful testing of the validity of the knowledge claim (see Chapter 11).

Take action

The researcher considers what needs to be done both in the situation under observation and in relation to the research question. In traditional research, the action is usually to conduct an experiment in which variables are manipulated to check whether it is possible to establish a cause-and-effect relationship. In action research, the action is usually to begin a process of

Figure 1.1 Pursuing a linear path to an end-point.

improvement in learning, with a view to influencing thinking and behaviours (see Chapter 5).

Gather data

All research involves observation, monitoring practice and keeping records of what is happening, using specific data-gathering methods. The data gathered go into a data archive, in the physical form of boxes or files, or documents or multimedia representations in a computer. First-hand data are 'raw' data about the immediate situation, such as diaries, photographs or tape-recorded conversations. Second-hand data are derivative and are contained in reports or other documents about the research (see Chapter 8).

Identify criteria and standards by which to make judgements about the quality of the research

Criteria refer to what we expect to see when we make judgements about something, and are set in advance. For example, you would judge the quality of a hotel in terms of its cleanliness and warmth. The criteria for judging

Figure 1.2 Stepping into risk.

the quality of a hotel would be cleanliness and warmth. These are the things you expect to see: you ask, 'Is the hotel clean and warm?' You continue to make judgements about the quality of the hotel in relation to how well the criteria are met: you ask, 'How clean is the hotel? How warm?' The ways you make judgements become your standards of judgement. In traditional research, quality is judged in terms of traditional criteria, such as 'Are the research findings generalisable and replicable?', and traditional standards, such as 'How well are the criteria addressed?' In action research, your values become your criteria, and quality is judged in relation to how well you can show that you are trying to live in the direction of your values (see Chapter 11).

Generate evidence from the data in relation to the criteria and standards of judgement

Evidence is not the same as data. The term 'data' refers to all the information you gather about a situation or a thing, whereas evidence refers to those pieces of data that are directly relevant to the research question and its transformation into a research claim. If you say, 'I aim to create a caring workplace where people are treated fairly and with respect' then you judge the quality of workplace life in relation to the values of care, fairness and respect. You extract from the data those pieces that show the demonstration of care, fairness and respect (see Chapter 10).

Make a claim to knowledge

Making a claim to knowledge means showing how new knowledge has been generated, and why the knowledge should now count as valid knowledge. In action research the claim is always related to whether you can show (from your evidence) that you have exercised your educational influence in your own or other people's learning. Can you show how you have interrogated and deconstructed your thinking, and made yourself open to new learning, and how you have influenced other people to do the same? If action is grounded in learning then the aim of action research is to improve learning in order to improve action. Improved action will be grounded in improved learning (see Chapter 8).

Link the claim with existing knowledge

All research aims to show how it has drawn on the thinking of others in the field in creating new knowledge. It does this by engaging critically with existing debates, usually in the literatures. Once validated (see next section 'What are the main characteristics of action research? How is it different from traditional research?'), the new knowledge is placed within the existing body of knowledge, usually in the literatures (the canon). The claim may now be perceived as a new contribution. It adds to the existing body of knowledge, usually in the form of a report that can be referenced by other researchers (see Chapter 13).

Test the validity of the claim

When you make a claim to knowledge you need to show that you have tested its validity; you ask, 'Is my claim believable?' If you do not show that you have done so, people may think your claim is your opinion or wishful thinking but not knowledge. In traditional research the validity of the claim can be shown when other people replicate your research by applying it to their own situations with the same results as yours. In action research the validity of your claim can be demonstrated when you show that you have moved towards a situation in which you are living your values more fully in your practice. You test the validity of your claim by referring to an authenticated evidence base, and articulating the specific criteria and standards, informed by your values, by which you make judgements about the validity of the claim and the quality of your research: can you show through authenticated evidence that you are trying to live in the direction of your values? (See Chapter 11.)

Submit the claim to critique

To prevent the claim being seen as your opinion or wishful thinking, you seek feedback from yourself and others about its validity. You do a personal validity check against your values: can you show to your own satisfaction that you are trying to live your values more fully in your practice? You also do a public validity check: can you show this to other people's satisfaction? In submitting your claim to critique, do you show that you are trying to speak clearly; to show your authenticity through trying to live in the direction of your values; that you are telling the truth in the production of evidence; and that you understand the wider contexts of your research? (These social and communicative criteria of comprehensibility, authenticity, truthfulness and appropriateness are drawn from Habermas 1976; see also Chapter 11.)

Explain the potential significance of the research and claim

All researchers explain the significance of their research. They say how and why it is relevant, which gives meaning to their work or to life in general, and offers potential development for themselves and other people. In action research, you can show the significance of your research in terms of how it has potential for contributing to the education of yourself, other people, and of social and cultural formations. You explain the potential of your research for cultural and social transformation, in your own and in wider contexts (see Chapter 13).

Generate theory from the research

The purposes of research include creating new knowledge and generating theory, but knowledge and theory are different. 'Knowledge' refers to what is known; 'theory' is an explanation that is grounded in what is known. Research always has to be connected with knowledge creation; if not, it cannot stand as research. Although all research traditions are steadfast about this, different research traditions have different views about what counts as theory. Traditional research defines theory as words on a page: the concept 'love' can be explained through words as 'a caring and compassionate stance towards another person or persons'. This words-based form of theory is termed 'theory' in the literatures, and usually takes the form of propositional theory (see p. 251 for a definition). Action research defines practitioners' theories in terms of the form that living practices take: the concept 'love' can be explained through how people act in caring and compassionate relationships. This practice-based form of theory is termed 'living theory' in the literatures, because the theory is embodied in the lives of real people. The distinctions between 'theory' and 'living theory' are important for current debates about what counts as knowledge and theory, especially in relation to decisions about who qualifies for recognition, with implications for issues such as research funding (see Chapter 12).

Modify practice in light of the evaluation

All research aims to show how it can lead to changed and improved practices, through validation and evaluation processes. In traditional research, the expectation is that users of research (practitioners) will improve their practices through applying other researchers' propositional theory. In action research, the expectation is that practitioners will improve their own practices through learning from existing practices, and will explain how and why the improvement has happened, and the validation processes involved. The research therefore becomes offering explanations for ongoing improvement of practice, and demonstrating the validity of the explanations. This is especially important: practitioners need to articulate how and why their claims and living theories should be seen as valid and not just their opinion. Validity comes to act as the basis of legitimacy, as discussed below (see also Chapter 12).

Write a report and disseminate findings

This involves making the findings of research publicly available, in order to:

- Establish the legitimacy of the claim to knowledge. You show how you have fulfilled publicly recognised research criteria, such as originality and critical engagement, in relation to your own thinking and the thinking of others in the literatures.
- Show how you have submitted your research to public critique.
- Show how you can potentially contribute to other people's practices. In traditional research you show how other people can apply your research findings to improving their practices; this fulfils the traditional criteria of generalisability and replicability. In action research, you produce your stories of research-based practice, and invite other people to learn from and perhaps adopt or adapt what you have done to their practices. This fulfils criteria to do with dynamic transformational potential, because other people can learn from you and can see new possibilities for their own research.

All these processes contribute to establishing the legitimacy of your research, i.e. that it is accepted in the public domain and qualifies as part of the wider body of knowledge. This is central to understanding where action research is in the world today (see below and Chapter 2).

We now turn to a discussion of the main characteristics of action research that make it different from traditional forms of research.

What are the main characteristics of action research? How is it different from traditional research?

The main characteristics of action research are that it:

- is practice based, and practice is understood as action and research;
- is about improving practice (both action and research), creating knowledge, and generating living theories of practice;
- focuses on improving learning, not on improving behaviours;
- emphasises the values base of practice;
- is about research and knowledge creation, and is more than just professional practice;
- is collaborative, and focuses on the co-creation of knowledge of practices;
- involves interrogation, deconstruction and decentring;
- demands higher-order questioning;
- is intentionally political;
- requires people to hold themselves accountable for what they are doing and accept responsibility for their own actions;
- can contribute to social and cultural transformation.

Action research is practice based, and practice is understood as action and research

Action research is conducted by practitioners who regard themselves as researchers. It therefore goes by other names such as practice-based research, practitioner research, practitioner-led research and practitioner-based research. It is also sometimes called action enquiry. It is not action learning, although it incorporates action learning, and the distinctions between action research and action learning are frequently blurred. Action learning is more about improving practice through collaborative learning and does not always emphasise research aspects. Action research involves improving practice through collaborative learning, and involves the research aspects identified above under 'What is action research? What it is not?', resulting in making public an explanatory account of practice. In health and social care contexts, terms such as 'user research' or 'service-user-led research' are used (see Winter and Munn-Giddings 2001). The practice base of action research means that all people in all contexts who are investigating the situation they are in can become researchers, regardless of their age, status, social setting, or social or professional positioning. The situations may be in virtually any context – in the workplace, in the home or in an aeroplane – and in any personal or professional arena. Because action research is always done by practitioners within a particular social situation, it is insider research, not outsider research, which means that the researcher is inside the situation, and will inevitably influence what is happening by their presence.

This stance is different from traditional research, which is usually conducted from an outsider perspective, for which an official researcher stands outside the research situation and observes what other people are doing. The researcher then offers descriptions and explanations for those other people's actions, so the researcher generates theory about other people. However, although much traditional research is outsider research, many research contexts require the researcher to become an insider researcher within the situation. The main issue, however, is always, 'Who creates the knowledge? Who generates the theory? Whose theory is it? What is the theory about?' In traditional research, the theory is usually the researcher's theory, and its form is propositional, about other people; the expectation is that the theory can be applied to practitioners' practices. Traditional research is therefore usually located within an asymmetrical power relationship between researcher and practitioner, which positions the official researcher as 'the one who knows' whereas the practitioner is positioned as an aspirant. This is one reason why action research is so popular: it puts practitioners in control of their own practices – but this also carries the responsibilities of offering explanations for those practices.

Action research is about improving practice (both action and research), creating knowledge and generating living theories of practice

Action research contains the words and concepts 'action' and 'research'. Although the two concepts always go together in practice, it can be helpful to look at them separately to appreciate how and why both are important, and the nature of their relationship with each other.

- 'Action' can be understood as activity – what we do. We take action when cooking or watching television or undertaking surgical procedures. However, considerable differences exist between 'activity', which is more to do with everyday 'jobs to do', and 'action', which is to do with purposeful, intentional practice (see McNiff and Whitehead 2009).
- 'Research' can be understood as how we find out about what we are doing and create new knowledge about those things; it involves everything described above under 'What is action research? What it is not?'

Action research therefore combines the ideas of taking purposeful action with educational intent, and testing the validity of any claims we make about the process. It becomes the grounds for other social and professional practices; professional development is understood as grounded in the capacity to offer explanations for our work.

The 'action' of action research is always about improving practice, however practice is understood. Processes of social improvement begin with personal improvement, and personal improvement is grounded in personal learning. Think about the idea of action, as outlined above. You can watch television; this is usually understood as 'activity', without involving ideas about improvement. When the action is about contributing to other people's learning, however, it must involve ideas about improvement. Investigating how the action has contributed to improvement becomes a process of knowledge creation; offering explanations for how and why this has happened becomes a process of theory generation.

Action research focuses on improving learning, not on improving behaviours

Action research is about individuals learning in company with other people. People are always in relation with one another in some way. Taking purposeful action with educational intent therefore involves a deep understanding of oneself in relation with others.

Action research is different from traditional social scientific research, which aims to understand and describe a social situation in terms of something 'out there'. It is a process that helps you as a practitioner to develop a deep understanding of what you are doing as an insider researcher, so it has both a personal and social aim. The personal aim is to improve your learning in order to use that learning to help you improve your behaviours. Its social aim is to contribute to other people's learning to help them improve their behaviours. Both are equally important and interdependent. When you make your research public by writing and disseminating your report and ideas, you offer an account of how your learning may or may not have influenced the situation, i.e. other people's behaviours (see Chapter 13). It does not matter if the social situation does not reach successful closure; it probably will not because any solution allows new questions to emerge. What matters is that you show your own processes of learning and explain how your learning has helped you develop your work within the situation.

On this view, action research focuses primarily on improving learning, not on behaviour. This stance is different from a focus on concrete behavioural 'outcomes', often expressed in terms of externally imposed targets, which potentially constrains learning and distorts the research process.

Action research emphasises the values base of practice

Values are the things we believe in and that give our lives meaning, such as love and fairness. When we value something it becomes a value. Action research begins with people thinking about what they value, and how they might act in the direction of those values, i.e. how they can achieve what is important to them. Action research is therefore value laden, different from the neutral stance required by traditional forms of research for the research to be value free.

It is important to clarify your values from the start because awareness of your values will keep you grounded throughout your project. You will find that your values form the basis of your conceptual frameworks and guide your reading. If your project is about finding more democratic ways of working, you will read up about issues of democracy. Your values will also come to act as your criteria for judging what you do (you believe that workplaces should be run in an equitable way) and they also become your standards of judgement (you judge your practice in relation to your values, to see the extent to which you are realising those values in your practices). A main characteristic of action research is that it turns the abstract concepts of values such as love and democracy into living practices. This point is central. John Rawls (1972), for example, writes about the practice of the value of fairness, yet he does not show how the abstract value of fairness can actually transform into the living practice of fairness. It is easy to talk about fairness, but talk does not necessarily encourage fair practices. Doing requires real-world intent, which is the domain of action research.

Action research is about research and knowledge creation, and is more than just professional practice

When people do action research for the first time they often say, 'This is what I do in any case.' To an extent, this is so. We act, reflect on our actions, and modify our practice in light of what we learn. This is good professional practice, which emphasises the action (often problem solving), but it is not research-based action. Action research is more than problem solving, and involves identifying the reasons for the action, as related to the researcher's values, and gathering and interpreting data to show that the reasons and values were justified and fulfilled. This goes beyond good professional practice, which emphasises the action but does not always question the reasons and motives. Action research is about showing that claims to improved practice must be interrogated and justified, and is about praxis. Praxis is informed, committed action that gives rise to knowledge as well as successful action. It is informed because other people's views and feelings are taken into account. It is committed and intentional in terms of values that you have examined and interrogated, and are prepared to defend.

Action research is collaborative and focuses on the co-creation of knowledge of practices

Action research is therefore never solitary. It involves individuals finding ways to improve what they are doing in company with others. Those individuals then claim that they have improved what they are doing, and test the validity of those claims against the critical feedback of others. So it becomes a cyclical process of improving practice, checking against other people's critical feedback whether the practice really has improved, and modifying practice in light of that feedback. Furthermore, it is not just one person who does this, but everyone, so all participants in the community of practice are involved in checking with one another whether they are justified in claiming that what they are doing is the best it can be. It becomes a case of people working collaboratively to improve their practices by improving their learning about those practices, and checking with one another that what they know is valid. Practice therefore becomes the site for the co-creation of knowledge of practice.

Action research involves interrogation, deconstruction and decentring

Knowledge of practice is a highly rigorous, and often problematic, process because it means interrogating what we are doing, beginning with our values and logics. 'Values' refers to the things we value, and 'logics' refers to how we think. Some people think in terms of cause and effect: 'If I do this, that will happen.' Some think in terms of 'this or that' categories, and often make judgements about other people from this basis: 'If you are black you go here; if you are white you go there.' Some people think in terms of connectedness and relatedness: they see the relationships between, say, the well-being of animals and the well-being of the planet. Some think in terms of transformations: they see everything involved in processes of evolution, one form transforming into a more developed version of itself. It may be worth stopping for a moment and thinking about what you value and how you think. Thinking about how you think can be difficult, because you will use your usual (normative) way of thinking to interrogate how you think. It can be difficult – often impossible – to step outside your form of logic to interrogate that form of logic, but it is important that you try.

The process of interrogating your thinking is called deconstruction (Derrida 1997). You deconstruct your usual ways of thinking. Many people find that they cannot deconstruct their thinking, because the experience can be destabilising. Other people welcome the opportunity. Your project is about how you can improve something and often it is enough to show that you have improved your thinking, in the sense that you see things from different, more educational perspectives. This reinforces the idea that action research is not about changing behaviours, but about changing the ways we think so that our behaviours are better informed.

Deconstruction usually involves decentring. This idea refers to the idea that 'I' am not necessarily the centre of the universe. Other people may see themselves as the centres of their own universes. Decentring therefore involves being aware that each person may claim to be their own centre, and others need to respect their views.

The ideas of interrogating, deconstruction and decentring are well communicated in the work of Richard Winter (1989), who speaks of the need for critical reflexivity (awareness of how one thinks) and dialectical reflexivity (awareness of the wider social, cultural, political, economic and other forces that influence how one thinks). Winter and others emphasise the need to ask interesting and important questions rather than focus on finding fixed answers. This brings us to ideas about different orders of questioning.

Action research demands higher-order questioning

Action researchers begin the processes of reflexive and dialectical critique by questioning the assumptions that underlie their practices and their social situations. Although it may not be problem solving (bringing an enquiry to closure), action research does imply problem posing, or problematising: that is, opening up the enquiry and not accepting things at face value. This involves questioning at several levels, which are often called 'first-, second- and third-order questioning'. First-order questioning refers to learning about a situation: for example, 'How many women managers are in the firm?' Second-order questioning is about questioning what has been learned: 'How can we involve more women managers?' Third-order questioning asks why the situation is as it is, and what one might need to do to change it, or change the way one thinks about it: 'Why is it necessary to ask questions about the involvement of women managers in the first place?' Developing this type of critical perspective means recognising that situations are not 'given', but are created by people with particular intentions over time. The research project might unearth issues that seemingly have nothing to do with its original aims, yet are important to understanding the situation with a view to changing it.

Action research is intentionally political

However, deciding to interrogate existing situations and to take action towards improvement is itself a political act, because what one person does invariably has consequences for someone else. Action researchers need to understand that they are frequently in potentially politically contested scenarios. When practitioners begin to question the current and historical contexts of a situation, and perhaps reveal injustices, they have to decide whether to follow their value commitments and try to influence the situation according to what they believe in, or to go along with the status quo. These are difficult decisions and can involve personal discomfort. The affirmation that you have contributed to social development, however, can be a powerful incentive to act in the interests of social justice.

*Action research requires people to hold themselves accountable
for what they are doing and accept responsibility for their own
actions*

Taking this stance brings special responsibilities. In traditional types of research, researchers usually carry out what is required by someone else, such as policy makers or funders, so, although those researchers may make decisions about research procedures, they do not necessarily make decisions about research aims. Action researchers, on the other hand, make their own decisions about what is important and what they should do. This is a massive responsibility, however, because researchers then base their decisions for action on how they understand what is good and how they think the world should be. They use their values as the basis for their actions. Because this is such a massive responsibility they always need to check whether theirs are justifiable values, whether they are living in the direction of their values, and whether their influence is benefiting other people in ways that those other people also feel are good. This involves rigorous evaluation checks to make sure that action researchers can justify, and do not abuse, their capacity for influence.

*Action research can contribute to social and cultural
transformation*

Perhaps the most powerful aspect of action research is that practitioners become aware of their capacity to influence the future, especially in relation to new forms of social and cultural practices. Because the focus is on improving learning to improve action, it becomes evident how one individual can influence the thinking of other individuals through collaborative working and making accounts of practice public so that other people can learn from those accounts and perhaps find ways of improving their own learning and practices.

The ideas of social and cultural evolution are important. 'Society' and 'culture' are problematic concepts. There is no one homogenous entity called 'society' and no one set of practices called 'culture'; neither is society a collection of individuals, nor culture a collection of practices. When we speak of social and cultural transformation, we are speaking about influencing people, acting in company with one another within given contexts, to rethink how they are with one another and with their environment, and find ways of improving what they are doing. It can be awesome to think that one person (you) has the capacity to influence the future through acting with purposeful educational intent in the present, but this is what action research enables us all to do.

Summary

This chapter has engaged with questions about what action research is and what it is not. Ideas are presented about action research as a way of improving practice through knowledge creation, within a broader discussion of ideas about research in general. A distinction has been made between traditional forms of research, which focus on manipulating variables in order to demonstrate a causal relationship between them, and action research, which focuses on improving practice. The point is also made that traditional research tends to be conducted from an outsider perspective, thus generating propositional theories about practices, whereas action research is conducted from an insider perspective, thus generating living theories of practices.

Checklist of reflective questions

This checklist of reflective questions will help you bear in mind the key ideas about action research, and you should make sure that you use them when doing your research and writing your report.

- Are you clear that action research is about improving practice and generating knowledge about what you are doing? Are you clear that this is what you are doing in your action research?
- Are you confident about where action research is located within all kinds of research?
- Can you say what the aims and purposes of all kinds of research are, and of action research in particular? Can you articulate your own aims and purposes as an action researcher?
- Can you explain the differences between traditional forms of research and action research?
- Can you explain the differences between 'theory' and 'living theory'? Can you relate this to your own practice, and say how you are generating your own living theory of practice?
- What are the main characteristics of action research? How do these relate to your own practice?

If you can show that you understand all these points, you are well on the way to conducting a good action research project.

In Chapter 2 we consider the significance of these ideas for today's world, and also make a case for why practitioners should do action research.

Chapter 2

Why should you do action research?

The question now arises, do you wish to do action research and, if so, are you reasonably sure and can you say why you wish to do it? Offering an explanation is key, especially in today's climate in which action research seems to be everywhere, and is in danger of becoming a bandwagon that many people are jumping on, some without necessarily knowing why, and some for the wrong reasons. Although it is heartening to see the high profile of action research it is also alarming that many policy groupings are introducing action research exclusively as a means of professional education, with a focus on achieving outcomes. This works on the assumption that action research is a panacea to fix all ills, which is a naive and dangerous practice. In this sense, action research becomes yet another grand theory to be imposed on practitioners from a disciplines perspective, rather than a way of enabling practitioners to generate their own living practice-based theories from an educational perspective. We authors, Jack and Jean, are all for practitioners doing action research, but for the right reasons – not because they are told to with the implication that action research could become yet another innovation to be implemented.

This chapter addresses these issues: first, by looking at where action research is in the world today; second, by considering why practitioners should do action research, for the right reasons; and third, taking into account what practitioners need to know to ensure that they realise their own potentials as action researchers and retain control over its real form as a means of theory generation for personal, social and cultural renewal.

The chapter is organised into three parts:

- Where is action research in the world today?
- Why should practitioners do action research, for the right reasons?
- How do you explain the potentials of your action research?

Where is action research in the world today?

If you had gone into the action research shop in the 1940s, in the US, it is likely that you would have been able to buy only one brand. This was the brand created by Kurt Lewin, who is generally considered one of the founding fathers of action research, although the values and concepts underpinning action research can be found in many historical records. Later, in the UK during the 1970s and 1980s you would have probably found two basic brands, each in one of two shops: one in East Anglia, presided over by John Elliott and his colleagues, and one in Bath, presided over by Jack Whitehead (see McNiff 2008a for a historical account). Elliott has since been influential in promoting interpretive approaches to action research, in which a researcher observes practitioners doing their action research and offers descriptions and explanations for what they are doing in the form of the researcher's propositional theories. Whitehead has been influential in promoting living approaches, by which individuals research their own practices and offer descriptions and explanations for what they are doing in the form of their own living theories of practice. From broader perspectives, things are different today from the 1940s. Action research seems to be everywhere, and much of what goes by the name of action research would probably not be recognised as action research by Lewin, Elliott or Whitehead. This situation raises considerable problematic issues, concerned with how action research is perceived and how it is used.

Addressing the problems involves first addressing the questions that are at the heart of all research, which are to do with knowledge and theory, and which inevitably give rise to power struggles about what is known, who knows and who says.

Questions of knowledge and theory

At the heart of debates about the nature and uses of action research are questions about theory: Which form of theory is most appropriate for offering explanations for how we come to know what we know? Who creates the knowledge and generates the theory? How is the knowledge and theory validated? Who says who is qualified to do so?

In traditional terms, 'theory' is seen as a set of statements, or propositions, and these propositions have normative status. 'Normative' means what is taken as 'normal', and also what should be taken as normal. The proposition 'Children should be seen and not heard' has informed the practices of generations of parents, schoolteachers and other professionals. The theory exists as a grand theory, to be imposed on people, who are expected to apply it to their practices.

It is not only what the theory says that is taken as normative, but also that the form of theory is as it is. Few people, especially those in power, question the form of theory, probably because it suits them. The form of theory is premised on a model whereby a researcher stands outside a situation, and observes, describes and explains what is happening within the situation; i.e. the researcher generates a propositional theory about that situation. Further, many theorists maintain that this is the only legitimate kind of theory; anything else is not 'proper' theory. In reality, this is not the case, as many different forms of theory exist. One form takes a living, in-the-moment form, in which people offer explanations for what they do as they do it; this book is premised on this view. Practitioners become researchers as they enquire into, and offer explanations for, what they are doing. They generate their own living theories of practice.

These power struggles around what counts as valid knowledge and who counts as a legitimate knower have emerged recently as several broad, linked sets of discourses within the wider domain of research. Here, we outline two of them, and explain where action research is located within them. They are:

- what counts as traditional scholarship and the new scholarship;
- what counts as education research and educational research.

What counts as traditional scholarship and the new scholarship

In 1990, Ernest Boyer wrote *Scholarship Reconsidered: Priorities of the Professoriate*, an influential book that said that it was time for a new form of scholarship to supplement traditional kinds of propositional scholarship. This new form of scholarship would focus on real-life practices, whereby practitioners would generate knowledge about their practices and have that knowledge legitimised by the Academy. In 1995, Donald Schön developed the theme by saying that the new scholarship required a new epistemology, a new way of knowing that was practice based and located within the everyday theories that practitioners generated about their practices. Concurrently, Jack Whitehead, since the 1970s, had been promoting the idea that practitioners need to generate their own living theories of practice, through which they offer descriptions and explanations for what they are doing, and show how they accept the responsibility of holding themselves accountable for their work. To help practitioners produce a strong evidence base that shows the living reality of real-life practices, they also need to find new ways of representing their research, perhaps by using new forms of multimedia. The production of their visual narratives of practice would help them communicate what ways of knowing are appropriate for generating living theories of practice, and for those theories to be understood and validated as educational. This brings us to the second point, about education and educational research.

What counts as education research and educational research

In 2005, Geoff Whitty, then President of the British Educational Research Association, formalised a debate that had been in process for decades (see, for example, Lomax 1994a), about whether and why a distinction should be made between 'education research' and 'educational research' (the original paper can be accessed at www.bera.ac.uk/files/2008/09/gwberapresidentialaddress_000.pdf). Whitty said that education research should be seen as the broad domain of research into education, whereas educational research should be seen as matters of policy and practice. He suggested that education research, which embraces much social science research, should be distinguished from educational research, which embraces practice-based research. This view has serious implications. First, it turns education into a discipline or subject, a field of study that can be studied and explained (theorised) from an externalist stance. There is no requirement for the researcher to become involved in their own research, or to show how the research has been educational for themselves. Second, those who position themselves as practitioners, who wish to account for what they are doing by offering explanations for their practices in the public domain, are positioned as of lesser worth than those who generate theories about their discipline, in this case, education. And so the form of theory is perpetuated by those whom the form of theory suits; and, because they are usually the people who are already in power, as they already possess the means of validating and legitimising forms of theory, the situation stays as it is. From a Marxian perspective, it becomes clear that established elites retain control over the means of production: the product in question is the form of theory.

This debate is relevant for other fields: for example, whether the basis for high-quality dentistry should be seen as 'dentistry research', i.e. research about dentistry, or as a form of educational research that enables dentists to account for their practices. These debates are on the horizon.

The significance of the debates

The significance of the debates is concerned with who gets to have a say in what the future looks like by acting in the present. The key questions are about what counts as knowledge, who counts as a knower, and who says so. Currently, the Academy is still positioned as the body that has greatest influence in these matters, so for many it becomes a question of influencing the Academy, so that the voices of practitioners can be heard. However, if practitioners wish to be heard, they need to make sure that what they have to say is worth hearing, and this is a key reason for doing action research and ensuring that the quality of the research will be such as to ensure that the practitioner is actually taken seriously. This brings us to the second point, about why practitioners should do action research, but for the right reasons.

Why should practitioners do action research, for the right reasons?

Two further debates have emerged that have direct bearing on your decision whether to do action research. The first is to do with economic globalisation and the part that practitioners' action research can play. This debate, for us authors, contains both the wrong reasons why practitioners should do action research as well as the right reasons. The right reasons are about how action researchers can contribute to social and cultural regeneration. The second debate engages with matters arising, and involves explaining why it is so important to establish the validity of practitioners' accounts.

Debates about economic globalisation

The first debate is about how universities can contribute to future economic sustainability, a crucial issue given the long-term outlook for economic regeneration and its implications for social sustainability. For example, the 2009 multimillion-dollar injection of cash into the US economy has a deliberate focus on renewing confidence in the public sector, including home ownership as a symbol of the American dream. Universities are caught up in these debates because they are seen as institutions for turning out employable citizens who will contribute directly to the economic regeneration. Hence, the idea of work-based learning becomes central. It is understood that universities will produce people who have the skills and capacities to implement fiscal policies. Some thought, however, leads one to see that these efforts are not far removed from efforts of previous times when workers were seen as implementing company policies, and judged in terms of efficiency and productivity (Callahan 1962). Because work-based learning is strongly associated with action research, action research therefore comes to be seen as a means of enabling practitioners to implement government policies, rather than a means of enabling practitioners to think for themselves. These, for us authors, are the wrong reasons for doing action research.

However, combating these wrong reasons and articulating the right ones means engaging with issues of demonstrating the validity of what you are doing as an action researcher. This brings us to the second debate, about validity in action research.

How the validity of practitioners' accounts may be established

Another debate arose during the 1980s and 1990s about how the validity of practice-based research could be demonstrated. This had a direct bearing on work in the field, and a new focus developed.

The situation is explained in influential papers by Furlong (2004) and Furlong and Oancea (2005). Their argument is that practitioner research has tended to be judged in terms of traditional research, because practitioner research has not yet worked out its own criteria and standards to judge the quality of practice-based research. If a field cannot articulate its own criteria and standards of judgement, it must expect to be judged in terms of associated fields: if rugby had not its own rules and standards, it could expect to be judged by the rules and standards of football. Hence it is crucially important for a person or field to be able to articulate their reasons and purposes for doing something (theorise it), and explain how their practices should be judged in terms of those reasons and purposes. In the case of action research, dominant assumptions were that it could continue to be judged in terms of the traditional yet inappropriate criteria of generalisability and replicability. Consequently, a good deal of work by the practitioner research community has gone into finding new forms of criteria and standards. The work in this book represents one school of thought about how validity can be demonstrated. This thinking revolves around the need for practitioners to do good-quality action research and be able to articulate how they make judgements about why their work should be understood as good quality; in this case, this is done through articulating the values-based criteria and standards of judgement used.

For us authors, practitioners do need to research their own practices to show how they have improved the quality of those practices (the action of action research) and also be able to articulate how and why those practices should be understood as high quality (the research of action research). We emphasise the research as much as the action. We also emphasise that accounts need to contain reasons and purposes, and not be seen simply as stories of action, which positions action research as a means of professional development but not as a means of generating new theory. Not to do so carries the consequences that practitioners will continue to be seen as implementers of other people's theories, who are not able to think for themselves, rather than creators of their own theories, informed by their capacity both to think for themselves and also to show how and why their thinking can influence other people's thinking. They can encourage others also to think for themselves and to realise their capacities for contributing to international debates about what counts as a decent society and how it may be nurtured.

This brings us to the final point about how it is possible to resist current moves that threaten to turn action research into an instrumental policy-oriented activity, and retain control over its real form as a means of theory generation for personal, social and cultural renewal (see Hymer *et al.* 2009 for a persuasive account).

How do you explain the potentials of your action research?

It is against this broad background of linking practice-based research with economic and environmental sustainability that this book offers ideas about how you can generate your claims about your own knowledge of practice, and place that knowledge in the public domain for critique, validation and ultimate legitimation. We maintain throughout that if you wish your knowledge to be seen as good-quality knowledge, worthy of contributing to public debates, you must show that you are aware of what is involved in generating and validating that knowledge, through demonstrating your capacity to conduct high-quality work-based research that is the grounds of your knowledge. You also need to be aware of the potentials of your research for informing new thinking and new practices. The most important of these is to show how practice-based forms of theory are methodologically valid and also have validity for contributing to other people's thinking, i.e. they have what Lather (1991) calls 'catalytic validity'. This means that the story of one person's research reveals its transformational potential for influencing other people's thinking, so that they also see the value of doing their action research and will be inspired to do so.

Many texts tell how cultural change happens. In our view, a key strategy in influencing normative cultures is to build a parallel culture that works alongside the normative one. Action research represents one such parallel culture. People investigate their practices and do educational research alongside those who maintain a subject focus and do research into education (or management, or leadership, and so on). Most of the time they live in peace, as do states that share the same territory, such as Israel and Palestine. Sooner or later, they need to learn to live together, not as separate entities, but as singularities who are willing to share their identities and influence the thinking of the other. This can be done through the sharing of stories, and the creation of a knowledge base that shows how people have improved the quality of their lives and are able to explain how they judge that quality in the interests of their own moral accountability.

These days are probably still a long time coming, both for Israel and Palestine, and for action research. In the meantime, it is up to the participants in all contexts to show that what they have to say deserves to be taken seriously, and to create a knowledge base that represents contemporary thinking in the field. This book constitutes one such knowledge base, to show how it can be done.

Summary

This chapter has discussed why it is important for practitioners to do action research, and to be aware of the need for theory generation as much as for improving practice. In offering a rationale to practitioners for doing action research, the chapter explains that the right reasons and the wrong reasons are often used by different agencies representing different interests. These reasons and interests are further grounded in the ways in which different agencies perceive education and research, as well as how they position other people. You should be aware of the associated debates and implications, so that you can offer your own rationale.

Checklist of reflective questions

The following checklist may help you to come to an appropriate decision about whether or not to do your action research project, and how deep a commitment you are prepared to make.

- How are you positioned as a practitioner? Do you perceive yourself as a researcher too? How do other people position you?
- Are you clear about why you wish to do your action research? What are your reasons for or against?
- How do you think about 'education research' and 'educational research'? Which kind do you wish to do?
- Do you see the need to do high-quality action research, which means generating theory, and not to stay only at the level of professional development? Why is it important?
- Are you confident that you can achieve the highest quality in your action research? (Of course you can.)

So, to address the themes raised here, we now turn to Chapter 3, which is about some of the key issues to bear in mind to communicate your practice as a valid form of theory.

Chapter 3

The main features of action research processes

In Chapter 1 we set out some ideas about how action research is different from traditional research, so that you can decide whether to use an action research approach for your project. In Chapter 2 we made a case for why you should do action research, improve your knowledge of your practice and articulate its significance as theory generation. In this chapter we outline some key aspects that will enable you to communicate your understanding of practice as generating theory.

First we introduce some key terminology for when you work on and write up your action research. These terms are as follows.

- *Ontology*. This refers to a theory of being, to do with how you identify yourself, especially in relation with others. We can speak about our ontological security when we feel our lives have meaning and purpose. We can speak of ontological despair in those times when we feel a loss of meaning and purpose.
- *Epistemology*. This refers to a theory of knowledge, and contains two parts: a theory of knowledge and a theory of knowledge acquisition or creation. It refers to what is known, and how it comes to be known. You say, 'I tend to use relational epistemologies, because I believe that people create knowledge together through conversation.' It is usual to distinguish an epistemology in terms of its unit of appraisal (what is being judged), its standards of judgement (how judgements are made) and its logic (the mode of thinking that is appropriate from within the epistemology for apprehending the real as rational) (Marcuse 1964: 105).
- *Methodology*. This refers to how things are done. You can use a range of methodologies, including systematic methodologies and haphazard methodologies. Sometimes action research appears

continued on next page

haphazard until an underlying order begins to emerge and become clarified (Mellor, 1998, speaks about how his methodology emerged out of the muddle).

- *Socio-political intent.* All research is political and socially oriented. In action research, socio-political intent is embedded within educational intent, so social renewal is grounded in people's commitment to taking responsibility for how they think and act, and how they are contributing to sustainable processes of personal and social renewal.

The chapter is organised as two parts. Part 1 contains ideas about key ontological and epistemological features of action research, and Part 2 contains ideas about key methodological and socio-political features. Although these ideas appear separately for purposes of analysis, they are inextricably entwined in reality and should be treated as such.

Ontological and epistemological issues

Keep these ideas in mind when thinking about your action research project. Action research involves:

- a commitment to educational improvement;
- a special kind of research question, asked with educational intent;
- putting the 'I' at the centre of the research;
- educational action that is informed, committed and intentional.

A commitment to educational improvement

Action research is about improving learning in order to influence improvement in the social context in which you, the researcher, are located. This idea is complex and contains four related ideas:

1   the idea of improvement;
2   the nature of processes of improvement;
3   the question of who improves what;
4   the nature of education.

Note: we now begin to use real-life examples to illustrate points. The examples in this chapter are drawn from Jean's work in different settings in South Africa.

The idea of improvement

The idea of improvement is often taken to imply that something is faulty and needs fixing. This is sometimes the case with practice. We experience aspects of practice as unsatisfactory and take action to improve them. However, a thing does not have to be faulty to improve; it can be the best and still be able to improve. Olympic athletes who are the best in the world continue to practise in an effort to improve. Improvement can therefore be seen as an ongoing process of changing for the better over time. You need to decide the direction you wish your action research to take. Some people see improvement as improving things for themselves, at the expense of other people; others see improvement as working towards the best interests of others. This is a problematic issue. You can improve your practice as a thief (usually to your advantage and someone else's disadvantage) the same as you can improve your practice as a nurse (usually to someone else's advantage as well as your own).

> Jean worked with ten previously disenfranchised teachers in Khayelitsha, a township near Cape Town, to achieve their masters degrees through studying their own practices. She did not see her involvement as 'improving' people, rather as enabling people to improve themselves in ways that were right for them. In an e-mail after the successful completion of his masters programme, Sundays Blayi wrote to her: 'Thank you for helping us to get our masters degrees. We are now people among other people. We are so proud of you.' The comment, 'We are now people among other people' was significant for Jean; its significance is discussed at the end of the chapter.

The nature of processes of improvement

Improvement does not imply an end-point where everything will be perfect. This is an assumption of traditional research, which suggests that (1) there is an answer for everything; (2) the answer can be found; and (3) everyone will agree on the answer (see Berlin 1998). This is a linear and two-dimensional view of change. A generative transformational view of change, however, sees everything in process of coming into being, whereby any thing at any point of time holds its potentials already latent within itself, which can move in any direction as influenced by its context.

This is an amazing idea that involves appreciating that you have the capacity to influence the future through acting intentionally in the now. It also carries the responsibility of ensuring that we act well, to create the kind of future we wish to live in.

Tsepo Majake wrote to Jean:

> After much reflection and introspection, I learned that 'I CAN'. The most difficult periods in my life have taught me that I am not alone and that I can do things for myself. I however have also learned that without your support and that of other people, I would not have come to this realisation as early in my life as I have.
>
>   (personal correspondence, 6 January 2009)

You can read Tsepo's (2008) presentation at the American Educational Research Association at www.jeanmcniff.com/khayelitsha/tsepo_AERA_2008.htm.

The question of who improves what

You can improve an object by acting on it physically. You can alter a coat to fit you better or add more salt to your cooking to improve its taste. You can also act on people physically to improve them: you can cut someone's hair or wash their face.

However, it is not possible to 'improve' someone's learning, or education, because all people are born with the capacity for originality of mind, i.e. the capacity to think for themselves, and will therefore exercise this capacity in deciding whether or not they wish to be influenced by you. On this view, you cannot 'improve' someone, or 'educate' them, because people improve and educate themselves. Individuals take intentional action in, and improve, their own learning. Whereas we might learn all of the time unintentionally, as when we learn to get bored or not to touch a hot stove again, the kind of learning we use to take political or educational action is intentional and purposeful.

> On 12 July 2008, the ten teachers on the masters programme presented their work to their peers, as part of a celebratory end-of-programme conference. The presentations can be found on http://www.youtube.com/watch?v=Llhn5WZJ mr8&feature=channel_page. The teachers speak about their confidence in doing action research, and how they are aware of their capacities to influence their own and other people's thinking.

The nature of education

This idea of intentionally taking action in your own learning can be understood as education. The idea of education is central to action research, and does not necessarily have anything to do with the discipline of education or with the teaching profession. It refers to intentional processes of learning, which you can do in a bus queue as well as in a classroom. Education is not what one person does to another; it is what people do to themselves when they decide to take action to improve their own learning.

This view of education raises interesting questions about the purposes of education. Different people have different ideas about this depending on their values position. We authors agree with people such as Chomsky (2000), Dewey (1938) and A.N. Whitehead (1967) that the aim of education is not to get a job or produce people with employable skills, but to enable mental, spiritual and physical growth; the aim of education is more education. It is your decision whether to get a job or make yourself employable.

When you decide to take action in your own learning, you would probably ask questions of the kind 'How do I improve this . . .?', which brings us to the next significant feature of action research.

A special kind of research question, asked with educational intent

The special kind of research question that practitioner researchers ask begins with:

- 'How do I . . .?'

They continue with questions that have educational intent:

- . . . understand my practice better?
- . . . help you to learn?
- . . . contribute to the wider body of knowledge?

Action research questions can take a variety of forms, such as:

- I wonder what would happen if . . .?
- Is it possible to . . .?
- How about trying . . .?

Any question in action research communicates that you wish to improve your learning about something, that you are trying something out for the first time, and that you are holding ideas lightly and provisionally. You do not expect concrete answers or solutions: you are experimenting with life and creating something new. It is not about encouraging behavioural outcomes; you are exploring your capacity for learning, and your new improved learning will inform new, improved actions.

This raises issues of acting with educational intent. Doing action research signals your intent to intervene in and improve your learning in order to improve your practice, and accept responsibility for doing so. You are not responsible for others' learning, or what they do, or whether they will decide to improve themselves. The most you can do is to exercise your educational influence in their learning, so they can decide, from the grounds of their capacity for original and creative thinking, whether or not to accept what you say and act accordingly.

This idea has significance for how people in all professions and settings, regardless of status, can understand themselves as educators. Your job as a manager or engineer or zookeeper is to exercise your educational influence in your own and other people's learning. Any form of work, therefore, can be located within the broader field of education; and action research undertaken in any field or workplace can be understood as educational research.

> Robynn Ingle-Möller supports the learning of staff, animals and the public within a broad programme of educational enrichment at the National Zoological Gardens in Pretoria. She tells many stories of how she helps people and animals to develop their self-confidence in their chosen identities. In a particularly moving story, Sonnyboy Modumu (keeper of lions) explains how he conducted his action research into his own learning as he helped a young male lion regain his self-confidence and develop appropriate social behaviours when introduced into a group of three lionesses. You can read some of Robynn's work at http://www.youtube.com/watch?v=Gr_7D86AhkA.

Putting the 'I' at the centre of the research

You are the person at the centre of your own research. You use 'I' as the author of your report, and it takes the form of your personal research story. Your report is an explanatory account, not just a descriptive account, in which you give your reasons and purposes for your actions. It is written in the first person ('I/we did . . .'), not the third person ('the researcher did . . .'), which is appropriate for traditional research reports. You can also use a range of innovative forms of research reporting, including multimedia representations (see below and Chapter 10), which show, often better than through printed text, the actions involved in producing the evidence base of knowledge claims.

The emphasis on the living 'I' shows how you take responsibility for improving and sustaining yourself, and for trying to influence the development of the world you are in. 'I' therefore have the capacity to influence processes of social change, because 'I' can influence my own learning and the learning of others in my immediate context, who in turn can influence their own and the learning of others in wider contexts. The circles of influence are potentially infinite. One individual, working collaboratively with others, can generate worldwide change.

> Mzuzile Mpondwana (2008) explains how he has learned how to influence the learning of the people in his community, in the interests of developing more sustainable social orders.

Remember that action research is about both taking action and also doing research with social intent, so think about these specific issues:

How do 'I' fit into the action?

- I show how I understand my practice as the central focus of my research through critical reflection and study.
- I encourage others to participate in a negotiated living definition of shared practices.
- I show respect for other opinions and other ways of doing things.
- I show humility and make myself vulnerable.
- I am open to challenge.
- I am willing to accept that I may be wrong and may need to change my ideas and thinking.
- I own my mistakes.
- I stand my ground when my principles are at stake.
- I take responsibility for my actions and hold myself accountable for what I do.

How do 'I' fit into the research?

- I am the subject and object of the research: 'I' study my 'I'.
- I gather data and generate evidence in relation to identified criteria and standards of judgement.
- I explain how I test the validity of my claims to knowledge against an authenticated evidence base.
- I am able to explain the significance of my research for my own and others' learning.
- I understand how I can disseminate my findings so that others can critique my work, and also learn from what I have done.

How do I influence wider social contexts?

- I accept responsibility for investigating how to improve my work for my own and others' benefit.
- I encourage others to do the same.
- We engage in collaborative practices to create cultures of educational enquiry.
- We co-create, share and disseminate our ideas to inform the education of other social groupings.
- We create ourselves as groups of critically reflective scholars and practitioners who are committed to securing freedom and fairness for all.
- Our aim is to contribute to the education of social formations through educational enquiry.

A paper presented at the American Educational Research Association annual meeting by Gerrie Adams, available at www.jeanmcniff.com/khay-elitsha/gerrie_AERA_2008.htm, shows how he included the above principles in his work as deputy head teacher in a large school. Gerrie successfully completed his masters programme in January 2009.

Educational action that is informed, committed and intentional

A fourth significant feature is that the action of action research is not mundane action such as watching television. It is action that is informed, committed and intentional, with a view to generating knowledge of practice for personal and social well-being; these elements turn practice into praxis. Let's look further at (1) informed, purposeful action; (2) committed action; and (3) intentional action.

Informed, purposeful action

The action of action research is always informed and purposeful. The action begins with a felt need to do something, which transforms into intent, which in turn transforms into action. Deciding to take action usually means actively deciding to question your own motives, and treating your findings and interpretations critically, suspending your judgements, and being open to other people's points of view. You need to accept that other people may be better informed than you are. Winter and Munn-Giddings (2001: 212) explain the need for reflective critique. They say that when people 'do not understand' us, a frequent reaction is to say that their lack of understanding is their problem. However, if we want to learn, we need to ask, 'What is it that I do not understand about them that leads me to perceive them as "not understanding" something?' We need to question the view that we know all the answers. Although we might passionately commit to our values, we always need to recognise that we may be mistaken (Polanyi 1958), and still have much to learn. Finding the balance between conviction and open-mindedness can be difficult and involves personal honesty.

Committed action

Having made a decision to act, you then need to get on with it. Your action stems from a personal conviction that things could be better. You are not acting out of a desire to have things your own way, or manipulate others or to implement a certain policy. You are committed to your values and how you might live in their direction. This means you constantly evaluate what you are doing and check, through rigorous validation procedures, that you are doing what you say you are doing, and acting honestly and openly for the benefit of others.

Intentional action

Action research is intentional. When you identify your research issue and formulate your research question, you imply that you intend to do something about it. Husserl (1931) says that intent informs social action; once something is intentional in the mind, it triggers the actor's capacity to take action. Said (1997) says that intent contains its methodology within itself – an unfolding of new beginnings. This is the nature of action research, which is not about aiming for behavioural outcomes (a feature of traditional research) but about generating new, interesting questions that open up new possibilities. Each step of the way contains new possibilities, so action research becomes a process of exploring life potentials. We authors try to communicate these ideas in a variety of ways; one of the most enduring is the diagram shown in Figure 3.1, which aims to communicate the nature of generative transformational processes that are in a constant process of realising themselves.

These ideas are communicated in Jean's writings about her learning from her work in South Africa: see, for example, McNiff (2008b) and www.jean-mcniff.com/aera08/JM_AERA08_Paper_final.htm.

Methodological and socio-political issues

We now move to Part 2, which addresses methodological and socio-political issues and contains ideas about the following:

- systematic monitoring of practice to generate data;
- describing the action: gathering data;
- generating evidence to explain the data and make knowledge claims;
- testing the validity of knowledge claims;
- communicating the significance of knowledge claims;
- making your action research public and disseminating the findings.

Figure 3.1 Representation of generative transformational processes.

Systematic monitoring of practice to generate data

Lawrence Stenhouse (1983) said that research is systematic enquiry made public. This definition can be modified for action research to say, 'Action research is systematic enquiry made public with educational intent.'

An action research project begins when you identify an issue and formulate a research question about that issue, such as, 'How do I encourage participative working in my organisation?' You move towards a point where you can claim that you have addressed the question, which could now take the form, 'I have encouraged participative working in my organisation.' You bridge the gap between question and claim by monitoring practice in the form of keeping records of what you do, and gather data about what you are doing, using a range of research gathering techniques (Figure 3.2).

Data refer to the information you gather about your research as you proceed with your project. The best data, and the data you will probably keep, refer directly to your research question, and show its transformation into action so that the question becomes a claim. 'How do I encourage participative working?' becomes 'I have encouraged participative working', and the

Figure 3.2 Bridging the gap between research question and knowledge claim.

data show the processes involved. The question, claim and data to do with improving participative working would be about people working participatively (or not, as the case may be). Any data that show things contrary to what you expected to see (perhaps people working in a non-participative way) would be disconfirming data. You would probably discard these data, though not before you had taken appropriate action, as suggested by the data, to try to turn things around so that the situation was more in line with what you wished it would be.

To gather appropriate data, you have to monitor what you are doing. It is wise to do so systematically, because you can then pinpoint those episodes when you develop new insights about your practice. Aim to keep systematic records, such as research diaries, so that you can make explicit when key learnings developed and you modified your actions. Also aim to keep your data and records in a data archive, such as a box or in one place on your computer. Although you should focus on those data that show your systematic engagement with your research issue, do not be in too much of a hurry to discard what appears initially as irrelevant, as many important insights develop over time and what you think is irrelevant today may become highly relevant tomorrow.

> Jean's archive of her work in South Africa contains her reflective diary; teachers' and other colleagues' e-mails, as they reflected on their learning; her e-mails back to them as she reflected on hers; evaluative comments from colleagues in other institutions who acted as observers in the project; videotape recordings of practices that constitute a visual narrative, for example when the teachers presented their work for accreditation, or at the end-of-programme conference; digital photos of significant episodes throughout the project . . . and so on. She is now collating her data, prior to writing up the project in a variety of forms.

Describing the action: gathering data

Be clear about the differences between descriptions and explanations. Descriptions refer to activities – what you have done: for example, 'I woke up, had breakfast, and left the house.' Often people write descriptive stories about what they have done for their professional portfolios, thinking that descriptions are sufficient: for example, 'I took my qualifying examinations, joined my present institution and began to encourage participative working.' However, although descriptive accounts are invaluable for helping others to see and learn from what you have done, they are not explanatory accounts, which is what you need to produce if your work is to be seen as research based or as a research report. Remember that research is about generating new knowledge and offering explanations for what you have done (theorising). Explanations are about the processes of making sense of what has happened, when you reflect on the reported action and give reasons for how and why it is happening. Think about what sports commentators or news reporters do. First they describe what is happening (the actions) and then they offer their analyses and interpretations of the actions (their explanations). Part of the explanations is about the reasons for the actions and their significance. The reasons and significance are often given in terms of values: 'The research report shows the realisation of the values of democracy through the demonstration of participative working: this has significance for new thinking about how to manage organisational development.'

> Teachers on the masters programme comment extensively on the analyses and explanations they give for their work. They speak openly about how they felt about one another at the beginning of their work together, and about Jean, who also speaks about how she felt about them. Participants and Jean explain how they have deconstructed their thinking to see 'the other' as 'you who are part of my life': see McNiff (in preparation).

Nevertheless, most reports do contain descriptions of action, and these can take any of the different forms that follow.

Factual accounts

Most descriptions of action are factual accounts. They are often based on transcripts of conversations and meetings, or summaries of data from interviews and questionnaires. Often statistical summaries are included to show the number and quality of events and phenomena, such as interactions between people at meetings, or individual opinions, or preferences and trends. Contrary to some opinions, statistical data can be important elements in action research accounts (see pp. 159–160 for examples).

> Sundays Blayi (Blayi 2008) gives a comprehensive account of how he helped students to become more respectful of property and the physical environment of their school. His reports contain statistical analyses, as well as photographic evidence, to show the situation before and during his involvement.

Multimedia approaches

Multimedia technologies such as video and audiotape recordings are important ways of gathering factual data, as the examples in this book testify. Developments in the use of multimedia technologies are setting new precedents, because visual narratives can often communicate the actions involved in the action research better than words on a page. Often it is impossible to capture the full significance of actions and events through purely verbal reports. For example, the idea that 'Mary was enthusiastic' might be communicated more effectively by showing a video-clip than the bare presentation of words. The websites www.actionresearch.net and www.jeanmcniff.com

are powerful resources to show these ideas in practice, and will also put you in touch with other websites around the world.

Subjective accounts

Descriptions may be based on subjective accounts taken from diaries, personal reflections and observations. These are subjective only in that they represent one person's viewpoint about the extent to which the practitioner–researcher has realised their values in their practices. During the course of the research, the validity of these subjective accounts will be tested against the critical feedback both of the researcher, as they reflect on the robustness of what they have done, and also of critical friends and validation groups, who examine the quality of the data and evidence recorded in the reports. In this way, subjectivity becomes objectified. There is nothing wrong with subjectivity, provided subjective claims can be shown as having been subjected to critical feedback, and their validity demonstrated as justified so that subjectivity does not sink into prejudice (see Explaining the action: generating evidence from the data and making knowledge claims, below).

> In the presentations at the end-of-programme conference, teachers explain how they learned to interrogate their assumptions and test the validity of their claims against the critical feedback of peers and students. Jean also learned to check her interpretations against colleagues' feedback. A favourite saying among the group was 'Jean, you do not understand', which was usually the case. An explanation always followed.

Fictionalised accounts

Many action researchers use fictionalised accounts when it is important to preserve the anonymity of participants, such as in projects that look at staff development or appraisal, or management meetings when the identities of people should be protected. Some researchers have written stories that enable them to open up to public discussion events that would be too confidential to report. These fictionalised accounts may be written so that the context is changed or the characters are given identities that mask their real identity (see Dadds and Hart, 2001, for accounts that adopt this approach). Presenting your work as fiction can often strengthen it in ways that cannot be communicated in more factual accounts. Stories are increasingly recognised as communicating the processes of research. For further ideas, have a look at narrative inquiry (Clandinin and Connelly 2004; Clandinin 2007).

Jean frequently uses story to communicate her learning from the experiences of South Africa and other places: see especially www.jeanmcniff.com/cagedbird.htm and www.jeanmcniff.com/Living%20with%20foxes%20paper.htm, where she speaks about the need to deconstruct outmoded disabling thinking and develop new life-affirming values and attitudes.

Generating evidence to explain the data and make knowledge claims

Having described the action, you now need to go on and explain it. This involves:

- sorting the data and looking for possible meanings, and linking with other work;
- making the descriptions problematic;
- theorising.

Sorting the data and looking for possible meanings, and linking with other work

Although action research can (but need not) include testing hypotheses and applying other people's theories and models to your work, aim also to read the literature and incorporate relevant insights into your explanations and analyses. If you are on an award-bearing course, you will be expected to engage critically with the literature. You should explain why you agree or disagree with other people's theories and do or do not use them in your work, and why you are developing theories of your own and why these are appropriate for you.

Making the descriptions problematic

Taking a critical stance towards your action and its outcomes is essential in offering an explanation, especially in action research, where, as noted, 'subjectivity' can be both an advantage and a limitation. It can be an advantage because you have an insider's knowledge of events. It can be a limitation because you may come to biased conclusions about what you are doing. Aim to be systematic in questioning your motives for action and your evaluation of its outcomes. To get a reasonably unprejudiced view aim to involve other people who will act as critical friends to critique your interpretations, as well as a formal validation group to test the validity of your findings, which you hope to communicate as knowledge claims.

> Jean asked many people to help her reflect on critical incidents. She did not initially appreciate the significance of developing a masters programme in Khayelitsha. Karin Hendricks, the Deputy CEO at False Bay College in Cape Town, explained to her in many informal meetings: 'Pre-1994, black people and people of mixed heritage were given an inferior education. By gaining academic accreditation, they now have legitimacy in their own eyes, and in the eyes of others.'

Theorising

Offering explanations is the ground for creating your own theory of practice, i.e. what you do as a human being who sees their work as contributing to social well-being. Your theory of practice is not static; it is living, part of your life. It is your own living theory of practice (Whitehead 1989, 1993). Your living theory of practice is your explanation of why you are doing things the way you are. You are making your practice problematic by questioning taken-for-granted assumptions (your own and others'), and by questioning whether you are living your values in your practice. You are stating your reasons for action in terms of your values, and showing how you can justify your action in terms of what you believe is a right way of living. You can then go on to show the potential significance of your living theory for wider social and political debates. Your living theory is created from within your work and represents your present best thinking. It is always developing because you are always in process of development. If your living theory shows how your work can be understood as educational, you can claim that you are creating your own living educational theory.

Testing the validity of knowledge claims

We have said throughout that research is about making knowledge claims and testing their validity, so validation processes are key aspects of doing all kinds of research. However, differences exist between traditional scholarship forms of validation and new scholarship forms, such as action research. In traditional scholarship, it is supposed that validity can be established objectively through formal procedures (Popper 1963, 1972), using a propositional form of logic (thinking) that sees things mostly in terms of causal relationships ('If I do x, y will happen'). This kind of formal logic is inadequate for action research, because action research emphasises the importance of the person's own interpretations and negotiation of events, which requires a form of thinking that sees all things in relation and accepts elements that often appear as contradictory. However, the relational kinds of logics of action research can, and should, incorporate formal logics, such as when a researcher includes the ideas of formal thinkers in their own developing and shifting thinking.

Validity in action research therefore involves several processes, which also involve other people in different ways, and works at the levels of:

- *personal validation*, to do with testing the validity of the knowledge claim against one's own espoused values;
- *social validation*, to do with testing the validity of the claims against the critical feedback of others;
- *public legitimation*, which is an ongoing aspect of social validation.

These ideas are developed further in Chapter 11.

In traditional research, the knowledge in question is knowledge about the external world. In action research the knowledge in question is knowledge of practice; knowledge claims are to do with how you have taken action to improve your practice. The validity (truthfulness) of the knowledge claim therefore has to be tested against the evidence of improved practice, in relation to identified criteria and standards of judgement.

Processes of validation therefore involve:

- making claims;
- identifying criteria and standards of judgement;
- critically examining the claims against an authenticated evidence base;
- involving others in validation processes.

Communicating the significance of knowledge claims

Making a claim to knowledge means saying that something is known now that was not known before. Action researchers make claims about new improved knowledge of practice because action research is about improving practice and coming to know about the processes involved. They make claims about what they have come to know through studying their practice. It is vital to make claims about the research (what you have come to know), and not only about the action (what you have done). Placing the action within a research framework adds a dimension of credibility that makes the claim different from what it would have been had the claim been regarded simply as the outcome of good professional practice. You can say things such as:

- I have improved my management capacity, and I have evidence to show what I have done and how and why I have done it.
- I have encouraged people to do things differently in ways that can be shown to be more life affirming than before.

Validation processes help action researchers to test the validity of their claims that they have improved their practice and that they understand better what they are doing and why they are doing it, such as enabling people to become more reflective about their work, or contributing to organisational learning and development (see, for example, Bosher 2001 and Delong 2002). Some action researchers explain how they are influencing organisational change in ways that represent organisational improvement, such as implementing a new policy successfully or for more participation in decision making.

Patrick Barnes (2008) explains how he is enabling organisational change through renegotiating the form of staff meetings, at which he invites colleagues to comment on his practices as deputy head teacher. Alice Nongwane (2008) explains how she is enabling parents to take a more active part in the school life of their children. Nqabisa Gungqisa (2008) explains how she has enabled her learners to develop greater self-discipline, and how she has developed a schools-based action research professional education programme for colleagues to help them learn how to develop their practices.

Identifying criteria and standards of judgement

In any process of making judgements, you identify certain criteria (what you expect to see) and standards by which you will arrive at those judgements (how well the criteria are realised in action). For example, you would expect a hotel to be warm and clean; your criteria for a hotel would therefore be warmth and cleanliness. You make judgements about the quality of the hotel in terms of how warm and clean the hotel is, i.e. how fully the criteria are realised in practice. The same principle applies in action research. You say, 'I aim to show how I realise my values (of fairness or participation) in my practice. My values become my criteria for good practice.' You judge the quality of your practice in terms of how fully you realise those values: you say, 'I think my practice is good because I can show how I have realised my values (of fairness or participation).' You can also say, 'I can claim that I have improved my practice because I can show that I am realising my values more fully now than before', and you produce evidence to show the situation as it was then and as it is now. This means that you have to produce an authenticated evidence base to show the development of action and understanding over time, as we now explain. The processes outlined so far are part of your personal validation procedures.

Critically examining the claims against an authenticated evidence base

To create an authenticated evidence base you would monitor your practice on a regular basis, such as recording personal reflections in a journal or keeping minutes of meetings. You now move into public validation procedures by subjecting this evidence base to the critical scrutiny of others in a validation meeting. In these meetings, people look at your evidence and consider the claims you are making in light of your evidence, and in relation to your identified criteria and standards of judgement. Validation meetings should never take the form of cosy chats during which everyone aims to reach agreement, although people should always be supportive; they aim rather to encourage researchers to think about their work critically, and find ways of improving it where necessary. Validation meetings therefore enable researchers to:

• test the robustness of arguments with a critical audience who will challenge any lack of clarity, and help identify weaknesses and suggest modifications;

- consider data and the way it is analysed, interpreted and presented;
- sharpen claims to knowledge and make sure the evidence supports them;
- see possible new directions for the research;
- draw on others' support and solidarity.

Always regard validation meetings as working meetings that you can learn from. Do not be defensive, but use the experience to move your thinking forward.

Especially watch out for the following:

- Make sure you are clear about the need for explanations as well as descriptions. Say what you did, why you did it, what you hoped to achieve, and what you have learned from the process.
- Aim to generate evidence from the data, and do not confuse the two. Show how you summarise the data and can show its relationship to your research question and identified criteria.
- Make sure you record the validation meeting, so it becomes an integral part of your data gathering and overall research processes.

Involving others in validation processes

Other people are therefore involved in helping you validate your claims to knowledge throughout the process of the research. These people can be:

- *observers*, who maintain a level of interest in what you are doing, but are not necessarily involved in the research process itself;
- *critical friends*, who listen to your ideas as you go and offer critical feedback;
- *members of validation groups*, who engage in more formal procedures of scrutinising your evidence and offering critical feedback on the research process overall.

The way these people operate is discussed more fully in Chapter 4, but here it is important to note that all people should:

- know the context of your work, and be able to empathise with your context;
- come from both inside and outside the context, to complement their different views as insiders and outsiders;
- be familiar with the values, logics and methodologies of action research, although not necessarily with the situation in which it is being undertaken.

External validators for the Khayelitsha project included Karin Hendricks, whose organisation provided the venue and logistical support for the programme, and members from the Nelson Mandela Metropolitan University (NMMU), who observed the teachers' presentations of work and offered critical feedback to help the teachers develop their thinking. Professor Lesley Wood from NMMU wrote the following report after she had observed the teachers presenting their work:

> *Practice*: Students on the whole demonstrated a good understanding of their practices and definitely have grown in terms of their self-perceptions as agents of change – they are more proactive and self-directed than before. They do understand the need to be self-critical and demonstrate evidence of this. Many gave examples of how they have influenced learners and the wider school environment. They certainly seem to appreciate the input from Professor McNiff and it is evident that they have learnt a lot from her. They can all articulate their ontological and epistemological values and can critically reflect on whether they are living them out or not. They demonstrate understanding of the systemic nature of the school environment and of the importance of acting in collaboration with others to improve the social good.
>
> *Research*: Although all students appeared to understand the process of action research and the theoretical foundation it is grounded in during oral conversations, few were able to demonstrate this in their presentation. Only one or two students referred to theory to explain their interventions and values. Many failed to present a clear evidence base. There was also a lack of contextual grounding of values – what does it mean to live out the value of commitment, for example in their specific context? There was also little explanation of their values as living standards of judgement, and, although they mentioned critical friends, they did not really show how they validated their claims. This may be covered in the assignments but was not clear from presentations.
>
> *Presentation*: The students are to be commended on their presentations, as most were clear and well communicated. Use of PowerPoint was well done, with a few exceptions who tended to go overboard. Students were confident and were both supportive, yet critical of each other's work.

The discussion about establishing validity continues in Chapter 11.

You now move into the wider aspects of establishing validity by showing how validation turns into legitimation, as follows.

Making your action research public and disseminating your findings

Making public means sharing ideas and findings with other people, particularly colleagues in your work context, and checking with them whether your findings are reasonably fair and accurate. Do not leave going public until the end of the project. Aim to go public throughout the process of the research to keep checking the validity of your accounts and help to keep your enquiry moving forward.

Making research public involves processes of validation, as noted above, and also moves the discourses from validation (establishing the truthfulness of the claim) to legitimation (establishing the acceptability of the claim in the public sphere: see Explaining the significance of what you have done, below).

Making research public is the first step in getting it validated. You can learn a great deal from listening to questions from people outside the research. These questions may help you strengthen your convictions about the claims you have made and find better evidence to convince others about them, or, as is more often the case, they may lead you to modify your claims because you are able to identify gaps in your arguments that you had not seen before. 'Going public' can be an exciting aspect of action research, because other people would share similar concerns to yours, and express their support and enthusiasm. Support can be important in research processes.

> Before the end-of-programme celebratory conference, the teachers were nervous. Most had never presented in public before. They had practised speaking in public when presenting their work for assignments, which had boosted their confidence and their capacity for articulating their ideas, but these presentations had been to their peer group, not a group of strangers, some of whom were from higher education. A great deal of effort went into the preparation for the conference, and members of the group worked together to plan and refine their papers. This work went on without Jean, who had returned to the UK, although she responded to drafts of the papers, as was her usual practice. On the day of the conference, despite their nervousness, the teachers presented their work well and were congratulated by colleagues who had attended the conference. You can see the visual record at http://www.youtube.com/watch?v=FNIK7BUHyFo. The teachers acknowledged that the experience of planning for the conference and delivering their paper gave them a new confidence in themselves and their work, and a considerable sense of pride that they had achieved something really significant.

Making research public also has its difficulties. You need to consider important ethical issues if you intend to publish information that involves others. It is particularly important to ensure confidentiality and anonymity in action research when and if required, although you should take every opportunity to celebrate other people's involvement if they wish (see Chapter 5). It is also particularly difficult because action research by definition is about yourself, and therefore others can identify themselves and one another through you. Being completely open about the research from the beginning can pre-empt many of the problematic issues that can arise when people are secretive about what they are doing. Sometimes researchers have found themselves unable to report some of their work because it involves colleagues who had no idea they were included and rightly refused permission for the research to go ahead when they found out.

> All of the examples in this book are in the public domain, or publication has been negotiated with their originators. All confidentiality has been respected and safeguarded.

Making public also involves finding appropriate ways of communicating your research, and this can involve different forms of technology, which we present here as:

- conventional print technologies;
- digital technologies.

Conventional print technologies

Conventional print technologies use forms of representation that involve mainly writing. The most common forms of writing are as follows.

Self-reflective writing

Self-reflection may be understood as a conversation with oneself. This often appears as diaries and logs. Diaries may be kept as records of events, and of reflections on those events and consequent learning. On p. 156 we offer advice about how to write and organise a self-reflective diary.

Using conversation and dialogue

We all have conversations all the time. Conversations take place in face-to-face encounters, and with people who are distant in space and time. We have conversations with people who write books and articles, create the buildings we live in, and appear on TV. These conversations are one-sided, not dialogical; we respond to people, but we get no response in return. Dialogical conversations are those in which all participants respond to one another in ways that will enable the conversation to continue. This form of dialogue can help in creating your own living theory of practice.

> Zola Malgas explains in a videotape at the end-of-programme conference how the group has learned with and from one another (see http://www.youtube.com/watch?v=G2HzXNwsm01). She emphasises that at the beginning of the programme that all participants were 'fed up and ready to quit'. Now they have organised themselves into an educational task force with a mission to contribute to the learning of other educators.

Using narrative and story

Stories are a valuable way of representing action research. Action research stories tend to resist closure. They tell the processes of coming-to-know, and share people's thinking, and they are generative, because they show the potential for further development. Stories may be presented both as formative progress reports (work in progress, theories in development) and also as summative reports, dissertations and theses (reports of current thinking, theories in action). When you present your progress report, whether orally or in writing, your data should be available to show how your personal development is always in relation to what other participants in the research are thinking and doing. Your final report will probably appear in written form, but should include the 'live' evidence of your interactions and conversations with other people, to show how you exercised your educational influence in their lives. This live evidence may appear in non-written form, such as in CD-ROMs and interactive texts, and these would be included as part of the written text and as appendices or archived materials.

Digital technologies

Throughout this chapter and the book we have referred to multimedia technologies. These can be web based as well as used in local settings. Multimedia representations can be particularly powerful for showing the living nature of an evidence base and, by disseminating them through public spaces such as YouTube, it is possible to establish the validity of knowledge claims in a rigorous way.

The Khayelitsha project is now being written up in a range of formats: in books and papers and on the World Wide Web. You can see further exemplars of web-based dissemination at www.actionresearch.net.

Explaining the significance of what you have done

Offering explanations for what you have done and why you have done it involves analysing its significance and showing how it can contribute to new thinking and practice at wider levels. This brings us to discourses about legitimacy, and how validity acts as a necessary first step in the process.

First, it is useful to clarify the differences between validity and legitimacy (see also p. 190).

Validity is to do with establishing the truth of knowledge claims, and explaining what this involves. The truth of a knowledge claim such as 'It is raining' can be tested and established by looking for concrete evidence – in this case, seeing whether it really is raining. Some knowledge claims take a form where the truth is not so easily established, such as 'I have toothache'. The fact that you cannot produce concrete evidence for these kinds of knowledge claim, however, does not invalidate them; it means you have to find different ways of showing their validity, perhaps producing secondary evidence such as a dentist's appointment card. Generally, however, you are expected to produce authenticated evidence to back up knowledge claims if you wish to claim validity for them.

Legitimacy refers to getting your knowledge claim accepted in the public sphere. This involves persuading people to accept what you say, and to authorise you to say it. Sometimes people run up against established ways of knowing and thinking, and so the establishment rejects their knowledge claims, even although these have been demonstrated as valid. Many examples exist to show these processes in action. James Lovelock (2009) and others involved in environmental lobbies have been speaking for years about the need for planetary care, informed by their research findings. They have not generally been listened to until quite recently. Throughout history, critical voices, speaking from the authority of their own experience, have cautioned against certain moves such as going to war or ignoring the need for diplomacy; but they are listened to only when it suits those in power to do so. Accepting critical voices and granting legitimacy to knowledge claims has nothing to do with truth telling and everything to do with power and politics.

Establishing validity therefore has to be seen as a first step in achieving legitimacy. You have to show that your knowledge claims are to be believed if you wish your work to be accepted in the public domain, and, as an action researcher, this means showing that you (1) have improved action in your contexts; (2) have undertaken quality research that justifies your claim that you have done so; and (3) are able to explain the significance of what you have done. This can be seen in how you are contributing to new learning that will inform new practices. The learning in question is the learning of yourself, of others, and of social formations, such as your professional community.

> The comment 'We are now people among other people' enabled Jean to appreciate the significance of her involvement in Khayelitsha, and to begin to develop new understandings of how validity has to be a prerequisite of legitimacy, an idea that permeates this book.

Summary

This chapter has set out the main features of action research processes. These are grounded in issues to do with ontology, epistemology, methodology and social intent. The advice offered in the chapter is supported by evidence that was drawn from data about work in South Africa.

Checklist of reflective questions

- Can you use the terms 'ontology', 'epistemology', 'methodology' and 'social intent' in speech and writing? Can you explain to other people what they mean, and show their meanings in your practices?
- Are you clear about the main features of action research? Can you explain what they are?

- Can you offer your accounts to show how you are realising these features in your action research?
- Can you ground your explanations in your values? Can you say what your values are? Are you clear about how your values inform your practices, and come to act as your criteria and standards of judgement?

If you can do all these things, your report should show your understanding of the main features of action research in action.

We now turn to Part II, which deals with planning your action research project.

Part II
Planning your project

Before you begin your project, think about how you are going to approach it, and why you need to approach it in certain ways. Your question transforms from 'What do I need to know?' to 'Why do I need to know it?' Your enquiry therefore becomes a feasibility study. You need to assess realistically where you are, what you hope to achieve, and how you think you might do so. This is a vital reconnaissance phase that will enable you to consider how you will involve other people in your project and what you need to know about working with them to ensure success.

The next two chapters address these issues.

Chapter 4 discusses how and why you need to develop your understanding of working in organisational contexts.

Chapter 5 deals with issues of ethics and influence, and raises questions about why these aspects are central to doing good-quality action research.

Chapter 4

Working with others in organisational and institutional settings

We said in the Introduction that there is an increased focus internationally on workplace learning, which is how action research is often positioned. There is also an increased focus internationally on practitioners studying their own practice, as demonstrated in the literatures of many agencies that support workplace and lifelong learning. The Teaching and Development Agency for Schools (TDA), for example, sets this as a core standard for judging the quality of the professional practice of teachers (TDA 2009).

This is all good news. However, the fact remains that action research projects are usually conducted in institutional or organisational settings, and this can be difficult, because working with people is more often than not problematic. The main way to manage difficulties, of course, is to avoid them; but sometimes this is not possible, and you have to deal with them in strategic ways to ensure that your professional contexts remain healthy and life affirming for all.

This chapter gives advice about working with people in organisational and institutional settings, so that appropriate relationships can be nurtured and maintained in order to ensure that your project remains sustainable and you can achieve your educational goals.

The chapter is organised into three parts:

- *Working with people at an interpersonal level*: basic principles of working successfully with others.
- *Working with people in organisational and institutional settings*: advice about what you can do to ensure that your project has a reasonably good chance of success.
- *Possible implications*: what you may decide about conducting your project.

Before you begin, be aware that certain basic principles relate to working with people at an interpersonal level and to working with people in formal settings. These are:

- *Be optimistic and be realistic.* You are probably doing your research because you believe it is possible to do something useful. Your sense of what is possible can be obstructed, however, by the realities of what is not possible. You may feel it is possible to influence a situation, but you may find that constraints prevent you from doing this. The constraints can be in the form of people and their interests, and also in the established structures and processes of organisational life. Have faith that you can overcome the constraints and realise the possible from within the seemingly impossible (see Joan Whitehead 2003 for an idea of making the possible probable.
- *Be sensitive to the situation and be strategic.* You need to develop a sense of what people are feeling, and how well your work is accepted within the organisation. Unless you are sensitive to your contexts, you are probably not going to get very far. Develop strategies that will help you deal with whatever situation arises. This means building up a repertoire of coping skills and strategies, and using them.
- *Be flexible and stay focused.* Aim to adapt to circumstances as they arise, both in terms of people's needs and wishes, and also of situational changes. If you cannot adapt to changing circumstances, you will probably go under. At the same time, stay focused on what you want, and find new directions if your initial plans are not successful. This idea is built into the methodologies of action research.
- *Have faith in yourself and others.* This is probably the best understanding anyone can develop. People do not need fixing; nor do you. People, including you, know what they are doing, and have extraordinary capacities and internal resources to enable them to grow and flourish. Have faith that people will deliver on their potentials; this includes you. Try to let things develop as they do. Good management often means managing to stay out of the way and let things evolve.

Many examples in this book show these processes in action, especially the following.

Je Kan Adler-Collins's (2007) PhD thesis explains how he designed and implemented a curriculum of the healing nurse at Fukuoka University in Japan. Je Kan shows great intercultural awareness in the development of his living theory as he asks, researches and answers his question, 'How do I clarify, live and explain my educational influences in my learning as I pedagogise my healing nurse curriculum in a Japanese University?' You can access Je Kan's thesis at www.actionresearch.net/jekan.shtml.

Jocelyn Jones's (2008) PhD thesis focused on 'Thinking with stories of suffering: towards a living theory of response-ability'. Jocelyn demonstrates

how thinking with stories of suffering in relation to child abuse and relationships between prisoners of war from different nations at war can be
expressed with values that carry hope for the future of humanity. You can
access Jocelyn's thesis at www.actionresearch.net/jocelynjonesphd.shtml

Eden Charles's (2007) PhD thesis explores the implications of the question
'How can I bring Ubuntu as a living standard of judgement into the Academy? Moving beyond decolonisation through societal reidentification and
guiltless recognition'. Eden offers a strategic approach to living the values
of Ubuntu in social contexts of intercultural tensions and violence. You can
access Eden's thesis at www.actionresearch.net/edenphd.shtml.

Working with people at an interpersonal level

This section sets out the main principles of working with others, and identifies (1) the main groups of people you are likely to work with, and (2) ways
of working, including the kinds of attitudes and behaviours you should
develop to keep them on your side.

Groups of people

The main groups of people you are likely to work with are as follows.

Research participants

These are often your colleagues, students or customers. Your research cannot
happen without your participants, so never abuse their goodwill. You are
researching your practice, and finding ways of improving yourself for the
benefit of yourself and your participants. You are the main source of data for
your project, because you are investigating your own work. You will ground
your claims to personal improvement in terms of how you have influenced
others in an educational way, so they also become sources of data. Pay close
attention to all matters of access and confidentiality. Keep your participants
informed about how your research is going. Invite their feedback, and let
them know it is valued. Thank them frequently; affirmation goes further
than any other incentive. You cannot afford not to let your participants know
they are valued.

Your critical friend(s) (or another term such as 'critical colleague')

These are also often drawn from the people you are working with, or they
may be external to your situation. Your critical friends should be willing
to discuss your work sympathetically but critically. You and your critical
friends choose each other, so you should negotiate the ground rules of your
relationship. They may turn out to be your closest allies, so never take them
for granted. As well as expecting support from your friends, you must also

be prepared to support them in return. This means being available, even in out-of-work hours, offering as well as receiving advice, even if it is painful or unwelcome, and always aiming to praise and support.

Your tutor (or adviser, mentor or supervisor, depending on whether you are on a formal course or in a workplace situation)

You may have more than one tutor. They are on your side, but their job is to challenge you to interrogate and extend your thinking (and, hopefully, theirs) by developing the capacity for reflexive and dialectical critique (Winter 1989). You probably know more about your subject area than they do, and they know more about research procedures than you, so listen carefully to their advice and act on it. Expect to receive critical feedback as well as praise. If you disagree with your supervisor, stand your ground and argue your case. You are expected to exercise your originality of mind and critical judgement, so go ahead and do so, but be prepared to change your mind in the light of better knowledge. Don't be defensive; the aim is not to score points but to improve practice and advance knowledge, mainly your own in this relationship, so keep the atmosphere friendly, businesslike and positive. If things go wrong, don't immediately blame your tutor. Assess the situation sensibly and, if it really was your fault, be open about it, look upon it as valuable learning, and start again.

Your fellow action researchers

If you are on a formal course or a professional development programme, you will be one of a group of action researchers. These people are key resources for sharing information on progress and insights, offering feedback, and providing support and challenge. Aim to work collaboratively rather than competitively. You all want to do well. Aim to build an atmosphere of trust and collegiality. This is essential in action research, which is informed by a collaborative ethic.

Your validation group

This group is made up of colleagues, participants, principals and managers, students, and other sympathetic people who you feel would be able to comment fairly but critically on your research. Look on them as you would someone who is assessing you. They want you to succeed, but they will not accept careless or uncritical research. You do not expect them to be hostile, but you also do not expect them instantly to agree with you. They expect you to justify any claims you make, so do not react negatively to criticism or challenge. It is their job to ensure that your research is valid, authentic and supported by reasonable evidence, and it is your job to learn from the experience and make sure that your work comes up to standard. You can find a good example of these kinds of procedures in the story of Martin Forrest (1983) (Chapter 11).

Developing ways of working, including appropriate attitudes and behaviours

Participants are key resources, and you need to relate to them well. Good interpersonal skills are fundamental to good relationships. Carry out some kind of audit on your own capacity in interpersonal skills. What are your strengths? Do any areas need improvement? In particular, aim to develop the following skills.

Listening

Aim to listen more than you talk. If you are not sure how good you are at listening, make a videotape of yourself in conversation, and count the number of times you speak and others speak. Watch the videotape first by yourself. You may want to share it later with someone such as your critical friend. Aim to say 'you' more often than 'I'. Above all, watch the use of 'no', which can be a powerful deterrent to conversation. Watch your body language. Being a good listener is far more important, in any walk of life, including research, than being a good talker.

Managing

Managing means managing yourself, not others. Aim to do whatever is required of you to achieve your goals: arrange meetings, carry out assignments, connect with other people. Make sure you attend all meetings and honour deadlines. Be punctual. Be aware of organisational procedures, and other people's sensitivities. Maintain a professional and business-like attitude throughout.

Collaborating

Action research demands that you work with others. You are doing your research into your practice, but your practice is about how you are with others, and is carried out in company with others. You need to be intellectually independent, but not an isolationist. Action research is always undertaken in social situations, with specific intent; your aim therefore is to help you understand your relationships with others as you try to influence them with educational intent. This does not mean trying to take over their minds. They have a right to their independence and space, as you do to yours. You may want to influence them in ways that you consider educational, but you must be respectful of their opinions and their capacity to think for themselves, even although it may be contrary to yours. You may aim to challenge but not destroy, and they have the same responsibility to you. This is a pluralist society that respects others' opinions and their freedom to think as they do. Aim to be comfortable with diversity and handle conflict in ways that enable the conversation to continue.

Intrapersonal ways of working

Your most precious resource is you. Personal relaxation and concentration are essential to high performance and personal fulfilment. Develop a positive attitude. Say to yourself 'I can' rather than 'I can't'. Keep negative experiences in perspective. It is not the end of the world if something goes wrong – more an opportunity to learn and create better futures. Doing research enables you to re-enter the world of learning, a world that many adults forget. Life is a process of constant learning, being in touch with what might be possible and daring to find ways to do it. Professionals often feel anxious that they may not know the correct answers. No one can know everything, and it is exciting to explore this amazing world of ideas.

Inclusional ways of working

Including means including everyone, not excluding anyone. People are different, hold different values and come from different backgrounds. They think in different ways (Belenky *et al.* 1986) and also learn in different ways (Gardner 1983). You need to use this understanding to make sense of your life with others. The people you are working with may see things differently from you. How do you ensure that all people, regardless of how they are socially positioned in terms of their ethnicity, colour, age, physical and intellectual capacity, sexual orientation or other 'differences', are treated respectfully and fairly? Will you include men as well as women, give as much weight to the voices of adults as of children? Will you report other people's opinions as well as your own? How will you check that you are acting fairly and respectfully throughout? These are difficult issues, but central to ensuring that other people see your research as meeting the demands of social justice. If you can show that you have addressed these issues, you can claim that you are living out the stated goals of your research. Throughout your research, aim to communicate the idea that you have interrogated and deconstructed your own thinking, and shifted your position from centre (Ngugi 1993) to allow others to become their own centres, with you perhaps on their periphery.

Style of language

When you present your oral or written accounts, try to develop an inclusional style of language in speaking and writing that has a clear sense of audience. People come to know in many ways, including through what they read or hear. If you want people to understand your ideas, you must express them clearly and unambiguously. Avoid language that is biased towards any group, such as academics or females. You can expect your audience to be educated and reasonably familiar with discourses of educational research, but you should avoid densely packed ideas and jargon (when you use a specialist term that you understand but other people might not). Aim to lead your audience easily and without fuss. Do not make great conceptual leaps, or use unnecessarily 'big' words: 'use' is as good as 'utilise'. Do not talk down to your audience or avoid using a professional tone. Regard your audience as an educated person you are partnering, and walk with them through your work, always checking that they are where you hope they should be. It is your responsibility to explain clearly, not theirs to try to work out what is in your mind.

Here is an example from the abstract of Karen Riding's (2008) PhD thesis 'How do I come to understand my shared living educational standards of judgement in the life I lead with others? Creating the space for intergenerational student-led research'.

> In this account I explain how the shared life that I lead with my husband Simon transforms itself into a loving energy that emerges in our educational practice. This loving way of being emerges as the energy that drives me to transform the social formation of the school to work alongside student researchers in an intergenerational and sustainable way.
>
> These living and loving standards of judgement are shared between us, asking the other to be the best that s/he can be and valuing the contribution that s/he makes. I live out an inclusional way of being that extends across the professional and personal domain, asking me to be responsive to the others with whom I share this life.
>
> This account attempts to explicate the emergence and significance of these standards between those in my life.
>
> The boundaries shared between participants on this journey are fluid and dynamic. They are permeable, yet also recognise the limitations of certain relationships into impermeable boundaries.
>
> In the current debate about personalised learning within education, I see a new language of education emerging, shared between school and student researchers that places learning at its heart. I am supporting Schön's (1995) call for the emergence of a new epistemology for educational knowledge with the expression and clarification of new living standards of judgment that can contribute to enhancing educational space.
>
> (Karen Riding 2008: retrieved 22 February 2009 from www.
> actionresearch.net/karenridingphd.shtml)

Working with people in organisational and institutional settings

If you are doing a formal action research project you are probably working as a member of an organisation, although not necessarily in an institution. Some published accounts of research in private contexts exist (for example, McCormack 2002), but most studies are written by people in an organisation, and most within institutional settings. If you are on an award-bearing course, you are working in two organisational settings: the workplace and the Academy. Both carry potential constraints. Be aware of these before you begin your project. If you are not, you could be in for an unexpected surprise.

Here are some things to look out for.

In the workplace

You are hoping that your work will be supported through appropriate conditions and resources. These come in the form of people, organisational structures and facilities. Here are some aspects you should consider.

People

Ask yourself the following questions:

Will the people you are working with support your efforts?

Once you have negotiated the base rules (for example, by distributing and receiving back your ethics forms – see Chapter 5), will you be able to go ahead unhindered? It is essential to get proper clearance and have everything in writing, so it is clear that you have conducted yourself professionally and with due courtesy and respect for conventions.

Will people be available to help you?

Will you find sufficient and appropriate people to be your critical friends, research participants, and validators? Be realistic. Sometimes researchers find they have to go outside the workplace to find participants.

What is the cultural climate like?

Are people open to new ideas? Margaret Cahill conducted her research into teaching marginalised children, including Traveller children (Cahill 2007), to find ways of enabling them to go on to further and continuing education. She found that prejudice permeated the attitudes and structures of the school. When she questioned her colleagues about this she encountered the same kind of prejudice and hostility to herself that had been reserved for the children she was teaching. While she could rightly claim to have influenced staff attitudes, and some staff became sympathetic to her work, others changed in the direction of becoming more entrenched and she found herself becoming as marginalised as the children she was teaching. Margaret's thesis is available at www.jeanmcniff.com/margaretcahill/index.html.

What is your line manager or principal like?

Managers tend to set what counts as cultural climates and expectations. Is your manager sympathetic to you? Are they interested? Do they want to be kept informed, or are they happy to let you get on with it? Does the manager have to report back to superiors? Will you encounter any problems? Is the manager open to the idea of professional learning? Is the manager publicly positioned as a learner?

Organisational structures

Think about these issues:

Where are you positioned in the structures of the organisation?

Do you work in a hierarchical structure in which you are directly answerable to a line manager? Do you need to check with your manager about your actions and opinions?

What is your functional role in the organisation?

Does your role carry specific expectations? Are you expected to conform to established rules and practices? Will your research compromise you in relation to your role? Or are you perhaps in a position to use your power to manipulate existing structures and create new ones to meet your interests?

What kinds of stories and scripts are used most throughout the organisation?

Who says what to whom? How do they say it, and how do they position you? Are you happy to speak the lines someone else has written, or do you want to write your own?

What will you do if your research reveals injustices, or you come to understand how things should change?

What happens if you find yourself in conflict with established norms and structures? What do you think could happen to you if you raise inconvenient questions? Many texts reveal what happens when people blow whistles (Alford 2001) or challenge established norms (Chomsky 2002).

Facilities and resources

Availability and uses of resources are often symbolic of underlying relationships and attitudes. Ask yourself the following.

Does the organisation commit to the professional learning of its employees?

Is time allocated for your study? How about money? Many organisations are willing to fund people's studies, provided the study can be shown to have significance in the workplace. If not, you will probably have to fund yourself. You would almost certainly have to do your study in your own time. Although action research is grounded in your practice, it will nevertheless take extra time. What will you take out of your already busy life in order to put the study in?

Will you be able to use the library, if there is one, or online resources? Will you get financial support for the purchase of books or equipment? Will you be able to use the workplace photocopier or networking facilities? Who expects to see a copy of your report, and what will happen to it? Ray O'Neill (2002) explains how the person with the keys is the person with the power.

If you use organisational facilities and resources, does this have implications for the ownership of your research? Will anyone else claim it as their property? Major dilemmas arise around issues of intellectual property rights, and some end up in court. Be clear about whose property the research is, and what the conditions are around its production.

In the Academy

If you are on an award-bearing course it means you have chosen, consciously and deliberately, to enter into a legal contractual agreement with an institution. This does not imply that you have to conform to expectations, but it does mean that you should be aware of existing structures and practices and, if you disagree with them, to work creatively from within. Many published action research reports show how practitioner researchers did challenge academic norms and standards, and created new ones that were then accepted by the Academy. These are problematic issues that always carry risk. Sometimes it can mean the difference between getting your award or doing things your own way (see Dadds and Hart 2001: 1–10). You have to weigh up the options and make your own strategic choices.

People sometimes experience difficulty when they assume that their action research will be accepted automatically as a legitimate form of research that can generate valid theory. In a famous metaphor, Schön (1995) speaks of a traditional high ground where academics generate conceptual theory, which is accepted as quality theory by everyone; and the swampy lowlands in which practitioners generate practical knowledge, which is perceived, also by everyone, as useful knowledge but not genuine theory. This metaphor still holds largely true for today, although, given the emphasis in recent years on the need for high-quality action research reports (Furlong and Oancea 2005; McNiff and Whitehead 2009), the situation is changing. Whereas, previously, only theoretical conceptual knowledge was regarded as valid and worthwhile, now, personal practical knowledge is also acknowledged as valid and worthwhile. The practical embodied theories of practitioners are now accepted as legitimate knowledge. The significance of this shift in perception is manifested clearly in the 2008 UK Research Assessment Exercise, through which funding that was previously allocated only to traditional research universities is now allocated also to teaching-led universities (Times Higher Education 2009). Teaching is finally coming to be seen as a form of research-based practice, as recommended by Boyer (1990) when he first promoted the idea of a new scholarship of teaching and learning.

Where you are positioned institutionally will depend on what precedents have been set at your institution through previously validated work. Sometimes higher education institutions have impressive databases of action research dissertations and theses, and these form a new knowledge base of scholarly enquiry, which are themselves seen as a potential means of social, cultural and economic renewal. We said in the Introduction that higher education is now seen as the means for economic recovery, especially through the new focus on the legitimisation of workplace research and theory. If you are in an institution where this kind of progressive and politically aware culture is the norm, few problems are likely to arise, and your research project will be welcome. However, if you are in an institution that has no established or emergent tradition of new scholarship work, you will have to draw on other knowledge bases to ground and support your efforts. You can find extensive and influential databases from the University of Bath at www.actionresearch.net; from Dublin City University at webpages.dcu.ie/~farrenm/; from the University of Limerick at www.jeanmcniff.com/reports.html; from Action Research Expeditions at www.arexpeditions.montana.edu/docs/about.html; and from Southern Cross University at www.scu.edu.au/schools/gcm/ar/arhome.html.

Your tutor is your best support and ally. If experienced, they will be politically aware and will guide you expertly. If they are relatively inexperienced, they will probably count as much on your support as you on theirs, as they work to transform the traditional epistemologies of their institution into a new scholarship of educational knowledge (Whitehead 1999), as well as the organisational structures that relay that knowledge throughout the organisation.

Possible implications

It is easy to flourish in a warm and friendly climate, and not so easy in a hostile one. If you work in an even mildly hostile climate, you may be tempted to give up, wondering whether the effort is worthwhile. The answer is yes, it is worthwhile. Foucault (2001) says it is the responsibility of all citizens who are capable of speaking for themselves to do so; and Chomsky (2002) and Polanyi (1958) say it is the responsibility of intellectuals to search for and tell the truth in spite of the hazards involved. If you remain silent and inactive, you will deliberately submit to the frequent exercise of disciplinary power (Foucault 1980), or perhaps watch other people doing so. If you take action, you stand a chance of achieving greater social justice.

However, if you do decide to take action, through doing your research, you should do the following.

Find allies and join networks

You cannot do it alone. Allies can offer support and comfort, propose alternative strategies, and help you check whether your thinking is on the right track. They can provide emotional and practical support, and help you find the necessary spiritual resilience with a loving dynamic energy (Walton 2008: 5) to keep you going. It is easy to join networks through the Internet, perhaps through JISCmail or the many special interest groups of larger organisations such as the American Educational Research Association or the British Educational Research Association, or other similar professional bodies. A search engine will help you find what you want, and you can access many of these networks through www.actionresearch.net.

Maintain high standards of scholarship and research

Make sure your work achieves recognised research criteria, such as those set out in the UK Research Assessment Exercise, of originality, rigour and significance. The more your action research is seen as high quality by the Academy, the more it will be regarded universally as valid knowledge, and the more it will strengthen you as you engage with issues such as reconceptualising the public sphere as a place where people may engage in communicative action with political and social intent. Your work must always demonstrate integrity, accuracy and coherent thinking, and be presented in an error-free way, so that it cannot be faulted on technical grounds.

Publish

Aim to publish your work and disseminate your findings wherever and whenever possible (see Chapter 14). Having work published is one of the highest markers of academic and organisational esteem. Aim to build up a track record of publications so that you have a recognised and legitimised platform to speak from. Create a space that is yours alone, and as inviolable as possible.

Work at all levels of the system

In organisational contexts, make sure to work at all levels of the system. Aim to talk with everyone, including senior and middle managers, as well as key workers. You cannot afford to privilege any one sector, otherwise you would alienate others and introduce a new kind of structural prejudice.

Support others

You have much to contribute, and others will benefit from your insights. Remember that doing action research is about learning, and we learn with and from one another. Be generous in all things.

Always keep a good sense of what is possible, and let that guide you as you encounter what is structurally not possible. Your vision of what is good and worth fighting for is stronger than life's constraints.

Summary

This chapter has discussed what it takes to work successfully with others in institutional and organisational settings, and the possible implications for you and your project. It has considered the different groupings you may work with, and the kinds of skills and capacities required. The success of your project could depend on your awareness of other people's sensitivities, and your capacity to act strategically and appropriately.

Checklist of reflective questions

- Have you thought through the different groupings that you may need to work with, and whether they will be sympathetic to you and your research? Write out whom you need to check with, and check with them as part of your planning.
- Do an audit of your interpersonal skills. What are your strengths? Do you need to refine any others?
- Are you confident about the different structures in your organisation and who speaks to whom? Are you aware of the different scripts in the organisation? Can you speak them? Do you wish to?
- Have you thought about how you might cope if people disagree with you, and how you could negotiate to reach agreement?

- Do you have a clear sense of what it takes organisationally to do a successful project?

The issues discussed in this chapter raise questions about ethical conduct, and this becomes the focus of Chapter 5.

Chapter 5

Influence and ethics

The idea of influence is at the heart of action research. Because action research is always conducted with other people who constitute social situations, and because those other people can think for themselves, the way to influence the trajectories of social change is to encourage them to act differently, through influencing their thinking.

This raises questions about the kind of influence we wish to exercise. It also means that, before trying to influence other people's thinking, it is vital to influence one's own, in the sense of deconstructing favourite ways of thinking, and checking whether they are indeed the kinds of thinking that will contribute to life-affirming and life-sustaining practices for all.

It is a salutary thought that every time we say or do something, we are potentially influencing someone somewhere. No one is ever isolated, even although we might like to think we are. We are always connected with others, in space and time, through our ideas and creations. This carries significant implications for what we do and say. It carries especial significance for the idea that you can exercise your influence in a way that is educational, so that you encourage others to think. A main theme of the work of Hannah Arendt was that the first responsibility of people is to think; a main responsibility of action researchers is to learn to think critically, and to use that capacity for personal and social betterment.

This chapter deals with the idea of influence and its educational potentials, and explains the kinds of checks and balances necessary to ensure, as far as possible, that the influence is educational. It deals with the following issues:

- What is meant by educational influence?
- What are the ethical principles of action research?
- How do you realise these principles?

What is meant by educational influence?

It is often assumed that influence is negative and sinister. This is not necessarily the case. Influence can happen in many ways. It is also often assumed that one person can directly influence another, especially their learning, as an act of transmission. We often hear people say things like, 'I said it; why didn't he understand it?' or 'She never does what I ask her to do'. The assumption here is that what is in one mind can directly be transmitted into another. Refusal or inability to accept what is said, or taught, is often put down as wilful disobedience; in reality it is more the exercise of originality of mind and logic, and independence of spirit. This idea is illustrated by the story of John Nash, the Nobel laureate for economics, who consistently refused, or was not able, to produce conventional proofs for complex mathematical problems, much to the frustration of his professors, and was frequently deemed obstreperous and even unteachable (Nasar 1998).

Said (1997: 14), drawing on a note from the poet Valéry, focuses on the importance of influence in saying that there is nothing in the critical field that should be of greater philosophical interest or prove more rewarding to analysis than the progressive influence of one mind by the work of another. He suggests that each person possesses independence of mind that acts as a filter for whatever they hear, so they can decide for themselves whether to accept it or not. On this view, we are all capable of mediating other people's influence in our learning through our own originality of mind and capacity for critical judgement. Not all learning is educational. Many return-to-learning adults often say that they need to unlearn some of the destructive learnings about themselves from experiences in the family and at school. Taking responsibility for one's educational influences in one's own learning, through the mediation of our originality of mind and critical judgement, is central to our understanding of what counts as 'educational'.

Therefore, we make choices about whether or not we will be influenced. This depends, of course, on whether we are subjected to the manipulative tactics of propaganda (Marlin 2002) or the hidden persuaders of advertising, which lead us to believe what we do not really believe and to deny our values in our practices.

Our own education helps us to make wise decisions about what we choose to believe. Educational processes refer to those processes that help others and ourselves to develop this capacity, to become critical through reflexive and dialectical critique (Winter 1989; see also Carr and Kemmis 1986). The idea of dialectical critique is explored also by Habermas (1976), as the need for people to make themselves aware of the different forces that constitute the normative background of the situation they are in.

The idea of educational influence, therefore, is when you influence other people to become critical in relation to values that carry hope for the future of humanity. This process is always transparent, because in order to encourage other people to become critical you have to demonstrate your own capacity for critical reflection on your own thinking. This realisation is demonstrated in the doctoral thesis of Mary Roche (2007), who writes about her developing understanding of the need to become critical if she was to encourage her primary school children also to think critically. You can access her thesis at www.jeanmcniff.com/MaryRoche/index.html.

Your job as an action researcher is, first, to learn to become critical yourself and, second, to exercise your educational influence in other people's learning so that they can also learn to become critical. This means asking yourself critical questions about your own practices, and acting on your responses to yourself. Some of the (uncomfortable and perhaps destabilising) questions you could ask are as follows:

- How do I see other people? Do I position them as 'It' in my space and time, or as 'Thou' with whom I am in deep relation (Buber 1970)? How do I view the world I am in? How do I treat the environment?
- Do I see myself as the centre, where everything revolves around me; or do I see other people as their own centres, and myself as part of the constellation of persons around them? Do I see the need for centres?
- What kind of relationships do I experience with other people? Do I encourage power relationships, in which other people look up to me as if I have all the answers; or do I insist on a dialogue of equals? Do I require others to think for themselves, or do I conveniently do their thinking for them?
- As a supervisor, do I tell others what to write, or do I expect them to do their own original thinking and writing? Do I spoon-feed them or require them to feed themselves? As an aid worker, do I give others aid without an expectation that they will learn to look after themselves? Do I see myself as giving charity or do I require others to learn to be independent of me?

These are issues that are grounded in our ontological values, and have as much bearing on our own capacity for critical awareness as for our efforts to encourage other people to develop the same.

What are the ethical principles of action research?

A good deal of work has been done over recent times into the ethical principles of action research (for example, Zeni 2001); but the basic principles are reasonably straightforward, and in line with the ethical guidelines of major learned societies and research associations: see, for example, the BERA ethical guidelines (www.bera.ac.uk/files/2008/09/ethical.pdf). Action research is of course different because it is not only about working with human participants, but also about trying to influence their thinking, so you need to be extra-aware of ethical issues.

At a practical level, here are some of the things you should think about.

Draw up your documentation

You need to prepare and distribute ethics documents to all participants. Your documents should include an ethics statement and letters of permission. If you are writing an account of your project, include blank copies of this documentation in your appendices, and make sure you conceal all the names of people or organisations. In letters of permission, check that you have blanked out names, addresses and signatures. However, check with your participants whether or not they wish their identities to be revealed. If they do, you should identify them, to celebrate their contributions and to acknowledge their participation. If you do this, make sure to put a note in a relevant place in your report to the effect that the person has given their permission for their identities to be revealed, otherwise examiners, most of whom still work from traditional perspectives, may get suspicious and refuse to assess your work.

Your documentation will include the following.

An ethics statement

This is your personal statement about how you are going to conduct your research, and should mention all of the points articulated in this section in some way. Make copies of this statement before you begin your research, and give everyone a copy as they become involved. Your statement should include room for your and their signatures; you and they should keep identical copies for your files. Don't be embarrassed at giving these documents even to close friends and colleagues. It is part of good research practice.

Letters requesting and granting permission

Draw up letters requesting permission to do the research for strategic managers, and requesting their involvement from all participants. As above, make copies of these letters and distribute them to people as they become involved. Always make sure they and you have identical, signed copies, and store your copy carefully. Keep in mind that we live in an age of litigation, and you have to protect yourself as well as your participants. If anyone has difficulty reading, give them a letter for their reference, and also explain things orally, and do so again at regular intervals. In your letters, say when the data about them will be destroyed and make sure you honour your commitments. Check who will need a copy of your report and give them one if they ask for it. At the end of this chapter you will find exemplars of an ethics statement and letters to principals, managers and parents/carers. You can adapt these to suit your own purposes. The principles and values involved extend to most contexts.

Negotiate access

You will need to negotiate access with the following people. Do not take it for granted that you may proceed without negotiation.

Principals and managers

Check with principals and managers before undertaking research that is connected with their (your) organisation. Establish boundaries about what you may and may not do. Make sure you get this agreement in writing. Be absolutely honest about what you plan to do. If your plans change during the course of the project, let the principal or manager know, and get their permission to proceed. You really should not go ahead without their permission.

With participants

Obtain permission from the people you hope to involve in your research. Keep them informed. Invite them to do their own action research. Make it clear from the start that they are participants and co-researchers, and not 'subjects' you are studying. You are studying yourself, in relation with them. Explain this carefully, and as many times as necessary for them to become comfortable around what you are doing.

With parents and carers

If you are working with children, or people who are vulnerable or under supervision, make sure you obtain permission from parents or other supervisors to involve those people in your research. Send a letter home, explaining what you are doing, or arrange an information meeting. If anyone is experiencing reading difficulties, explain things orally. Get people on your side from the start and keep faith with them.

Promise confidentiality

You must explain that you will be true to your word and protect people's interests. This involves the following.

Confidentiality of information

Give a firm undertaking that you will report only that information which is in the public domain and within the law. You will not reveal anything of a personal or compromising nature. If you wish to use information that is in any way sensitive, seek and obtain permission from the originator to use it.

Confidentiality of identity

As noted, you should not reveal the real names of people or places unless you have specific permission to do so in writing. Do not give people fictitious names; those names may belong to other people elsewhere. Allocate initials, numbers or other symbols to identify participants. If the organisation gives full written permission to use its real name (and many organisations are delighted to do this), go ahead, but you must obtain written permission first. Place a note in your report to say that you have done this.

Confidentiality of data

If you wish to use first-hand data such as transcripts, or excerpts from video recordings, always check that this is acceptable to the originators and obtain their written permission. Ensure that your perceptions of the data are accurate. Ask the originator to check and approve transcripts, and edit their contribution as they wish. Encourage others to read your versions of events before you publish them.

Ensure participants' rights to withdraw from the research

You must check continually to make sure that participants are comfortable with procedures and are always in full command of their own involvement in your research. You must let your participants know that their rights are protected, that they may withdraw if they wish, and that all data about them will be destroyed at a time you negotiate with them.

Ensure good professional and academic conduct

When you gather your data and produce your report, make sure that your practice is academically and professionally sound. When in a lecture or group setting, do not tape-record anything without permission. When interviewing people, make sure that you explain how the data will be used and stick to your commitment. When you write your report, always acknowledge your intellectual debts, and do not use other people's words without acknowledgement. Do not expect your tutor to provide references, or to read your drafts umpteen times. Doing research is a professional practice that requires commitment to hard work and personal responsibility.

Keep good faith

Establish right from the start that you are a person to be trusted, and that you will keep your promises about negotiation, confidentiality and reporting. Never take anything for granted. Always check back with people if there is any doubt. In matters where there is some possibility of misunderstanding, write down what you are hoping to do and get that approved. Although you have a duty to protect others, you also need to protect yourself.

At the end of the day, having observed all of these issues and demonstrated your integrity and authenticity, keep faith with yourself and go ahead and publish your work. Claim your work as your intellectual property, and be aware that you are contributing to a body of knowledge that is of great worth in the world.

How do you realise these principles?

You can realise these principles by ensuring that you act in a way that is in accordance with your values. To repeat, values are those things we value – the things that give meaning to our lives. Most people hold a range of values, relating to different areas of experience: for example, ontological values, about how you see yourself, especially in relation with others; epistemological values, about what you see as valuable in issues of knowledge and knowledge creation; and methodological values, about forms of enquiry and how enquiries should be conducted. You can also have values around other issues such as social justice, the need for all to feel valued, the environment, an understanding that all have the right and a duty to speak for themselves, and so on. What makes one value more important than another is how the person understands what is important to themselves as persons, and the priority they give to that particular aspect in a particular context.

It is important to remember the distinction between speaking about values and living them. It is easy to speak about values; many philosophers do. For example, Rawls (1972) speaks about the values of social justice. Grayling (2003) speaks about the need for, and different perceptions of ethical conduct. Murdoch (2001) speaks about the sovereignty of good. Raz (2003) speaks about the practice of values. These philosophers and researchers speak about values, in an abstract, propositional way. They tell us about values, but they do not show us how to live so that those values may be realised. This is the domain of action research; it is about identifying and being aware of the values that inspire your life and give it meaning, and then finding ways of living in the direction of your values. It is unlikely that you will ever fully achieve all your values, but you will achieve some and you can definitely move nearer to their achievement in general. There is abundant evidence to show the processes in action; furthermore, the accounts that show the processes involved in the realisation of values have been academically recognised, as the examples throughout this book show, and this example in particular:

Geoffrey Suderman-Gladwell (2001) explains how he engaged with 'The ethics of personal, subjective narrative research' after his research proposal had been rejected by a university ethics committee:

I use narratives from my personal experiences both in teaching and in theo-
logical education to explain my reactions to the document (Tri-Council Policy
Statement) and the implied world view. I explain why my vision of research and
teaching is not compatible with that of the Tri-Council Policy Statement: Ethical
Conduct for Research Involving Humans, and I propose an ethical understanding based on the realities of my understanding of research and teaching.
(Suderman-Gladwell 2001: retrieved 17 February 2009 from www.
actionresearch.net/values/gsgma.pdf)

So the response to the question of this section, about how you achieve
your ethical principles, is equivalent to articulating how you realise the
good. Ethics is about how to live a good life; in other words, how to live
a life that is conducted in accordance with our values. If you can show, as
those cited above, that you are living according to your values, you can say
that you are acting in an ethical fashion. This is not easy, often because values are in conflict. You may feel, for example, as many people do, that you
wish to be both free and loved; these desires are often in conflict and cannot
be resolved, in the same way, for example, that the values of freedom and
justice are often in conflict (Berlin 1969). In these cases you need to draw on
another value, which is finding ways of living with dissonance, that do no
violence to your own integrity.

If you can stay true to your values of what contributes to others' benefit, and make every effort to show how you are doing this, you can claim
your integrity as your main justification. We are justified when we act with
honesty in the direction of the well-being of others. Doing your research,
which involves generating evidence from authenticated data and testing the
validity of your emerging claims to knowledge, will enable you to check
whether or not this is the case, or if you need to rethink and act differently.
Do the best you can, with honesty and humility, which is all you or anyone
else can ask of you.

Examples of ethics statements

Your ethics statement can be simple or complex, depending on what you
wish to achieve. A simple ethics statement is:

ETHICS STATEMENT

I, [name], promise to ensure good ethical practice in conducting my research. I promise at all times to negotiate permission to conduct the research, respect confidentiality, and ensure participants' rights to withdraw at any time from the research.

[Your signature] ....

[Your name] ....

A more complex statement is:

ETHICS STATEMENT

Dear [Name],

I am undertaking an action research project to study my own practice as a [type of work]. This ethics statement is to assure you that I will observe good ethical practice throughout the research.

This means that:

- the permission of my Principal and Board of Management will be secured before the research commences;
- the permission of the children and their written consent will be secured before the research commences;
- confidentiality will be observed at all times, and no names will be revealed of the school, children or staff;
- participants will be kept informed of progress at all times;
- participants will have access to the research report before it is published;
- I will report only that which is in the public domain and within the Law;
- all participants have the right to withdraw from the research at any time and all data relating to them will be destroyed.

[Your signature] ....

[Your name] ....

Examples of letters requesting permission to do your research

Example letter to parents or carers

[Your institutional address]
[date]

[Name and address of parent or carer]

Dear [name]

Requesting permission to undertake research

As part of my work with the [organisation, or name of project], I am conducting a piece of action research into studying how I can encourage children to improve their word skills using computers. I would be grateful if you would give your permission for [name of child] to take part.

My data collection methods will include audio and videotape recordings of the children and myself in conversation, photographs, diary recordings, field notes and reports. I guarantee that I will observe good ethical conduct throughout. I promise that I will not reveal the name of your school, colleagues, parents or children at any time, unless you inform me in writing that you wish me to do so. If you wish I will keep you informed of progress throughout. My research report will be available at [work, school] for scrutiny before it is published.

I would be grateful if you would sign and return the slip below at your earliest convenience.

I enclose two copies of this letter. Please retain one copy for your files.

[Your signature] ....

[Your name]

✂_ _

---

continued on next page

To [your name],

I, [name], give my permission for [participant's name] to take part in your research.

[Parent's/carer's signature] ....

[Parent's/carer's name]

Example letter to principal or manager

[Your institutional address]

[date]

[Name and address of principal/manager]

Dear [Name]

Requesting permission to undertake research

As part of my work [with name of project where appropriate], I am conducting a piece of action research into studying how I can encourage children to improve their word skills using computers. I would be grateful if you would give your permission and support for this project.

My data collection methods will include audio- and videotape recordings of the children and myself in conversation, photographs, diary recordings, field notes and reports. I guarantee that I will observe good ethical conduct throughout. I will negotiate permission to work with the children. I will secure permission from parents and children to involve them in the research. I guarantee confidentiality of information and promise that no names of school, colleagues or children will be made public without your permission and the permission of those who wish to be named.

continued on next page

I promise that I will make my research report available to you for scrutiny before it is published, if you wish, and I will make a copy of the report available for your files on its publication.

I would be grateful if you would sign and return the slip below at your earliest convenience.

I enclose two copies of this letter. Please retain one copy for your files.

Yours sincerely

[Your signature] ....

[Your name]

✂_ _

I, [name], Principal of [name of school], give my permission for [your name] to undertake her/his research in her/his classroom and in the school.

[Principal's signature] ....

[Principal's name]

Summary

This chapter has discussed issues of ethics and ethical behaviour. The success of your project depends on your attending to all aspects of appropriate conduct. You must seek and obtain permission to do your research before you commence, and resolve to keep people informed throughout the process. Exemplars of letters requesting and granting permission are given.

Checklist of reflective questions

- It is essential that you attend to all matters of ethical conduct before doing your research, and throughout its process. Have you made yourself aware of what the key issues are?
- Check that you have sought and obtained permission to go ahead with all relevant parties. Do not proceed until you have done so.

- Are you reasonably confident that you will get the permission you are looking for? Are there any especially tricky areas you need to attend to?
- Write out the persons you need to get permission from, and tick the names off when you have distributed your ethics statements and letters requesting permission.
- Have you a supply of ethics statements to distribute as and when appropriate?
- Anything else?

If you feel that you have attended to all aspects of ethical conduct as fully as you can, then start to think seriously about designing your project. Detailed advice is given in the next chapter.

Part III
Designing your project

This part invites you to ask, 'How do I come to know what I need to know?' It is about designing your project, which means thinking about the methodological aspects of what you are going to do and how you are going to do it, and includes Chapters 6 and 7.

Chapter 6 is about planning what you are going to do, and what it could look like in action. This also involves thinking about the conceptual frameworks you intend to use. These are explained fully in the chapter.

Chapter 7 is about the logistical aspects of the project, and asks questions about the practicalities of when and where the project will be carried out, who will be involved and how it will be implemented.

Both aspects are vital in designing a successful project.

Chapter 6

Designing your project: action planning

There are two parts to designing a project:

1 Planning what you are going to do and why you are going to do it this way, which means you will offer a rationale for your actions. These issues are discussed in this chapter.
2 Thinking about the logistical and practical aspects involved. These include considering when and where you will conduct the project, and who and what will be involved. These issues are discussed in Chapter 7.

Here we address the first set of issues, i.e. planning for action and saying why the action is necessary. Said (1997) says that intent contains its whole methodology within itself. Once you think about it, you can imagine the entire project unfolding. Offering a rationale like this is vital, because it communicates the idea that you intend to take action in a purposeful way, and not simply on an *ad hoc* basis. This meets the criteria of doing quality research, which involves giving explanations for action (theorising) as well as describing the actions.

Planning therefore involves two sets of issues:

1 Why you intend to do something (take action): 'why' involves identifying which issues you will take as the basis of the project – *why you intend to do your project*.
2 How you intend to do it: 'how' refers to the methodology you intend to use – *how you will do your project*.

continued on next page

'Why' and 'how' are closely related because they are grounded in your values. Your values inform everything you do. Shortly we will discuss the ideas of ontological values and methodological values, which is another way of saying that what we value about ourselves and our ways of living informs both what we study and how we study it.

This chapter deals with the 'why' and 'how' of doing your research, which are elements of designing it. It is helpful to think of these as two complementary frameworks, so the chapter is organised as two related parts: (1) conceptual frameworks and (2) methodological frameworks.

Conceptual frameworks: why you intend to take action

The words 'conceptual frameworks', also known as theoretical frameworks, refer to the underpinning ideas and concepts that inform and permeate the research; your choice of ideas and concepts are informed by the values you hold. If you believe in justice then you will take justice as a conceptual/ theoretical framework. If freedom and independent enquiry are things you value, or a passion for lifelong learning, or deconstructing gender stereotyping, then these will become conceptual frameworks.

Your conceptual/theoretical frameworks will be linked with ideas in the literatures, so you will look for key authors who have something to say about the concepts. Ray O'Neill (2008) draws on the work of Hannah Arendt (1958, 1977), and her ideas of the importance of thinking for oneself, and the value of each individual. He develops these ideas into a framework of Information and Communications Technology (ICT) as political action (see www.ictaspoliticalaction.com). Margaret Farren (2005) draws on the work of John O'Donoghue (1997) and his ideas of a web of betweenness. She develops these ideas into a framework of a pedagogy of the unique in a web of betweenness (see http://webpages.dcu.ie/~farrenm/).

The kinds of values identified so far tend to be ontological values: they give meaning to your identity in relation with others. Bullough and Pinnegar (2004) say: 'The consideration of one's ontology, of one's being in and towards the world, should be a central feature of any discussion of the value of self-study research' (2004: 319). As well as ontological frameworks, you will also develop *epistemological frameworks*, informed by values around knowing and coming to know, *methodological frameworks*, about how to organise your study and writing, and perhaps other frameworks that are related to other sets of values.

In a real sense, then, your values transform into your conceptual and theoretical frameworks. You can also use these values to judge the quality of your action research in relation to the extent to which you can show that you are living your values in your practice. Your values – kindness or justice or freedom – then also come to act as your criteria and standards of judgement. You say that you wish to see the practice of kindness or justice or freedom in your work (you identify them as your criteria, what you perceive as signifying quality), and you say that you will judge the quality of the action in relation to the extent to which you can show kindness or justice or freedom in action (your standards of judgement, how you judge quality).

Here is an example of how these ideas are used in practice. The example is from the abstract of Barry Hymer (2007), who articulates how he uses his values as conceptual frameworks and living criteria and standards of judgement in his research programme into 'How do I understand and communicate my values and beliefs in my work as an educator in the field of giftedness?'

I articulate in narrative form the meanings of my embodied ontological values through their emergence in my practice – specifically in my practice of philosophy with children, in creating webs of meaning through dilemma-based learning, and in seeking to unmask (Foucault, in Rabinow, 1984) the concept of giftedness – by asking whose interests the concept serves. In the process of living, clarifying and communicating the meanings of these practices are formed, I argue, living epistemological standards of judgement for a new, relationally dynamic epistemology of educational enquiry. I record also how through my professional activity, my reflections on and revisions of this activity, and the process of creating this account, I have moved in the direction of creating and living my core personal and educational values and realising the critical standards of judgment which are both consisting in and attendant on these values. These include the value of individual intellectual respect as a contributor to the creation of generative-transformational giftedness – i.e. giftedness which is co-constructed (not identified) in a social, relationally respectful, activity-oriented, dialectical, tool-and-result (Vygotsky 1978) manner and context. I make a claim to originality in scholarship in articulating the emergence of the value-laden concept of generative-transformational giftedness and its latent fecundity in and relevance to the field of gifted and talented education. To this end, I suggest an inclusional, non-dualistic alternative to the identification or discovery of an individual's gifts and talents by arguing that activity- and development-centred (not knowing-centred) learning-leading-development (Vygotsky, ibid.) environments lead not to the identification of gifts and talents but to their creation.

(Hymer 2007: 4 – retrieved 19 February 2009 from www.actionresearch.net/hymer.shtml)

You can also see Jane Renowden explaining how she holds herself accountable for her work in relation to her identified values at:

- www.youtube.com/watch?v=yND2Ra7vdhQ
- www.youtube.com/watch?v=QSK1lI3sMVE

- www.youtube.com/watch?v=kBOKMlVPDRo
- www.youtube.com/watch?v=sIpJsXyhvm4
- www.youtube.com/watch?v=tg4zos6St-0

Remember that the more academically advanced your studies are, the more you will need to articulate your understanding of these ideas as conceptual frameworks. If you are involved in a non-accredited work-based project it would probably be sufficient to explain to your readers that you know why you are doing your action research, and relate your reasons to your values. For example:

- I decided to find ways of encouraging participative working in my organisation because I believe that participation enables all to feel involved and lifts morale.
- I want to find ways of encouraging people to trust one another because trust is at the heart of quality relationships, which are central to effective working practices.

If you are doing a project as part of your higher degree work, you would explain these things to your reader in more theoretical terms; for example, Jocelyn Jones (2008) explains how she holds herself accountable to the following:

> In the thesis I develop a living theory of responsibility, movement, engagement, withdrawal, and self care with a living standard of judgement of response-ability toward the other.
>
> (Jones, 2008, p. i)

Marian Naidoo (2005) explains how she holds herself accountable to her value of 'a passion for compassion':

> I believe that this original account of my emerging practice demonstrates how I have been able to turn my ontological commitment to a passion for compassion into a living epistemological standard of judgement by which my inclusional and responsive practice may be held accountable.
>
> I am a story teller and the focus of this narrative is on my learning and the development of my living educational theory as I have engaged with others in a creative and critical practice over a sustained period of time. This narrative self-study demonstrates how I have encouraged people to work creatively and critically in order to improve the way we relate and communicate in a multi-professional and multi-agency healthcare setting in order to improve both the quality of care provided and the well being of the system.
>
> (Naidoo 2005: 9)

To get yourself started on showing how you can make judgements about what you are doing, try the following exercise, which explains how to identify conceptual and theoretical frameworks.

Identifying conceptual and theoretical frameworks

Think about what gives meaning to your personal and professional life. In your personal life, perhaps you value loving relationships and kind attitudes. In your professional life, perhaps you value efficient working practices or strong professional commitments. These personal and professional values come to act as your criteria (what you consider significant about your work) and standards of judgement (how you judge your work in relation to how well you achieve the criteria – in this case, your values).

Now think about the week you have just spent, perhaps at work. Was there any episode when you felt that your work was really worthwhile? What happened? Why was it so worthwhile? Perhaps two colleagues who have been at odds with each other have suddenly begun to work together? Perhaps the dog you operated on and thought would never recover has suddenly picked up? Can you say that your values of, in this case, collaborative working and determination to survive, have been realised? Further, can you see how you have influenced these situations? If so, do you feel justified in claiming that you have realised your values in your practices?

In this example, you can see how collaborative working and determination to survive become conceptual or theoretical frameworks. If you are on an award-bearing course, you would now link these ideas with the literatures, and find authors who write about the same matters. For example, Brown and Duguid (2002) speak about the need for collaborative working, whereas Frankl (1959) and Todorov (1999) speak about the will to survive in the face of terrible odds.

However, it is frequently the case in life that we do not manage to realise our values in our practices. One of the key theorists in this regard is Jack Whitehead, who speaks about the experience of oneself as a living contradiction when one's values are denied in practice.

Experiencing oneself as a living contradiction

Jack understands the experience of oneself as a living contradiction when one's values are denied in one's practice as a clear starting point for an action enquiry; that is, episodes when you experience dissonance between your values and beliefs and your actions (see Whitehead 2008). For example, we may say we believe that people should speak for themselves, yet we often find ourselves in family or workplace situations where we actively prevent people from speaking for themselves. Jack has expressed his ideas as follows:

- I experience a problem when some of my educational values are negated;
- I imagine a solution;
- I act in the direction of the imagined solution;
- I evaluate the actions;
- I modify my actions/ideas in the light of my evaluation.

(Whitehead 1993: 38)

The 'I' exists as a living contradiction in the sense that values are denied in practice. Sometimes it is easy to see ourselves in situations in which our values are denied by external agents and forces acting on us. Perhaps the institution we work in holds different institutional values from our own personal values, and the situation then becomes a conflict of values (Sowell 1987). At other times, we may deny our own values, by believing in one thing and doing another. It is easy to listen to messages communicated through the culture about what we should think and how we should act, without bringing our capacity for critical thinking to bear. A vegetarian colleague tells the story of how they bought a can of chicken soup from being influenced by an advertisement. Many people are often persuaded to act by the subtle messages of politicians, communicated through the media. The most insidious messages persuade us that we cannot think for ourselves, and need other people to make decisions for us. Calderisi (2007) suggests that this could be the basis of dependency cultures. We often use sophisticated defences or excuses to hide from ourselves the realisation that we may not be living in the direction of our values; in this case we fool ourselves. These ideas are key for you as an action researcher, because you need to demonstrate the exercise of reflexive critique and dialectical critique in your report. An examiner would be concerned if they were missing.

The whole question of values, and realising values in practice is complex, and always needs to be problematised, even to the extent of asking whether it is always possible, or desirable, to aim to realise values in practice. These more complex issues are discussed in our other books, such as McNiff and Whitehead (2009).

We now turn to the methodological frameworks you can use for your action enquiry, still on the understanding that values inform your choice of methodology, which we explain below.

Methodological frameworks: how you intend to take action

The methodologies of action research mean that individual people enquire into their own practices in a systematic and rigorous way, so they can show how they hold themselves accountable for what they are doing. This stance is different from much traditional research, which works from an outsider perspective, and does not foreground personal accountability in doing research or taking action.

You choose your methodological framework on the grounds that you have a clear sense of how an action research project may be conducted. It needs to demonstrate your capacity to ask critical questions, to refuse to come to closure in the form of definite answers, and to see the end-point of one part of the research as the beginning of a new aspect. Your choice of methodology communicates your values of openness to new possibilities, the need for systematic enquiry and the continual need for critique.

The processes of action research tend to take a cyclical form. Most people agree that it involves a continuous process of acting, reflecting on the action and then acting again in new ways in light of what you have found, so that it becomes a cycle of action–reflection. When the work appears as an ongoing process, it can be seen as a cycle of cycles.

Here is a set of critical questions that will help you to reflect on how you can improve an aspect of your practice, and theorise (offer explanations for) what you are doing in a rigorous and systematic way. It can act as a methodological base for your enquiry.

- I review my current practice;
- I identify an area I wish to improve;
- I ask focused questions about how I can improve it;
- I imagine a way forward;
- I try it out, and take stock of what happens;
- I modify my plans in light of what I have found, and continue with the action;
- I evaluate the modified action;
- and I reconsider the position in light of the evaluation.

Different writers have found ways of representing this process. Some represent it as cycles of reflective action (Lewin 1946; Griffiths 1990); some as flow charts (Elliott 1991); and some as spirals (Kemmis and McTaggart 1982). The most useful models using a print form of representation are those that communicate the idea of practice as non-linear, showing that people are unpredictable and creative, and that life seldom follows a straightforward pathway. Multimedia forms of representation, however, have revolutionised the field forever. It is possible to show the live action of non-linear dynamic processes, which are far more appropriate for representing the realisation of values in practice than words on a page. You can see such multimedia representations in the contributions to the first issue of the *Educational Journal of Living Theories* (EJOLTS) at http://ejolts.net/. Look at Branko Bognar's and Marica Zovko's writings on 'Pupils as Action Researchers' and Jack's writings on 'Using a Living Theory Methodology'.

Bear in mind that action research is not only about problem solving, although it involves problem solving. Action research is about identifying what we want to achieve in terms of the values we hold, and offering justification for the actions we take, which is more than problem solving. It does, however, always involve problematising, and, as an action researcher, you should be aware of the need to ask awkward questions. For example, how do we identify an aspect that we want to improve, and why do we want to improve it? Although action research is not necessarily about 'problems', and may start from the point where we are simply interested in something and want to follow it through systematically, it always involves a sense of tension that inspires us to take action, even if the tension is a sense of wonder about the way things are.

Action planning

The action plan above can now be turned into a set of critical questions that will help you to plan for action, as follows:

- What is my concern?
- Why am I concerned?
- What is my research question?
- How do I show what the situation I am in is like at the moment?
- What can I do about the situation? What will I do?
- What is my research question?
- How will I show the situation as it develops?
- What kind of evidence can I produce to show that what I am doing is influencing someone's learning?
- How do I evaluate what I am doing?
- How do I communicate the significance of what I am doing?
- How do I ensure that any judgements I make are reasonably fair and accurate?
- How do I modify my practices and ideas in light of my evaluation?
- How do I evaluate the experience of doing the project?
- How do I write a good-quality report?
- How do I disseminate my findings, so that other people can learn from me and I from them?

   Let's look at the questions in turn.

An action plan in detail

Here is some more detailed information on the steps involved in planning an action enquiry and some of the possible problematics.

What is my concern?

As well as asking this question, you can also ask, 'What am I interested in studying?' or 'What do I need to investigate?' Your answer could be broad or narrow in focus: perhaps you need to manage your time better or do an overall review of organisational effectiveness. It is important to focus on only one issue at a time, if possible, even although other issues are pressing. You may find that the one issue you identify is symptomatic of other issues, or may contain other issues within itself. You may also find that if you explore any solutions to one concern, during one cycle of action reflection, it will probably develop into other research questions to form the starting point of another cycle. 'How do I manage my local football club more efficiently?' may contain the embedded question, 'How do I encourage new recruits?' and then develop into a new cycle that asks, 'How do I maintain a team spirit and a desire to become the best?' Sometimes action researchers feel overwhelmed by the complexities of their situations, but a focus tends to emerge through reflection and conversation with others.

You can communicate an initial research focus through the question, 'What is my concern?', but this does not imply that the situation you wish to investigate is a problem. It implies that you wish to pay attention to something, with a view to improvement. Remember that improvement does not mean that you are going to 'improve' someone. It means you will find ways of exercising your educational influence in someone else's thinking, starting with yourself, so that they can improve themselves. The main point at this stage is to identify an area you wish to investigate, and be reasonably confident you can do something about it.

Some key reminders

Here are some other reminders to help make your project a success:

- *Identifying a research concern.* Sometimes, especially on an award-bearing course, people find it difficult to identify a specific research issue. To get you started, think of the hundred things on your desk and choose one, with the following conditions: (1) you *can* do something about it; (2) you *must* do something about it; and (3) you *will* do something about it, starting tomorrow. Make sure you can meet these conditions. Sometimes people choose an area they cannot do anything about, such as remodelling the organisation, or trying to persuade people with entrenched attitudes to change their minds. Your keywords are to keep your project small enough for your resources, stay focused and keep it manageable.
- *You and your research.* Keep in mind that you are the focus of the research. You are investigating your work with others. You are not investigating them. That is their responsibility. You are hoping to influence them so that they learn how to deal with their own situations and lives. You are researching your educational influence in their learning, as well as your own. Also remember that, although many action research literatures speak about investigating 'a social situation', the 'situation' is made up of people: in your case, yourself and others. This means investigating

the kind of relationships between you and other people that influence how you are with one another and how you act towards one another.

* *Beginning from where you are.* All research begins with a latent hypothesis of sorts. Traditional social scientific hypotheses tend to work on a cause-and-effect basis and take the form, 'If I do this, such and such will happen'. Action research hypotheses are not so much hypotheses as working hunches, and take the form, 'I wonder what would happen if . . .'. This means that action research begins from where people are and real-world situations become the area of interest.

Why am I concerned?

You need to be reasonably clear why you wish to get involved in this area. Action researchers always hold a value commitment to improving the quality of life and learning for all. Make yourself aware of your own values position; this can be difficult, as noted on p. 21, because sometimes we do not always understand our motives. It may also be the case of deconstructing your own thinking, which can be painful. Also, we may have doubts about how our values can be justified or worry that we are imposing our values on other people, which denies a key value of honouring the other person's capacity and right to think for themselves. You can find good examples of how people articulate and deal with these kinds of dilemmas in the following reports:

* Amy Skuse's (2007) Educational Enquiry: 'How have my experiences of Year 2 SATs influenced my perceptions of assessment in teaching and learning?' (retrieved 22 February 2009 from www.jackwhitehead.com/tuesdayma/amyskuseeeoct07.htm)
* Claire Formby's (2007) Educational Enquiry: 'How do I sustain a loving, receptively responsive educational relationship with my pupils which will motivate them in their learning and encourage me in my teaching?' (retrieved 22 February 2009 from www.jackwhitehead.com/tuesdayma/formbyEE300907.htm)
* Claire Formby's (2008) Educational Enquiry: 'How am I integrating my educational theorising with the educational responsibility I express in my educational relationships with the children in my class and in my school and wider society?' (retrieved 22 February 2009 from www.jackwhitehead.com/tuesdayma/cfee3April08.htm)

Bear in mind also the idea of possibility of experiencing oneself as a living contradiction when your values are denied in your practice. For example, you may be a manager who believes in collaborative working, yet do not involve others in decision making. As a parent you may be committed to the idea that your children should lead independent lives, yet expend a lot of energy in trying to keep them at home. Further, institutional constraints may prevent you from living in the direction of your values. If you are a doctor, you may wish to spend more time with individual patients, yet be prevented from doing so because of your administrative workload.

Most people do not manage problematic issues on their own, or instantly, but they can engage with others and take small steps, one at a time, towards a more satisfactory situation. Action research is a means of explaining how we work together, systematically and collaboratively, to help us achieve the things we believe in; and then testing the validity of what we have done to show that we were justified in taking the actions we did.

What is my research question?

Having identified your research issue, you now formulate it as a research question. This is important because your question will transform into your claim to knowledge, and you will gather data and generate evidence specifically in relation to this question. You will test the validity of your eventual knowledge claim by producing an evidence base that shows how you have engaged with the question and have transformed it into a knowledge claim.

Action research questions are generally expressed as 'How can I . . . ?' or 'How do I . . . ?' or 'What can I do . . . ?' You should also be practical and ask, 'Can I actually do something about this issue? Can I hope to influence the situation, or am I out of my depth?' Be realistic. You cannot change the entire world but you can change yourself, beginning with your thinking. Keep it small, focused and manageable. For example, you may want to investigate reductions of funding for the adult education service in your community. You can do nothing on a large scale because it is probably connected with the wider political–economic situation. However, you could mobilise the adult learners in your institution to lobby the local policy makers to present their views about the importance of adult learning. This is a small step that could contribute to a better understanding by politicians. You would express your research issue as 'I am concerned that the level of funding for adult education is falling', and your research question could be 'What can I do to raise the level of funding?' If you and others share the same research intent, you could ask, 'How do we raise the level of funding?'

Here are some more examples:

- How do we evaluate whether our student care programmes are working for the benefit of the students?
- How will I manage my work schedule better?
- How can I persuade the management to introduce new consultation procedures in this organisation?
- How do I help Mr X to raise his self-confidence?

Keep the following ideas in mind:

- I am the central person in my research. I am investigating how I can help others learn to make their own wise choices.
- I am asking a real-world question about a real-world issue, and I am hoping to find an imaginative way forward.
- I am starting from where I am. I am starting small and focusing on a local issue with wider educational intent.
- I am trying to influence people's learning so that they see ways in which they can manage and improve their own situations.
- I remember that 'the situation' is not an abstract entity, but comprises real people in interaction with one another. Therefore I am not trying to improve 'a situation' but trying to help people see that they can help themselves.

How do I show what the situation I am in is like at the moment?

It is important to show the current situation as it is, so that you have a base line for demonstrating progress and explaining the processes involved. At this point therefore you begin thinking about gathering baseline data and generating evidence. 'Data' refers to the information you gather about a situation (remember that data and evidence are different things – see below p. 102 for a full explanation).

When you begin your project you may not be sure which data to gather. You may need to gather a lot of data before your main issue emerges. It can be difficult to decide which data to use for particular purposes. Aim to gather your data and store them in one place: in a box or on your computer. As you progress, learn how to manage and organise your data. Detailed advice about gathering and managing the data appears in Chapter 9.

Gather data according to what you wish to show. This means you have to make decisions about what you wish to show and how you will show it through the use of data. To help you, keep in mind what action research is about and why you are doing it. Action research is about taking action in your own thinking in order to help you find ways to influence other people's learning in an educational way, so that they in turn investigate their practices and find ways of helping others. A key issue then becomes how learning informs actions, and how one person's learning can inform their own and other people's actions. You need therefore to gather data to show how your learning informs your actions, which can in turn influence other people's learning for future action. The most powerful action research accounts show these transformational relationships in action. The very best action research accounts show the relationship between how your learning has influenced the development of other people's actions. These ideas are discussed further in Chapter 8.

Examples of what these relationships look like in action, and the processes involved in developing them, can be shown in the accounts of researchers such as Julie Pearson (2008) and Alex Sinclair (2008 – see also http://www.youtube.com/watch?v+THua6Ywoswc), who worked in similar areas for their masters studies. Their enquiries showed how they learned how to encourage reflexive thinking and the capacity for independent enquiry among early-career teachers. You can also see the accounts of a group of academic practitioners from St Mary's University College (see below, p. 104).

At a practical level, you need to ask some specific questions:

- Which participants?
- Which data?
- Which criteria?

Which participants?

You probably work with many people. Your research is an aspect of your wider work, so you would aim to work initially only with those people who are involved in your research, with a view to influencing practices in the field. However, even in your narrowed field you still need to be selective. Identify a small group of people as your research participants and representative of your wider work. Be reasonably sure they will help you to generate the kind of data that will enable you to make judgements about your developing work together.

Don't feel pressured into choosing a large group. It is perfectly feasible to do a piece of good-quality action research working with one person; for example, Erica Holley (1997) explains how she influenced the writings of one of her students and includes a dialogue that shows how this influence was worked on by the student. She also shows how she made a creative response to the constraining influences of government policies on appraisal (see www.actionresearch.net/erica.shtml). The focus of your work is you, and you are your main source of data. Your research participants are sources of data that show how you are trying to exercise your educational influence in your own and their thinking. Perhaps they will also begin researching their work, and you would become a source of data for them. Always negotiate access and permission with your participants; don't take anything for granted.

Which data?

You are the main focus of your research. You are not trying to show a cause-and-effect relationship between you and others in the sense of 'If I do X, they will do Y'. You are trying to show an improvement in your practice, beginning with your learning. The evidence for this lies in the extent to which you are having an educational influence on others' learning. They need to say whether or not you are influencing them in ways that help them to learn. It might be argued that they will agree with you, just to please you (or perhaps because they are afraid of you). You can never avoid this situation entirely, but you can produce reasonable evidence to show that you are acting with honesty for their benefit. This evidence may be found in any data that show you in interaction with others in ways that help them improve their learning (see p. 179). You and your participants would share records of practice, negotiate your perceptions, and come to a collective agreement about your findings. These processes provide strong sources of data to show how you are holding yourselves individually and collectively accountable for your work.

Which criteria?

You need to identify criteria and standards of judgement for you and others to judge whether you are achieving your goals. Your criteria will be related to your values (see above p. 93). If your values include ideas that people should think for themselves and make their own decisions, your criteria will be whether people do think for themselves and make their own decisions. Your values, which you hold at a tacit level, become your living criteria when they emerge within and through your practice. If you can show that you have enabled people to think for themselves and make their own decisions, you can say that you are living your values and meeting your criteria.

This then acts as the basis for generating evidence.

Turning data into evidence

Evidence refers to those pieces of data that relate directly to your research question and claim to knowledge. Remember that the claim to knowledge is a transformation of the research question, and it is possible to show how this transformation happened. You will tend to gather lots of data, much of which may turn out to be irrelevant. Relevant pieces of data that show these processes of transformation will become evidence. On p. 182 you can find detailed advice on the steps involved in generating evidence from the data.

Note: Remember that data and evidence can confound, as well as confirm, our expectations. Sometimes they can show that things are not going according to plan; this is called disconfirming data and evidence. Disconfirming data give a powerful steer that helps you check whether you are on the right track, or need to change course; and disconfirming evidence would indicate that you may be seriously mistaken in the conclusions you have drawn. Either way, it means you have to rethink what you are doing and, perhaps, start again.

What can I do about the situation? What will I do?

First, you should question your own interpretation of your data. Imagine different ways in which they could be interpreted, and talk with others about what you could do. Remember that any decisions for action should be your decisions, not other people's. It is also your responsibility to ensure that whatever you decide to do does not involve organisational upheaval for others.

Sometimes researchers feel that if they don't immediately 'solve' an issue, or they don't achieve an anticipated 'result', they have failed. This is not the case. Things do not often work out as anticipated. Nor can you 'change' situations, other than in relation to changing yourself and trying to influence others to change themselves. Change happens in people's minds and this mental change then transforms into actions. Look on your project as an opportunity to develop your thinking and practice as you try to influence others. If you can show that you have developed your thinking and have learned then that is enough. Your improved thinking is an outcome of your research, although your claim to knowledge is more robust if you can show that your improved thinking has helped others to learn. Be clear about what you are claiming and produce appropriate evidence to support your claim.

In your report, you need to show the process of the development of your own and others' learning. Evidence for this will be found in your collective records of practice (see also p. 179). Try to show the possibly chaotic and punctuated processes of learning: how the unexpected happened – how you came to see that issues you believed existed only at a surface level were in fact symptomatic of underlying matters. Studying your own communication skills may reveal that you fidget or don't look people in the eye. Or perhaps you put people down in subtle ways. A concern such as 'How do I improve the way in which people of mixed heritage are perceived in this organisation?' could show that there is structural prejudice throughout the organisation. This kind of 'explosion' is common. Stay focused, and remember that this is a small-scale project. You may come to regard it as the first cycle of a project that develops into several progressive or developmental cycles. It may also be the first cycle in what will become a larger project or an ongoing feature of your everyday work. Whatever the overall shape of your project, stay focused on the issue that you have identified for this stage.

How will I show the situation as it develops?

Aim to gather data on a regular basis. Keep records of how you are monitoring and evaluating each cycle. These become your case records and show the developmental nature of your work. It is not quite the same as 'before' and 'after' data, because you should be able to show a progression of events that include your own changing understandings of the situation and a re-evaluation of the position you held at the beginning of the research.

You may choose to use the same data-gathering methods throughout your research, or you can mix and match them as appropriate. For example, during your reconnaissance phase, you may wish to interview people to hear their reactions to what is happening in the organisation, whereas at later stages you may choose to video interactions among people. You may also use different kinds of data and data analysis: you can use quantitative and qualitative data and evidence to support and test the validity of your knowledge claims (see p. 176).

For example, James Finnegan (2000) was able to show the use of both qualitative and quantitative data in the development of his enquiry 'How do I create my own educational theory in my educative relations as an action researcher and as a teacher?' (retrieved 22 February 2009 from www.action-research.net/fin.shtml)

Monitoring the research, gathering data and generating evidence are technical activities that should improve as your research goes on. Aim to triangulate the data, i.e. obtain data from more than one source to use as evidence to support a particular explanation, and show how the data from these different sources all go towards supporting the explanations you give of your situation (see also p. 179). This is important in getting other people to validate your claims to knowledge. You need to show how the findings from your research can be useful for other people, because action research is about learning to improve learning in order to inform new thinking and new practices.

What kind of evidence can I produce to show that what I am doing is influencing someone's learning?

Remember that action research is about improving your learning, so that you can bring that learning to bear on your actions. Your learning and actions then have the potential to influence other people's learning and actions. These are all transformational and mutually informing aspects of practice. The question of the production of evidence to show the validity of these interactive processes then becomes somewhat complex. It is straightforward to show the process of improving your own thinking and actions: you can produce your reflective journal, and your 'before and after' videotapes of you interacting with others. It is not so easy to produce evidence of other people's learning, so you have to ask the people themselves. They will have recorded their learning in their journals or they can point to instances on videotapes that they claim are manifestations of their learning. This emphasises the collaborative and dialogical nature of action research, where people negotiate their meanings with one another as they seek to produce evidence to test the validity of their individual or collective knowledge claims.

For example, a group of academic staff from St Mary's University College have been working collaboratively on their masters and doctoral programmes for several years. They have formed themselves into a committed group of educational researchers who wish to influence others' learning through improving their own. They actively disseminate their work through conference presentations, books and scholarly papers, as well as through the programmes they deliver. An evidence base is available at EJOLTS (http://ejolts.net/node/136). A new book in preparation shows how their underpinning relational and dialogical values and logics inform the collaborative processes involved.

How do I evaluate what I am doing?

Evaluation is grounded in the idea of values, that is, what is to be counted as good. It involves making judgements about the quality of something to establish what is good about it. Value judgements are always subjective, because different people have different ideas about what counts as 'the good'. It is therefore up to the participants in the discourse to negotiate their understandings of what is 'good', and how agreements can be reached.

It is generally agreed that there are at least two forms of evaluation: self-evaluation and external evaluation. In external forms of evaluation, an external observer makes judgements about something, usually using specified criteria and standards of judgement. In self-evaluation, the person usually makes their own judgements about the thing in question, using both externally identified criteria, and also their own criteria, where permitted. An action research approach allows and encourages practitioners to make their personal subjective judgements about their practices, using their own nominated assessment criteria, and present their subjective judgements to the critical scrutiny of others (see below). They use their values as their criteria and standards of judgement, and judge the quality of their practices in light of the extent of their realisation of their values.

Therefore, in evaluating your research and establishing its potential worth, you need to show what has improved, and how. The whole of your action research is an evaluation process because you:

- gather data;
- identify criteria and standards of judgement;
- select pieces of data to act as evidence of the validity of your claim that you have influenced improvement in learning;
- test the evidence against your initial concern and research question;
- articulate the significance of what you claim to have done;
- present your work for others to judge whether or not you are justified in making your knowledge claim.

These practices are now well established in many universities and other award-granting institutions. A significant knowledge base exists in which practitioners have identified their values as their living criteria and standards of judgement, to act as a powerful precedent for new academic works within a self-study action research tradition. Some examples can be found at:

- Hartog, M. (2004) 'A self study of a higher education tutor: how can I improve my practice?', PhD thesis, University of Bath. Retrieved 19 February 2009 from www.actionresearch.net/hartog.shtml

- Lohr, E. (2006) 'Love at work: what is my lived experience of love and how may I become an instrument of love's purpose?', PhD thesis, University of Bath. Retrieved 19 February 2009 from www.actionresearch.net/lohr. shtml
- Charles, E. (2007) 'How can I bring Ubuntu as a living standard of judgment into the academy? Moving beyond decolonisation through societal reidentification and guiltless recognition', PhD thesis, University of Bath. Retrieved 19 February 2009 from www.actionresearch.net/ edenphd.shtml
- Glenn, M. (2006) Working with collaborative projects: my living theory of a holistic educational practice', PhD thesis, University of Limerick. Retrieved 19 February 2009 from www.jeanmcniff.com/glennabstract. html

How do I communicate the significance of what I am doing?

Most research processes, including action research, involve the following:

- *observations* (seeing what is happening);
- *descriptions* (describing what is happening);
- *explanations* (offering explanations for what it is happening).

Explanations are probably the most important, because explanations contain both observations and descriptions. Furthermore, explanations involve articulating the significance, or importance, of what you have done. Significance in action research refers to the implications of your research for other people's thinking and practices, as well as the transformation of your own. It is your responsibility, as an action researcher, to point out to others why they should take your work seriously and listen to what you have to say. However, other people may see the significance of our work before we do, and help us to see its importance. This can be a key function for a validation group (see p. 199).

To help you perceive the significance of your practices, try the following exercise. As part of your regular journal keeping, try dividing the page into four columns, each with their own headings: (1) What I did; (2) Why I did it; (3) What I learned from what I did; and (4) The significance of my learning (Figure 6.1).

Explaining the significance of your practice and your research encourages you to reflect critically on your practice and identify its strengths and limitations. It also allows you to claim validity and legitimacy for what you are doing. By making explicit what you feel implicitly, you are able to (1) speak with the authority of your own practice; (2) defend your arguments from an informed standpoint; and (3) claim with justification that your work has potential significance for other people's learning.

What I did	Why I did it	What I learned from what I did	The significance of my learning
I prepared my public lecture in advance	I wanted to be well prepared because I owe it to my audience to deliver a good lecture	I learned that it is necessary to be prepared as this prevents feelings of panic	I will bring my learning from this episode to other similar episodes, and be prepared for any public performance

Figure 6.1 Organising a reflective diary.

The best example available of the procedures and experiences of a validation group can be found in the work of Martin Forrest (1983). You can access this directly from www.jackwhitehead.com/writeup/alval.pdf; you can also see a summary on p. 198–9 of this book.

How do I ensure that any judgements I make are reasonably fair and accurate?

We said above that evaluation in action research is about reaching inter-subjective agreement about the validity of knowledge claims. This process has two parts: personal validation and social (public, external) validation.

Personal validation

Personal validation involves testing your provisional knowledge claim against the critical feedback of yourself. You scrutinise your evidence against your own critical judgement of the extent to which you can truthfully say that you are living in the direction of your values. If you feel your evidence is not sufficiently robust then it is your responsibility to strengthen it, perhaps by re-analysing your data, or gathering more meaningful or relevant data.

Social (public, external) validation

This is where you subject your provisional claim to knowledge to the critical scrutiny of others and invite their feedback. You also invite them to test the validity of your claims in relation to criteria such as those identified by Habermas (1976), as follows:

• Is the claim comprehensible? Do you use language that others can follow?

- Is the claim truthful? Do you show, through the production of an evidence base, that you have done what you claim to have done?
- Is the claim authentic? Do you show how, over time, you are to be trusted in living your values in your practices?
- Is the claim appropriate? Do you show that you have done your research with a full understanding of the political, economic, social and cultural (and other) forces acting upon your context: that is, the normative background in which you are writing, living and working?

You can also draw on work from researchers such as Lather (1991). She speaks of the need for ironic validity (i.e. explaining how your critical self has stood to one side of your researcher self, so that you are able to comment critically on your present thinking and actions) and how these may be improved.

How do I modify my practices and ideas in light of my evaluation?

If your new way of working appears to be more in line with your educational values and visions, continue with it and also continue the evaluation process. If the new way does not seem to be working, try something else.

You may not be entirely satisfied with your practice, although you have made progress. You will probably never reach perfection, because as soon as one issue has been addressed, other issues seem to arise in its place. We live with the paradox of the ideal: we imagine the way things could be, but as soon as we have an answer, new questions arise. Your present thinking is your best thinking yet, but you know it is going to develop, as it has already developed, and improved. Each day you have is the best, and tomorrow will be even better. Life is always dynamic and changing, even to the moment we die. It is what we do with that life that counts.

How do I evaluate the experience of doing the project?

As part of your overall evaluation, as communicated in your report, you need to say whether the entire experience of doing the project was beneficial to your own learning, and whether your learning has influenced your actions. You should also say whether you believe it was a success, or could have been a greater success if you had done things differently. You may already have decided that during the next cycle of your action research you will do things differently, perhaps by articulating a different research question or inviting different participants to be involved. Perhaps you found that you were acting in ways that did not encourage learning, or that the institutional constraints were too big to handle. By explaining that the research was perhaps not as successful as it could have been, you are showing your willingness to be critical of your own learning and actions.

Sometimes researchers feel that by saying things could have been better they are admitting to mistakes. This is not the case. By explaining how things could have been better, we are actually engaging with our critical capacity to reflect and find ways of improving. Action research is about learning, and action research reports need to communicate this process of learning. If you produce a report where you communicate that everything went smoothly and came to a happy ending then your readers will become suspicious, because life seldom has entirely happy endings. It is what you do with the problematic issues that counts. So feel confident in stating what some of the problematic issues were, how you learned from engaging with them, and how you will bring your new learning into new action reflection cycles.

How do I write a good-quality report?

All researchers need to make their research public and they do this usually by producing a report. There are many different kinds of report. Information about these kinds, and also how to write a good-quality report, is provided in Chapter 13. It is essential to ensure the good quality of your report, because what people know of you is what they read or hear about you. If your report is of less than the highest quality, people will not take your work as seriously as you wish. It is your responsibility to learn how to write well and address the technical aspects of producing high-quality writing. You can find comprehensive information in McNiff and Whitehead (2009).

How do I disseminate my findings so that other people can learn from me and I from them?

As soon as possible into your project you should begin thinking about how you can make your findings public. Chapter 14 gives ideas about how you can do this.

Summary

This chapter has looked at the idea of conceptual frameworks, which are formalisations of the main ideas underpinning your project, and methodological frameworks, which are formalised ways of doing your project. The chapter gives detailed information on the steps involved in how to do an action research project. Awareness of these should help you design and carry out your action research successfully, and offer reasons throughout for what you are doing.

Checklist of reflective questions

Think about the following:

- Are you clear about what 'conceptual frameworks' means? Have you thought about which concepts inform your project, and why these are important? Can you relate them to your values, and explain the relationship?
- Have you a reasonable idea about the overall methodology? Can you say why you have chosen this methodology, and not another? Especially at masters and doctoral levels you would have to justify your choice of methodology.
- Are you confident about the different steps involved in doing an action research project? Do you think you can fulfil each of the steps? You don't have to follow them slavishly, but you do need to show understanding of the issues involved and show that you have addressed them.

In the next chapter we continue with the theme of designing your project, now from the perspective of drawing up checklists for action, built around the questions that form the basis of this action plan.

Chapter 7

Designing your project: checklists for action

This chapter continues the theme of designing your action research project. In the previous chapter we spoke about the kinds of conceptual and methodological frameworks that you need to think about and develop. In this chapter we discuss the logistical and practical aspects of how you intend to take action. The checklists here will help you to see what needs to be done, whether you have done them, and, if not, to plan for when you will do them.

Before you begin

Forward planning

Draw up a provisional forward planner to give you a rough idea of what needs to be done. The sample planner below is for a sixteen- to twenty-week project. It shows how you can organise tasks into manageable chunks. You should adapt it to your own needs and insert new items as appropriate. Your planner may well change as your circumstances change, and new issues may emerge during the course of your project. Also take periodic advice from others such as critical friends to make sure you are still on task and on the right track.

Example of a forward planner

SCHEDULE FOR ACTION RESEARCH PROJECT

Your name ....

Task undertaken	*Weeks*
Planning and preparation	
Identify research area and issue	1–3
Initial reading and literature search	1–5
Draw up ethics statement	1–5
Plan and design project	1–5
Resourcing	
Draw up budget	1–3
Submit request for funding	1–3
Negotiate use of multimedia and Internet facilities	1–5
Working with other people	
Discussions with management and policy makers	1–2
Invitations to potential groups of participants	3–5
Invitations to critical friend(s)	2–5
Invitations to potential validation group	3–5
Send out letters requesting permission to do the research	3–5
Doing the project	
Identify research issue/concern: check with others	3–5
Articulate research question	3–5
Data gathering (first round)	3–5
Identify working criteria and standards of judgement	3–5
Imagining solutions/brainstorming with colleagues	5–7
Try out possible actions/solutions	5–12
Data gathering continued (second and further rounds)	5–12
Generate evidence from the data	10–12
Articulate knowledge claim and test its validity through specific validation procedures	10–13
Articulate the significance of the project and your findings	10–13
Convene validation group	7–13

Evaluating the significance of the project

Produce working document about the significance of your project for your own learning	13–16
Produce working documents about its significance for others	13–16

Writing up the report

Draft report produced and sent to colleagues for approval	13–16
Final report produced and disseminated to key persons	13–16

Dissemination of findings

Think about how to disseminate your findings through conferences, scholarly papers, books and journal articles, appearances on local radio and television, convening special interest groups, liaising with existing networks, and convening new ones . . . and so on. All this to be done in the near future.

You will probably draw up a more detailed planner than this. You would identify critical friends and groups of participants. The more thought you put in at this stage, the more successful your project is likely to be. Further, if you give this kind of information to managers and principals, they will be more likely to endorse your plans. Time spent in planning is well invested.

Beginning on the next page you will find useful checklists for your action plan. Use them to help you keep track of progress. Aim to develop them for your own situation. Create new items that are especially relevant to you, and draw on the advice of your supervisor and critical friends about what needs to be done. The boxes will help you check what has been done, and what is outstanding.

The checklists are organised broadly into the following sections:

- getting started;
- planning and designing the project;
- doing the project;
- evaluating the project and articulating its significance;
- modifying practice;
- writing up the research report,

This section is particularly useful for first-time action researchers. If you are more experienced, go to Chapter 8.

Getting started

Identifying a research interest

What aspect of your work are you going to investigate?

Have you:	Yes!	When?
• Identified an area you wish to investigate?	☐	....
• Related it to your work?	☐	....
• Kept it small, focused and manageable?	☐	....
• Thought about how you can improve your own learning?	☐	....
• Considered whether you will use this learning to improve your practice?	☐	....
• Considered whether you will be able to influence other people's learning?	☐	....
• Begun to think about a research question ('How do I . . . ?')	☐	....
• Anything else?	☐	....

Tips

- Aim to complete the question 'How do I improve . . .' as the starting point for your research. Don't worry if you can't formulate your question precisely. Researchers tend to have an idea about what they want to investigate and the idea begins to take shape as new insights develop through action and reflection. This can take a long time, and sometimes a new question, or several new questions, will emerge.
- Stay with one question only. Leave the others for later. You may decide to abandon your original question and choose a new one; or focus on a new one and come back to the original later.

Tasks

In your work file, write out:

- The area you hope to investigate. Put this as a question: 'How do I improve . . . ?' Show how this is related to your work.
- Give a brief outline of your context and why it is important to address your identified issue. Say how you intend to influence new thinking and new practices in some way.

Your values

Have you:	**Yes!**	**When?**

- Thought about the idea of values and how these need to be transformed into real-world practices? ☐ ....

- Thought about your own values? Thought about which values you do not subscribe to? ☐ ....

- Thought about whether your values are commensurable with institutional values, and how? If not, have you thought about what you can do about the situation? ☐ ....

- Considered whether you can realise your values in your daily practices? ☐ ....

- Considered how you might do so? Considered what you will do if you cannot do so? ☐ ....

- Thought about how you can show the realisation of your values in practice, and what kind of evidence you can generate to show the processes in action? ☐ ....

- Anything else? ☐ ....

Tips

- Think carefully about which values give meaning to your life. Is it possible to realise them in your practice?
- Consult with managers and colleagues about how your values might inform wider institutional practices. Is this achievable? How?
- How will you exercise your educational influence in your own and other people's learning?

Tasks

- Remember that discussions about values can be delicate. Always tread lightly and negotiate.
- Do not think other people necessarily share your values. Check with them and talk things through. Be prepared to negotiate your position as appropriate, but continue to stand up for what you really believe in.

- Write down your values, and if possible analyse them into ontological, epistemological, methodological, social and political values. Create your own categories for analysis of how you give meaning to your life, and how you may wish to influence other people's thinking and practices.

Your conceptual frameworks

This section is important if you are on an award-bearing course. It is not so important if you are on a non-accredited work-based learning programme, but even so aim to engage creatively and critically with the writings of others.

Have you:	**Yes!**	**When?**
• Identified the values that give meaning to your professional life, and begun to think of them as conceptual and theoretical frameworks, such as justice, independent learning, participation and warm social relationships?	❐	....
• Are you clear about which conceptual frameworks will act as the grounds for your project? Have you negotiated these with other people and sought their critical feedback?	❐	....
• Have you checked with potential participants that they are comfortable with the focus you have chosen?	❐	....
• Are you reasonably confident that you can show the realisation of your values in your practices, and therefore justify your choice of conceptual frameworks?	❐	....
• Anything else?	❐	....

Tips

- It is important to begin thinking about the frameworks that will inform your studies. What issues drive you? What are you prepared to stand up for? Think in these terms to help you to identify potential frameworks. Remember that they will become clearer and take on new meanings as your study progresses.

- Don't choose too many concepts in the first instance. In a workplace programme, one or two would be sufficient. On a masters programme, choose three or four major concepts, and on a doctoral programme, choose as many as you can reasonably handle. One key framework may be sufficient, with other embedded frameworks appearing from time to time.

Tasks

- Write down your conceptual frameworks, and relate these to your identified values. Write down why these are important frameworks; for example, you may be denying the concepts/values in your practices and need to do something about the dissonance.
- Discuss with critical friends how one framework may transform into another over time. Be as creative as you like.
- Doing this will help you offer a rationale and a justification for doing your research, and also enable you to articulate the significance of what will be your original claim to knowledge.

Background reading

Have you: **Yes!**   **When?**

- Read enough subject literature to give
  you a reasonable foundation, especially
  in relation to identifying your conceptual
  frameworks?   ❏   ....

- Done a literature search so that you know
  what other people say about your area?   ❏   ....

- Read enough methodology literature to
  give you a reasonable foundation and to
  articulate a methodological framework?   ❏   ....

- Kept a notebook with key ideas and
  authors?   ❏   ....

- Kept an index file with references –
  authors, title, date, place of publication,
  publisher? Kept a page reference for any
  quotations you intend to use? Remember
  that it will save you hours, if not days,
  looking up references at a later date.   ❏   ....

- Identified which literatures you still need
  to read, and when you will do so?   ❐   ....
- Identified where you will get them?   ❐   ....
- Identified who can advise you with
  different aspects of literature?   ❐   ....
- Read Internet dissertations, theses and
  other reports?   ❐   ....
- Anything else?   ❐   ....

Tips

- Ask your supervisor (if you have one) for reading lists to guide you.
- Use the library. Ask the librarian for advice on conducting literature searches.
- Find out the necessary computerised databases and abstracting and indexing services.
- Buy key texts for yourself. Share these among your study group (put your name in them if you lend them out).
- Don't feel you have to read a text cover to cover. Be selective.
- Access Internet resources for further contacts and examples of validated reports.

Tasks

- Read actively. Keep notes as you read.
- Write on your own books if you wish. Never deface library or other people's books.
- Keep a computer database or a card index system of books and papers. File them under author's name or theme. Organise your own system, and stay consistent with it. Write down key sentences as you read and always include the page number.
- Use your database to build up your references systematically. When you write up you must get your references accurate. Do not ignore this warning!
- Keep a file of important hard copy papers. Respect copyrights and intellectual property rights.

Ethical issues

Have you:	**Yes!**	**When?**

- Negotiated access with, and negotiated permission to do your research from:

  - principals/managers/others in authority? ☐ ....

  - your research participants? ☐ ....

  - parents/carers? ☐ ....

  - colleagues? ☐ ....

  - others? who? ☐ ....

- Produced your ethics statement and distributed it? ☐ ....

- Checked who wishes their identities to be made public, and who does not? ☐ ....

- Demonstrated good faith throughout? Do you need to go back and check, and perhaps put a few aspects right? ☐ ....

- Anything else? ☐ ....

Tips

- Do not skip this stage. You may find you cannot complete your project if you do not have the necessary permissions.
- Read other people's ethics statements to see how to write your own. Make sure you write yours in relation to your own context, and take organisational sensitivities into account.
- Seek advice if you are unsure of any aspects. Better safe than sorry.
- Tread very lightly around issues of ethics. Aim to keep people on your side, and respect their wishes at all times, even if this means you have to abandon a favourite element of the project. Try not to upset anyone!

Tasks

- Write out your ethics statement and give a copy to everyone involved in your research. Especially give a copy with every letter requesting permission to do the research. Write letters asking permission well in advance.
- Keep all letters in a file to show that you have negotiated issues of access and confidentiality as part of your evidence base. Have ready blank copies to place in your appendices. You can later refer to your

documentation to show that you were serious about ethical issues, and give to anyone who queries your authenticity or conscientiousness in addressing matters of ethical conduct.

Resourcing

You may find that you do not need any financial or logistical support for your project, but, if you do:

Have you:	Yes!	When?
• Planned and drawn up a budget for your project?	☐	....
• Secured the necessary funding, if any?	☐	....
• Catered on a shortfall of funds, and allowed a safety margin?	☐	....
• Considered aspects such as printing and other logistical factors?	☐	....
• Checked that all necessary technology is available, especially if you are intending to gather multimedia data?	☐	....
• Negotiated its use with others?	☐	....
• Worked out a time-line for your project?	☐	....
• Anything else?	☐	....

Tips

- If you are looking for funding you will need to apply well in advance. Make sure you have budgeted for the duration of your project, so that you don't run out of money.
- Obtain quotations from reputable typists and printers in good time. Check the availability of reproduction facilities.
- Checked that you have access to multimedia technologies, and that you can use them. Check the availability of technical support if appropriate.
- If you do all of your own typing, get a good computer and ensure Internet access. Learn to type using all of your fingers.

Tasks

- Draw up as detailed a budget as possible. Aim to stick to it.
- Keep a file of correspondence to do with finance.
- Keep a monthly record of accounts. This can be time-consuming, but is essential.

Working with others

Have you:	Yes!	When?
• Established a working plan and drawn up a schedule of work?	❐	....
• Negotiated and agreed it with your supervisor and manager/principal?	❐	....
• Identified your critical friend(s)?	❐	....
• Negotiated and agreed your joint responsibilities, and a schedule of meetings with them?	❐	....
• Established who your research participants will be?	❐	....
• Talked through your ideas with your proposed participants?	❐	....
• Identified your validation group, negotiated their responsibilities, and agreed a schedule of meetings with them?	❐	....
• Anything else?	❐	....

Tips

- Aim to do most of this in advance, although some aspects can be done as the project develops. Never assume that people will automatically be available, or will do what you want them to. Ask in advance – like you, they have busy schedules.
- Aim to keep your participants involved by producing regular written mini-reports or give them frequent verbal feedback.
- You must produce formal progress reports for your supervisor and your validation group, to let them see the progress of your project and to show them evidence of progress (or not as the case may be).
- At the end of the project, send a copy of the final report to any members of the group who request one, and thank them for their involvement. It is important to maintain courteous conduct at all times.

Tasks

- Negotiate a working schedule with your supervisor and write it out. This is your responsibility, not your supervisor's. Give them a copy and keep it as a reference point for your work together.
- Once you have identified all your participants, write to them, inviting them to be part of your research. Let them know what will be involved:

how many meetings, what their responsibilities are. Negotiate times, dates and venues with them. Do not take their availability for granted; check in advance. Always say please and thank you.

- For your validation group, draw up a schedule of meetings. The number of meetings will depend on the length and duration of the project. Aim to meet at critical points of your research, such as when you are presenting the evidence, or outlining a turning point in your research (this means having a research schedule yourself that you are working with).
- Produce regular progress reports and send them in advance of any validation meetings. Draw up a list of key questions you would like your group to discuss.
- Keep all of these records in your data archive.

Planning and designing your project

Organise your thinking and actions drawing on the set of critical questions on p. 96, for example, as follows:

What is my concern?

Have you:	**Yes!**	**When?**
• Identified an area that you feel needs to be addressed, and that you are reasonably confident you can do something about?	❒	....
• Discussed it with your supervisor?	❒	....
• Discussed it with other colleagues?	❒	....
• Ensured that this is an area where you can probably show improvement?	❒	....
• Kept the issue reasonably small and manageable, bearing in mind contextual issues?	❒	....
• Made yourself aware of any political, cultural, economic and social aspects of the wider context?	❒	....
• Anything else?	❒	....

Tips

- Check with your supervisor that the area you have chosen is appropriate as an action research project.
- When doing your preliminary reading, identify a few keywords and check who else is doing research in this area. There may be some valuable

research you can draw on and incorporate into your own theorising. Try to show that you are up to date in the field.

- Check what key policy recommendations exist around the area. Will your research contribute to new thinking, and possibly new policy? In what way?

Tasks

- Write your research issue in your workbook. It will act as a reminder that this is the focus of your research and help you stay on task.
- Write out a brief description of your context. Say what is going on in terms of social, cultural, economic, historical or political factors that may have a bearing on your choice of topic.
- Write out who you are, what your job is and where you work, and what the conditions are like. Keeping a record like this will act as vital data for when you write up your project.

Why am I concerned?

Have you: **Yes!   When?**

- Identified the values you hold as a
  person and a professional that inform
  your work?   ❏   ....

- Thought about whether they are they
  being realised or negated in your
  practice? In what way?   ❏   ....

- Imagined what your situation would
  be like if it were in keeping with your
  values?   ❏   ....

- Considered what it would take to
  influence people's thinking so that your
  social situation was in keeping with your
  values?   ❏   ....

- Checked your own perceptions of what
  is happening against other people's
  feedback? Are you justified in aiming to
  take action?   ❏   ....

- Interrogated your own thinking about
  the situation, and wondered whether
  you need to do some reflexive critique or
  deconstruction on yourself?   ❏   ....

- Made a record of your own values
  statement for future reference?   ☐   ....

Tips

- Think carefully about why you have chosen this particular area. What
  are your personal values that contribute to your professional identity?
  What are your professional values, the motives that drive you to do the
  job you do?
- To what extent are you working in the way you wish? What do you need
  to do in order to achieve that position?
- Can you justify your planned intervention in this situation for
  educational reasons?
- How do you plan to engage in your own thinking, and record your new
  learning?

Tasks

- Write out your personal, professional, educational and social values.
  You could write this as your personal mission statement.
- Give a brief description of your work situation, and say whether you are
  living in the direction of your values and why, or if not, why not.
- Say why you feel you are justified in intervening in the area you have
  identified. If possible, show that you have checked your perceptions
  with someone else. Take care that you are not just interfering and really
  can justify your intent to take educational action.

What is my research question?

Have you: **Yes!**   **When?**

- Formulated a research question of the
  form 'How do I improve what I am
  doing?'   ☐   ....

- Related it directly to the research issue
  you identified earlier?   ☐   ....

- Kept it focused, small, manageable and
  relevant?   ☐   ....

- Considered whether it is feasible to
  engage with the question in light of
  wider political, theoretical, historical,
  cultural and other contextualising
  factors?   ☐   ....

- Taken due account of recognising that
  you need to begin with interrogating
  your own thinking about what you are
  doing?   ☐   ....

- Considered whether your research
  question is justified and checked with
  critical friends?   ☐   ....

- Anything else?   ☐   ....

Tips

- It is easy to imagine that you can change the world overnight, which is
  simply not possible, although you can often influence people's thinking
  in a short time. The place to begin is with your own thinking, by asking
  yourself, 'Am I justified in thinking and doing the things I do? How do
  I check this out?'
- Test the justifiability of your research question against the critical
  feedback of critical colleagues. Listen to what they say, and take action
  appropriately.
- Be aware that your question may well change into a new question, as
  your thinking develops, especially through dialogue with critical others.
- Remember that you are aiming to transform your research question into
  your claim to knowledge. 'How do I improve my practice?' will become
  (hopefully) 'I have improved my practice.'

Tasks

- Write out your research question and keep it high in your mind.
- Write out what you think your knowledge claim will be by the end of
  your project.
- Check with colleagues whether they think they can work with you on
  this question.
- Check whether they think you are sufficiently informed about wider
  contextual issues, so that you can take action, from the grounds of your
  question, to make the whole thing feasible.

*What logistical and practical factors are involved in doing
my project?*

Have you: **Yes!   When?**

- Identified a time-scale, with a start and end
  date, and key dates for completion of tasks
  between?   ☐   ....

- Identified a location for your project? If this is your workplace, have you negotiated with appropriate personnel as to whether you may do it?   ❑   ....

- Considered whether you will have time to do it properly? Will this involve eating into personal time? If so, are you prepared for this?   ❑   ....

- Ensured that sufficient funds are available if needed?   ❑   ....

- Ensured that you have appropriate technical support on hand if needed?   ❑   ....

- Ensured that you can offer a cogent rationale for your project for anyone who wants to know?   ❑   ....

- Identified potential participants and negotiated their involvement with them?   ❑   ....

- Anything else?   ❑   ....

Tips

- Many logistical and practical issues can be planned for in advance, but not all. Be prepared for new eventualities to arise. At worst, be prepared for the entire project to fall apart but also be aware that you can use the experience as the basis of a new project, about what you have learned from the experience.
- Maintain an optimistic attitude throughout. The main reason that projects fail (and they do) is because the researcher lost confidence, and decided to give up. It is important to say 'I can' and keep 'I can't' in reserve. Sometimes it really does become impossible to continue with a project, and you simply have to change focus and begin again. But make sure you do begin again.
- Always negotiate logistical and practical issues. These tend to be aspects of organisational practices, and it is important always to check with others before taking action. Avoid taking unilateral action unless absolutely essential.

Tasks

- Write down a list of jobs to do and other logistical aspects under the following headings: Who? Which? When? Where? What? Why? How? It can be helpful to draw up columns across a page and show how different factors may impinge on other factors, because all issues in your project are related.

- Check with others that everything is feasible. Do not skip this aspect of designing. Also make sure you negotiate their involvement whenever possible. People appreciate being involved or at least having the opportunity to refuse.

Doing your project

Doing your project involves the aspects we have already discussed above, namely identifying a research issue, formulating a research question, and considering the values that inform your work. These are key aspects of working towards making your original claim to knowledge. Further key aspects of that process involve monitoring your practice in order to gather data and generate evidence, and these are the aspects that we consider now.

How do I show what the situation I am in is like at the moment?

Asking this question involves thinking about monitoring your practice and gathering data.

Have you:	Yes!	When?
• Decided what kind of data you can gather to act as your baseline data to show the situation as it is? What are you looking for?	☐	....
• Discussed with others the kinds of criteria you are going to use to make judgements about what you should look for?	☐	....
• Chosen which kind of data-gathering methods and instruments you will use?	☐	....
• Selected whose practice you will focus on?	☐	....
• Decided on initial categories for the data?	☐	....
• Made sure that any necessary technology is available (and technical support if required)?	☐	....

Tips

Gathering data

- There is always a temptation to gather any and all data. Be selective. You should identify key areas that will help you to show that you are improving your learning, and bringing that learning to improve your practices. Aim to gather data around these things initially.

- You can then go on to gather data about how you are influencing learning.
- Make a list of possible data-gathering techniques you can use, and put them in order of preference. This will help you identify what you would be most comfortable with (see Chapter 9).
- You can mix and match all these techniques. Do not feel you have to use them all, and certainly not all at once.
- Remember that data are not evidence (see next section).
- Keep data boxes, or files, in hard copy or on your computer. If you are gathering data for several different areas, use different coloured files or boxes, and put all your data into these boxes. Your stored data becomes your data archive.
- Never throw away any data until your project is finished; and even then be selective, because data that you thought to be irrelevant may turn out to apply to new emergent situations.

Storing data

- Check beforehand that technology is available. Make sure you liaise with colleagues about its use.
- If you are storing your data on your computer, make sure to back up your files. Losing your data could be catastrophic. Save your work at frequent intervals.
- Re-sort your categories at frequent intervals, too. Your categories of analysis may change as the project progresses.

Ethics

Always get permission before you do any audio or videotaping or distribute questionnaires. If people refuse permission, you must not go ahead. Respect others' sensitivities.

Evidence

This is dealt with on p. 131.

Tasks

- Identify the group(s) you are going to work with. Seek and obtain everyone's permission before you begin your project.
- Choose your data-gathering methods and instruments. Make sure that any necessary multimedia technology is available.
- Identify and write down your initial categories for the data. Put this information on your files or boxes, and label everything clearly, whether

as physical or electronic storage. You may need to change your categories as your project develops.

- Keep in touch with your supervisor and other colleagues at this stage. Get their feedback on what you are doing and let them see your ideas. Work out with them the criteria that are going to help you to generate evidence.
- Imagine what the evidence could look like.

What can I do? What will I do?

This question involves thinking about how you are going to take action.

Have you:	Yes!	When?
• Imagined at least one possible way you can begin to work differently, in order to address your concerns?	❏	....
• Written down ideas for other possible strategies?	❏	....
• Planned a systematic overall strategy for a possible intervention?	❏	....
• Checked with colleagues that your proposed action plan will not interfere with their schedules?	❏	....
• Invited them and other critical friends to talk through ideas?	❏	....
• Anything else?	❏	....

Tips

- Think about possible action plans. Draw up Plans A, B and C.
- Imagine possible future scenarios in which you will be working more in the direction of your educational values. What will be different then? How are you going to get there? Who will you walk with to get there? (Remember the saying: *If you want to walk fast, walk alone; if you want to walk far, walk with others.*)

Tasks

- Write down your ideas in response to your general question, 'What can I do about this?'
- Make these ideas available to all participating colleagues. Ask their advice and feedback. Ask them for their ideas about what to do.

- Draw up a route map. Brainstorm ideas with colleagues. Draw up diagrams and visuals about possible maps and strategies.
- Check with colleagues that your plans will not cut across theirs. Remember good ethical conduct.

How will I show the situation as it develops?

This question involves thinking about generating evidence, because, although you continue with data gathering, you should also by now be thinking about generating evidence (see p. 131).

Have you:	Yes!	When?
• Decided on the kind of data you hope to gather for your second and later rounds?	☐	....
• Decided on data-gathering methods and instruments?	☐	....
• Decided on categories for your data?	☐	....
• Identified the values you will transform into criteria and standards of judgement, and how you will do this?	☐	....
• Identified the kinds of critical incident that are going to show the values/ criteria in action?	☐	....
• Talked through your ideas with critical colleagues and friends?	☐	....
• Anything else?	☐	....

Tips

- This will be your second set of data. You can gather further sets of data later. You can use the same methods and instruments as in the first round, or different ones.
- You may want to organise a second set of colour-coded boxes or files to compare the first set of data with the second. If you go on to gather further sets of data, you may want to reorganise your sorting and storage systems altogether.

Tasks

- In the same way as for the first round, allocate data to different physical or computer files or boxes. Focus on the values that turn into criteria and standards of judgement to provide evidence that shows that something has improved in some way. Discuss these with critical friends and keep notes of the discussions.

- Ask colleagues how they would judge the quality of your practice and your research. Ask them how they would make judgements. Tape-record these conversations, and highlight those utterances in your transcripts that indicate real movement in the direction of your values. These will constitute some of your evidence. The rest of the data can stay in your data archive.

Evaluating

What kind of evidence can I produce to show that I am influencing someone's learning?

This question involves considering how you transform your values into criteria and standards of judgement to ensure that you are doing your best to realise your values in your practice, in terms of achieving both high-quality actions and also high-quality research.

Have you:	Yes!	When?
• Thoroughly developed your understanding of the difference between data and evidence, and how you turn data into evidence?	☐	....
• Shown in your action research how you use your values as your living criteria and standards of judgement?	☐	....
• Been courageous in identifying disconfirming data and evidence, and modified your actions accordingly?	☐	....
• Gathered sufficient high-quality data from which you will be able to generate evidence?	☐	....
• Articulated your understanding of the processes involved in judging quality?	☐	....
• Checked your judgements against those of critical colleagues, and modified any in light of their and your evaluation?	☐	....
• Anything else?	☐	....

Tips

- It is crucial that you are on the inside of ideas to do with data and evidence, and can speak with understanding and insight.
- Never ignore disconfirming data and evidence. These can act as powerful steers to make sure you are on the right path.
- Talk things through and write them down. This can contribute to the development of your own understanding, because you make explicit what is implicit, and tell yourself what you need to know.

Tasks

- Write down in your notebook how you have established which criteria and standards you are going to use for judging quality.
- Talk through the processes involved with critical friends. If possible, videotape your conversations, and use your videotapes as evidence of how you worked to ensure the quality of what you are doing.
- Constantly test the rightness of your understanding through your own critical engagement and critical engagement with others.

How do I evaluate what I am doing?

Evaluation involves making judgements about quality, about the extent to which criteria denoting quality are realised in practice. In your case, quality is contained within your values, which come to life through your practice.

Have you:	**Yes!**	**When?**
• Identified the values that will act as your living criteria and standards of judgement?	☐	....
• Found ways of representing the processes involved, such as multimedia representations that show the live action?	☐	....
• Negotiated with others how you will do this, and tested the rightness of your actions against your own critical feedback and that of others?	☐	....
• Shown how you incorporate the ideas of other thinkers in the literature into your decisions about your processes of evaluation, and tested the rightness of your ideas against theirs?	☐	....
• Anything else?	☐	....

Tips

- Evaluation in action research begins with your personal evaluation of your practice. Remember that you are making judgements about the quality of your actions and your research. These judgements have to be made public in the form of subjecting them to the critical scrutiny of others (see p. 135).
- Be prepared to be challenged about the subjectivity of your judgements. They are inevitably subjective (all judgements are), but you will lend objectivity through the processes of external social validation (see pp. 107–108).

Tasks

- Write down the processes involved as you find ways of evaluating the quality of what you are doing. Write down how you evaluate the quality of your actions and your research. Explain to yourself how you see both as your practice, and therefore how you are making judgements about your practice. You can use your informal jottings as part of your final report, or as evidence of your improving thinking.
- By writing down, we make our implicit understandings explicit to ourselves. This is an essential first step in processes of explaining things to others. Be aware of the need to externalise internal insights: it is a crucial aspect of explaining (theorising) your practices.

How do I communicate the significance of what I am doing?

This question involves thinking about the significance, or importance, of what you are doing in the sense that you are making contributions to new thinking and new practices.

Have you:	**Yes!**	**When?**
• Articulated for yourself the potential significance of what you are doing, for your own education, for the education of others, and for the education of social formations?	❏	....
• Clarified your understandings of the importance of the processes involved in demonstrating quality in your practices; and developed confidence in communicating these to other people?	❏	....

- Explained to your own satisfaction how you are improving practices and how, through the production of your living accounts, people are able to learn with and from you?   ❐   ....
- Made links between improving practices and creating knowledge? Made links between the quality of your action research and your contributions to the social good?   ❐   ....
- Anything else?   ❐   ....

Tips

- Articulating the significance of what we have done is a crucial yet often overlooked step in processes of explaining (theorising). It is vital that you do communicate your understanding of the significance of your practice, both to yourself and to others. If you are not prepared to take responsibility for your work, you cannot expect other people to take it seriously.
- Articulating the significance of what you are doing is equivalent to showing how you give meaning to your life. Through the process of making public, you could be contributing to other people's capacity to give meaning to their lives too.

Tasks

- Write down the significance of what you are doing. Give your accounts to critical colleagues for their evaluation, and act on any feedback they give.
- If you have the appropriate skills and technologies, make mini-documentaries about your practice with a voice-over indicating to your viewer what they should be looking out for and what you feel the significance of your work is.
- Make these multimedia representations available to a wider audience, for example through YouTube or other distribution agencies. Do not think that you are vaunting yourself; you are in fact showing your accountability to yourself and others by making your work public and inviting critique from others.

How do I ensure that any conclusions I come to are reasonably fair and accurate?

This question involves thinking about the processes involved in testing the validity of your claims to knowledge, and putting in place processes to enable you to do this.

Have you:	Yes!	When?

- Identified your validation group and organised a schedule of meetings with them? ☐ ....

- Organised your data so that you can produce evidence to test the validity of your claims that you have improved your practices? ☐ ....

- Identified possible criteria and standards of judgement, drawn from your values, to test the validity of your claim that you have improved your practices? ☐ ....

- Considered other possible criteria and standards of judgement? ☐ ....

- Tested the validity of your knowledge claims (that you have improved the quality of your practices) against your own values, which now transform into living criteria and standards of judgement? This fulfils your obligations to carry out personal validity checks. ☐ ....

- Tested the validity of those same knowledge claims against the critical feedback of others, both critical friends and validation groups? This fulfils your obligations to carry out external validity checks. ☐ ....

- Indicated to your judges and assessors the criteria and standards you would like them to use, i.e. making judgements about the extent to which you have realised your values in your practices; also on the understanding that, for award-bearing courses, they will make judgements also using normative institutional criteria and standards of judgement? ☐ ....

- Suggested that they use criteria such as those proposed by Habermas (1976) in processes of social validation (pp. 107–108)? ☐ ....

- Drawn up briefing documents for your validation groups (p. 199)? ☐ ....

- Presented sufficient evidence of progress,
  alongside your progress reports? Have
  you organised your multimedia evidence
  to show the living reality of your
  improved practices?   ☐   ....

Tips

- Now you are aiming to present evidence to test the validity of your claims to knowledge, and you are going to ask people to agree or suggest modifications.
- Be clear about what you are claiming to have achieved. What improvements do you think have taken place? How are you going to justify your claims? By what criteria do you want your work to be judged? Who will set those criteria? Will you be able to negotiate the criteria? Which data will you select as evidence to show the criteria (values) in action? Will you include disconfirming data that will possibly refute your claims? If so, you will be demonstrating the highest levels of research capacity, because you show your accountability to yourself and others.

Tasks

- Make sure you organise yourself and your materials well in advance of any formal validation meetings. It is your responsibility to guide your assessors.
- Produce reports and summaries that will guide people's thinking to enable them to get on the inside of your practice. Distribute these documents well in advance, electronically or in hard copy. Draw up briefing documents for the meeting.
- Make sure you have the appropriate technology for validation meetings. Organise technical support if necessary.
- At the meeting, produce your evidence and invite critical feedback. Listen, and resolve to act on advice.
- Record the meeting, in writing or on videotape, and put the record in your data archive.
- Send a note of thanks to all participants after the event. Always acknowledge people's efforts on your behalf.

How do I evaluate the experience of doing my project?

This question involves reflecting critically on your own learning from doing the project, and communicating that learning to a wider public in the interests of demonstrating your accountability.

Have you: **Yes!**   **When?**

- Considered what doing the project
  has meant for your own learning?   ☐   ....

- Considered how your learning
  may now influence other people's
  learning?   ☐   ....

- Tested the validity of your
  provisional perceptions against
  those of your research participants
  and others in your organisation?   ☐   ....

- Considered how you could have
  done things differently?   ☐   ....

- Considered how you could do
  things differently in new phases of
  your action enquiry?   ☐   ....

- Articulated how this phase can be
  seen as one cycle of action reflection,
  to transform into new cycles?   ☐   ....

- Anything else?   ☐   ....

Tips

- Remember to consider two aspects of your learning: (1) what you have learned about the area you are researching and (2) what you have learned about yourself through doing the project.
- Was it worthwhile? How can others learn from your experience? Make sure you include these issues when you write your report.

Tasks

- Write out how the experience of doing the project has helped you to understand your own practice, and yourself, better.
- Write out how you think you have influenced others' learning in an educational way.
- Reflect on the responses of others and consider how you will incorporate these into your report.
- Think about how you are going to communicate your new learning about your subject area and also your learning about yourself.
- Say how you intend to share your learning, so that others can learn from and with you.

Disseminating

How do I write a good-quality report?

This question involves demonstrating your awareness that high-quality reports and communication are central to establishing the validity and legitimacy of knowledge claims.

Have you:	**Yes!**	**When?**
• Set aside enough time to write the report?	❐	....
• Organised a writing schedule?	❐	....
• Arranged for binding and reprographics?	❐	....
• Arranged for typing if the work is going out?	❐	....
• Organised your work folders, disks and data archives so that you can access your material quickly?	❐	....
• Aimed to produce a report that:	❐	....
• fulfils all of the nominated criteria of your workplace or, if you are on an award-bearing programme, the accrediting institution?	❐	....
• demonstrates your knowledge of what is required at different levels, for example workplace/ undergraduate reports, masters dissertations, PhD theses?	❐	....
• demonstrates your awareness of the need for testing the validity of knowledge claims?	❐	....
• fulfils the general criteria of readability, as well as academic criteria of demonstrating originality, rigour and significance?	❐	....
• is error free, with a full bibliography and accurate referencing?	❐	....

- Read as widely as expected for your level, and incorporated the ideas of key theorists into your writing?   ❐   ....

- Included your multimedia narratives as appropriate, and explained their significance?   ❐   ....

- Anything else?   ❐   ....

Tips

- People approach writing tasks in different ways. Some are highly disciplined, putting in so many hours every day. Others go on inspiration. Decide what is best for you, but always be honest and do not find excuses to put off the writing.
- If you find writing difficult, tell your story to a friend and talk into a tape recorder. Then transcribe the talk.
- Check with your supervisor if the accrediting institution will accept multimedia forms of evidence, and present your DVDs or other materials with your written report in a back-flap or other accompanying folder.
- Make sure you know what a report at your level involves: expected criteria, how you achieve these and how the report will be judged.
- Write your report in draft and give it to critical colleagues for their comments. Act on their feedback.
- Do not expect your first draft to be the final draft. Spend time editing and refining your text. Pay attention to any academic conventions, such as including page references for quotations.

Tasks

- Your main job now is to produce a high-quality report. Some good books are available that tell you how to do this. A key text is McNiff and Whitehead (2009) *Doing and Writing Action Research* – see also Chapter 13 in this book.
- Writing involves a small amount of talent and a great amount of hard work. Try not to skimp the writing time. It is crucial that you produce a report that does justice to the quality of your action research.
- Arrange your workstation in a friendly way. Have everything you need to hand. Try to keep it tidy.
- Think about who will get a copy of your report and how you can disseminate it more widely. Aim to submit the full report or extracts for publication in journals or as a book. Aim to present at conferences.

Finally . . .

This now marks the completion of your first action–reflection cycle. You have come full circle, but you have not closed the circle. Any provisional answers you have reached will already transform into new, more interesting and problematic questions.

If you feel that the way you are working now is better than before, you will probably stay with this new way of working. However, there is still room for improvement, and to address the new emergent questions. You can say with justification that you have improved your learning, and have brought that learning to improve an aspect of your practice, and this can be a tremendous incentive for new action.

Summary

This chapter has given summaries of all the steps involved in an action enquiry, in the form of checklists for action. Each checklist sets out what you should do, and ideas about how you can develop the project. You can add further checklists as appropriate to your project. The main idea here is to organise your thinking and resources in advance, to ensure the success of your project.

Checklist of reflective questions

If possible, make sure that you have done the following:

- Have you thought about all the issues that were identified in designing and doing an action research project? Have you analysed what needs to be done and when? The checklists here should help you do so.
- You could tick off the 'jobs to do' once you have done them. Other jobs may emerge during the course of your project, so add these to your lists.
- The checklists ensure that you will conduct your project rigorously, so try not to skip any elements. Demonstrating methodological rigour is a key aspect of high-quality research.
- Use your imagination in adopting or adapting the advice offered. Everyone's situation is different so don't feel you have to follow everything to the letter. Do show, however, that you have thought through how you are going to conduct the project, and your awareness of the need to give your reasons why you have done things as you have.

We now turn to the practicalities of doing your project, with a specific emphasis on monitoring practice; gathering, analysing and interpreting your data; and generating evidence.

Part IV
Doing your project

This part deals with the practicalities of doing your action research project, and your question becomes, 'How do I use my knowledge?' The practical issues are mainly to do with monitoring and documenting practice, gathering and interpreting data, and generating evidence. These are all key research practices, and all work towards demonstrating and testing the validity of claims to knowledge.

The part is organised into three chapters.

Chapter 8 deals with how you monitor and document the action of your practice. This involves asking questions such as 'How do I observe what I am doing, in company with others? How do I keep records of what I am doing? What data am I looking for?'

Chapter 9 deals with how you gather data about what you are doing and how you deal with the data. This involves asking questions such as 'How do I gather data? How do I categorise and sort it? How do I store and retrieve it? How do I interpret and make sense of it?'

Chapter 10 deals with how you generate evidence from the data, with a view to testing the validity of your claims to knowledge. This involves asking questions such as 'Which procedures are involved in turning data into evidence? Which data do I select from my data archive? On what basis?' This in turn means identifying criteria and being clear about which standards you are using to judge the quality of what you are doing and also to judge the validity of your knowledge claims.

Chapter 8

Monitoring the action, looking for data, and documenting the processes involved

This chapter is about looking for data, thinking about where you might find it, and keeping records of it once you have found it. Remember that one of the aims of research is to produce knowledge, so 'data' refers to all of those pieces of information that help you find what you are looking for as you make your claims to knowledge and test their validity. In action research, your claims are to do with how you have influenced new actions by influencing learning, so the kind of data you are looking for is in the learning and action, both your own and other people's.

Action research is about how you can improve your learning to influence new actions, and then bring your learning and actions to influence the learning of other people so that they can use their learning, in turn, to inform their new actions. You are therefore looking for data that show the transformational relationships involved in how your learning informs other people's actions, as set out in Figure 8.1.

The data you are looking for, therefore, will be in those episodes that show (1) how you are exercising your educational influence in other people's learning, so that (2) they can use their learning to inform new actions, (3) inform the kind of actions that they take, as influenced by their learning, and (4) inform their feedback that you have influenced their learning.

The chapter is organised around these ideas and offers advice about how you monitor, gather data about, and document the processes involved in the following practices:

- Your learning
- Your actions
- Other people's learning
- Other people's actions

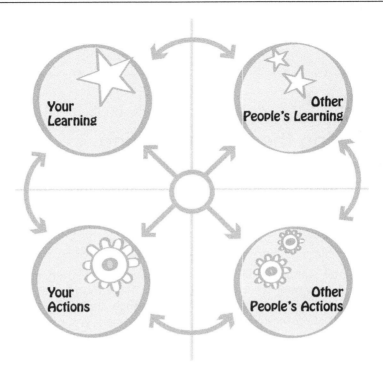

Figure 8.1 Transformational relationships.

Bear in mind the following

Your action is at the centre of your action research but it is not just any kind of action. It is action that is informed by your learning, so it is action to which you, the researcher, are *committed* by your personal and professional values; action that is *informed* by your careful considerations about its appropriateness; and action that is *intentional* and undertaken by you to achieve the goals you have set.

Also remember that monitoring is more complex than simply collecting data about how you perform something. It involves three distinct operations:

- collecting data about the action so that it enables you to produce the clearest possible description of what has happened;
- interpreting the data you have collected so that you can develop a tentative explanation of what has happened;
- evaluating what you have done so that you can explain the significance of your actions, and re-plan in light of your evaluation for further action.

These issues are dealt with in this chapter, and also in Chapters 9 and 10.

We now turn to what kind of data you look for, where you look for it, and how you monitor the processes of gathering it, as set out above.

Monitoring and gathering data about your learning

Look first for those data that show how your learning has improved. This means that you understand or know things better than before. You can gather data about your improved learning from other people's feedback, as well as from your own reflections.

Gathering data from other people's feedback about your improved or improving learning is relatively straightforward. Someone could comment on something you say or write. They could write you a note, saying, 'Mary, it is clear to me that you understand this concept better than you did.' This kind of note is often written at the end of assignments, to give you critical feedback on your learning.

Possibly the most powerful form of data, however, is in those instances when you are able to comment critically on your own processes of learning, when you demonstrate reflexive critique, and show how and why you have deliberately changed your thinking, informed by your values. Doing this involves a different form of data gathering, which usually takes the form of self-reflection.

Possibly the best way of monitoring how you are developing the capacity for self-reflection is by keeping a learning journal. Aim to keep your journal in a systematic way. Most people write an entry every day or every other day. Some people choose to carry their journals with them, like a workbook, and enter ideas as they occur, or record critical incidents on the spot. Often learning appears as 'Aha!' moments, and when least expected, so it is a good idea to keep your journal with you at all times.

Your journal may be a traditional paper kind, or it could be an audio or videotaped journal. Many people carry a tape recorder with them, and speak their ideas and thoughts into it as they move along. Some people maintain a video journal every day, or every few days. You could keep a multimedia journal, in which you insert pictures and video-clips to support your written text. You could build up a professional portfolio in this way, to show the progression in your learning, and the transformational episodes between different aspects of your learning.

Jane Spiro uses these kinds of techniques extensively in her doctoral enquiry 'How I have arrived at a notion of knowledge transformation, through understanding the story of myself as creative writer, creative educator, creative manager, and educational researcher'.

She writes in the abstract to her thesis:

> How I have arrived at a notion of knowledge transformation, through under-
> standing the story of myself as creative writer, creative educator, creative

manager, and educational researcher. My aim in this thesis is to tell the story/ stories of how I arrived at a living theory of creativity which I shall call 'knowledge transformation'. I explore this theory through 'story' as a methodology that connects both the creative writer and action researcher, and raises questions about self, reflective process and voice that are central to my enquiry. In telling these stories, I ask the question: what does it mean to be creative, as a writer, an educator and a manager? Is the nature of creativity transferable across each of these roles? How has this knowledge improved my practice as an educator? My examination leads to a theory of learning called 'knowledge transformation', which suggests that deep learning leads to change of both the learner and what is learnt.

> (Spiro 2008: retrieved 20 February 2009 from www.actionresearch.net/
> janespirophd.shtml)

Jane's thesis also includes a CD of her enhancing her violin playing in a master class. She explains the importance of music, with the music, in her narrative.

By monitoring your learning in this way, you are able to use the diary entries as data that show the processes involved in your learning, and how they potentially influence new actions.

Monitoring and gathering data about your actions

You can monitor your actions by inviting other people to observe and comment on them, and also by observing and commenting on them yourself. You are looking for key actions that show the influence of your learning, that is, how your new learning has led to new actions. It is also vital to remember that what you learn is informed by your commitment to certain values, and this involves moral choices, whether you act in your own interests or other people's.

Who gathers data about your actions, and what data they look for, is for you to decide and negotiate with others. You also need to negotiate how the data will be gathered. All these things involve choices, as follows.

What data do you look for?

Traditional action research literatures say that you would look for data that show how you have improved a social situation. We take the view in this book that 'a social situation' is constituted of people acting with collective purposes, so trying to improve a social situation means trying to influence people's thinking about what they understand as meaningful actions. You would look for data that show the processes involved. For example, if you were trying to help young people see that antisocial behaviour is not a good idea, you would look for data that show the processes involved in you trying to influence their learning – in this case, trying to find ways to enable them to become more critical of their own thinking. This would also involve showing how you are trying to arrange optimal conditions for influencing their learning, such as respecting the young people's right to speak and be heard. The idea of people speaking for themselves and being heard, and becoming more critical of their own thinking, can be understood as your educational values. You are also looking, therefore, for data that show how you are realising your educational values in relation to influencing learning and organising the conditions of learning for others and yourself.

For example, in her masters enquiry 'How do I improve my leadership as a team leader in vocational education in further education?' Daisy Walsh writes:

> Using a reflective journal I recorded my thoughts on significant events through-out my practice. Using narratives I constructed representations from the data gathered. I traced and explored my journey as a team leader in Further Educa-tion. My concern was to improve my understanding of my leadership practice for the benefit of my team and my students. In examining my self-development, I have extended my own professional knowledge. I aim to be a better team leader for the formation of a more effective team.
>
> (Walsh 2004: retrieved 20 February 2009 from http://actionresearch. net/walsh.shtml)

Daisy's account includes an engagement with a racialising discourse that enables her to be true to her values.

Who gathers the data?

You should negotiate with others who will gather the data. The following people could gather data about your actions.

Interested observers

These are people who are interested in how the research is going but do not have sufficiently vested interest to become participants. They may include managers, or the carers and parents of your research participants, or patients or customers. You could invite them to write you letters and notes to give you critical feedback on any aspect of your practice; or be involved in a dis-cussion group about a particular topic. Some may not wish to be formally included in your research, and you will need to negotiate with them whether or not they feel it is necessary to receive an ethics statement from you.

Your colleagues and research participants

Colleagues and research participants are centrally involved in your research, and they will be able to give you critical feedback on your actions. You may invite them to monitor what you are doing and to gather data about your actions. Remember that your actions are always in relation to improving learning in order to improve action; so the data you would ask your colleagues and participants to gather would be in relation to whether your actions had actually influenced their learning. The best data you could gather here would be data that showed the reciprocal relationship between your learning and their learning and actions. For example, Kevin Eames (1995) included dialogues with Jack on dialectics in his doctoral thesis. Jack was able to draw on these dialogues to show the reciprocal learning between Kevin and himself as Kevin enhanced his learning about dialectics and Jack enhanced his understanding of his educational influences in Kevin's learning (Whitehead 1999).

As noted on p. 102, always be alert to disconfirming data, that is, data that show you things you would rather not see, when for example the research is going in directions you do not wish it to. Perhaps your actions are not influencing learning in the way you wish. Perhaps people do not wish to listen to you, or to accept your ideas. These kinds of negative feedback can be powerful indicators for you to change direction and rethink what you are doing and how you are doing it.

You

You can of course gather data about your own actions. You can monitor what you are doing using a range of data-gathering techniques (see next section), and you can gather data in a systematic way about whether or not you are influencing learning for improving action. Be aware that many people can be suspicious about claims that are grounded in personally gathered data, such as journals or field notes or photographs, on the grounds that the data may be fabricated or personal opinion, so make sure your data are authenticated wherever possible, with the date and signatures of any persons involved in the action. If you are using multimedia technology, ask your participants to give their agreement on video. Multimedia technology can be the closest thing to real live action, as we explain shortly.

How are the data gathered?

You can use a range of data-gathering techniques, as appropriate to the situation. These can include any or all of the items below. Note: a more comprehensive list appears in Chapter 9.

Written methods

These include the following:

Field notes

These are the notes you make in the field, in the social situation you are investigating. As previously suggested, aim to carry a notebook with you at all times, so that you can record your ideas and actions, and write them up systematically at a later stage.

Personal logs and diaries

These are used to record your ideas and observations about actions. They can be powerful strategies for offering explanations for actions, and for showing the development of reflexive critique and dialectical critique.

Surveys and questionnaires

These can take a variety of forms and need to be treated with caution. It is important to construct good questions that will get the specific answers you are looking for, or indicate trends and patterns. It is important to have a working notion of what you are looking for in advance.

Record sheets

These are records and analyses of action that enable you to see at a glance what is happening, and to analyse the action. You may draw up tables and charts, for example, or bar charts and histograms to show percentages and qualities. Remember that you can use quantitative data as well as qualitative data as part of your action research.

Live methods

These include the following:

Interviews

Here you interview people to get their impressions of what is happening and their responses to it. You can track progress using paper and pen, or tape-recording, or you can videotape proceedings. Aim to develop good interviewing skills so that people will be able to say what they wish, and so that you can show that you are exercising educational – not coercive – influence on their thinking. The same principles apply in situations in which you conduct surveys and distribute questionnaires. These should be constructed to show the educational processes involved in dialogical encounters, not how you are manipulating people's thinking or engaging in a form of social engineering.

Critical conversations about the research

Critical conversations about the research take place at all stages of the process. 'Critical' in action research never implies negative criticism. It refers to the process of critique, when we problematise issues and unpack them for hidden meanings and assumptions. In any critical conversation you could talk about your plans and intentions; how you could share your data about your learning and action; and how you could invite criticism of your interpretations and evaluations, and act on the critical feedback. It is important to document the critical conversations. Doing so will enable you to:

- celebrate and record significant moments of change in thinking and practice for yourself and others over time;
- show the ongoing exercise of educational influence over time, and how this is possibly enabling the development of more life-affirming situations for all;
- provide information that shows how validation processes have been continuous and informative.

Bear in mind the need to perceive others, and act towards them as co-researchers who are contributing a critical perspective that informs your research; otherwise they may position themselves as respondents who see their task as supplying answers to questions you raise. This will not move you beyond your present way of seeing things. Their contribution to your project will help you show that they are active participants and not providers of data.

Role-play

A new genre has developed out of role-play, which has become known as performance text. This is a powerful means of revealing the hidden assumptions in people's thinking, including your own. By acting out real-life situations, all participants are able to reflect critically and discuss new ways of acting, within the safe space of assumed roles and experimental persona, prior possibly to bringing these into the real world as well-formed personal and social identities. A good example of performance text can be found in the video of Jack's 2008 keynote presentation to the International Conference of Teacher Research at mms://wms.bath.ac.uk/live/education/JackWhitehead_030408/jackkeynoteictr280308large.wmv (the sound takes a few seconds to clear at the beginning of the video). The text can be accessed at www.jackwhitehead.com/aerictr08/jwictr08key.htm.

In this keynote (Whitehead 2008), with the help of the video-reconstruction of a meeting with a Senate Working Party on a Matter of Academic Freedom (see www.youtube.com/watch?v=MBTLfyjkFh0), Jack explains how, through humour, he rechannelled the energy in the truth of institutional power relations into the creative energy of the power of truth. This can be seen within the time-slot of 51:39–53:24 minutes of the video of the keynote.

The clip on YouTube at www.youtube.com/watch?v=MBTLfyjkFh0 begins with Jack explaining to the audience the moment when he was leaving a meeting with the Senate Working Party, feeling defeated and without energy, because the draft report being prepared for Senate concluded that his academic freedom had not been breached. Although Jack agreed with this, he knew the effort that had gone into overcoming pressures that could have constrained his academic freedom. These were not mentioned in the draft report. As he got to the door to leave the meeting he felt a flow of life-affirming energy as he turned back to the Senate Working Party to explain, with passion, why the working party would be denying their responsibility as academics if the report they were preparing for Senate did not contain a recognition of the pressures Jack had been subjected to that could have constrained his academic freedom. The final report to the Senate contained this recognition.

Multimedia data

Websites, blogs and Internet exchange

The digital age has generated an entirely new response to issues of gathering data and generating evidence (see also Chapter 10). Multimedia technologies enable you to see and record the live action as it happens, and to show the live transformational actions and reflections involved in how learning influences new actions, and how those new actions then become the site for new learning. Multimedia technologies not only provide the means for developing powerful data archives that contain the evidence base of claims to knowledge, but also can act as the media themselves for developing and communicating this knowledge as forms of social and political action. In his thesis, Ray O'Neill (2008) shows how, by using ICTs, young people were able to develop their capacity for taking political action, and how ICT itself became a form of political action (see www.ictaspoliticalaction.com). The use of multimedia can be communicated through websites, blogs, e-mails and other forms of digital technologies.

Visual narratives

Researchers are beginning to explore the potentials of multimedia technologies for producing their visual narratives. These include video diaries, which, as noted in Chapter 9, are explanatory accounts of practice, that contain the living evidence that shows how practice has improved. You can find examples of video narratives in the first issue of the *Educational Journal of Living Theories* at: http://ejolts.net/node/82 and http://ejolts.net/node/80.

The book you are reading can also be seen as containing a powerful evidence base, through its referencing of paper- and Internet-based materials, and through drawing on the multimedia representations of the research programmes of dozens of practitioner–researchers. These researchers have deliberately given themselves the task of trying to exercise their educational influences in the thinking of themselves and others as they seek to make the world a better place for all.

Monitoring and gathering data about other people's learning

It is questionable whether you actually can monitor and gather data about other people's learning, or whether you can simply make tentative judgements about the quality of their learning through what they say and do. You can definitely make judgements in a crude way from your positioning as an external agent who is observing them. You can say, for example, that John is demonstrating greater understanding of key concepts, such as how to manage workplaces, or how to teach English as a second language. You can also comment on the degree of criticality demonstrated in speech and writing. It is possible to read the accounts of researchers such as Sally Aston (2008) and Dot Jackson (2008), whose masters assignments demonstrate both a significant development in their capacity to be critical of their own practices, and also a capacity to bring critical reflexivity to bear on their understanding of how practice can be improved. Generally speaking, however, making valid judgements about the quality of their learning has to be done by learners themselves. (This raises questions about the form of assessment practices that aim to judge progress in learning, and, by default, the teaching that aims to support learning, but this discussion is for another day.)

The question arises how learners can monitor and record their learning, and how their learning takes place. They can use much the same research methods as you when you monitor and gather data about your own practice. They can use traditional paper and pen methods such as journals, as outlined above. You could ask them specifically to comment on what they are learning and how they are doing so, and perhaps how you are encouraging and enabling their learning. You would negotiate access to their journals as data that would articulate how your influence had informed their thinking and actions, and how and why they had responded to you as they did.

This raises new questions, however, about the dialogical base of learning, and also about the co-creative nature of learning. Many theories, such as those of Bakhtin (1981) and Krashen (2003), specifically note that learning can be understood as a social practice as much as grounded in the individual mind–brain, which is a view held by Chomsky (1986) and others. These theories are especially important when you are researching, for example, how you are encouraging new dialogical practices in organisations.

Gathering data about the co-creative processes involved in dialogical learning can be best achieved through the use of multimedia technologies that show the live actions involved, as well as people's reflections on their actions. Especially powerful are videotapes of people watching themselves on videotape. For example, through watching a video-clip of her presentation at the 2008 Annual Conference of the British Educational Research Association on YouTube at www.youtube.com/watch?v=FNJnmjHQrBY, Marie Huxtable was able to clarify the practical principles she used to explain her educational influences in her own learning and in the learning of others. These included loving recognition, educational responsibility and respectful connectedness.

Monitoring and gathering data about other people's actions

Similarly, you can use multimedia technologies to monitor and record other people's actions as they use their learning to inform their practices of working collaboratively. Many examples of these practices are available to show the processes involved, and many higher degree dissertations and theses show how practitioner–researchers can produce their multimedia-based evidence to test and strengthen their claims to be exercising their educational influences in learning.

For example, Je Kan Adler-Collins, in his preparation for his doctoral viva voce, worked at improving his responses to questions on his thesis by viewing video-clips of his responses at a pre-viva voce meeting convened by his tutor in the Department of Education of the University of Bath. You can view one of these video-clips at: www.youtube.com/watch?v=bDFxigRjErc.

Another example is Alan Rayner responding to Eden Charles's questions in a video-clip of his preparation for a radio interview on inclusionality at: www.youtube.com/watch?v=Ap06AxMQbkg.

It is important, as these practitioner–researchers do, to remember that action research is not about making judgements about other people: it is more about making judgements about yourself and the quality of how you influence others to make judgements about themselves. They should be able to explain how they make such judgements, by using their values as their living criteria and standards of judgement (Chapter 11). You would invite people to document their own practices for two reasons: (1) so that they can make judgements about the quality of their own learning and practice and (2) so that you can use their documentations, with their permission, to show the educational nature of your influence in their learning as they ask, like you, questions of the kind, 'How do I improve my practice?' or 'How do we improve our practices?' They would provide data for your research and you would provide data for theirs. You and they would be researching your individual practices collaboratively. Your questions would transform from 'How do I . . . ?' to 'How do we . . . ?'

Summary

In this chapter we have considered issues of data gathering from the perspectives of which data to gather, and which actions may be monitored. We have specifically asked questions about what we are looking for when gathering data, and how we might find it. The data sought will refer to the transformational relationships between your learning and its influences in other people's learning and actions.

Checklist of reflective questions

When you gather data, bear these things in mind:

- Before gathering data, be as clear as possible about what you are looking for, otherwise you may waste a lot of time. Are you clear about the relationships between your own learning and other people's learning, and how these potentially inform your and their actions?
- Are you reasonably clear about how you are going to gather your data? Further ideas are given in Chapter 9.
- Before gathering any data about other people, make sure you have negotiated procedures with them, and refer back to your ethics statement about respecting their sensitivities. Have you addressed all the issues outlined in this chapter?
- When you collect your data, begin to think how you are going to categorise it and where and how you will store it. Be systematic in categorising and storing. It will pay dividends in the long run.

We now turn to issues to do with managing and making sense of the data, and what you have to do to accumulate a strong database that can be the grounds for generating good-quality evidence. These issues are dealt with in Chapter 9.

Chapter 9

Collecting and managing the data

This chapter addresses the issues of collecting and managing the data. Chapter 10 deals with analysing and interpreting it. These processes act as the precursors to generating evidence from the data. The chapter provides a guide for building an archive of data that may be used as evidence within action research case studies. Be aware that many books offer advice on data gathering, analysis and interpretation; for example, Bell (2005); Cohen *et al.* (2000); Costello (2003); Hopkins (1993); Koshy (2005); and you would do well to look at these.

This chapter is organised into two parts:

- collecting the data;
- managing the data.

Collecting the data

You can collect data using a range of data-gathering techniques or methods, some of which are listed below. The only sensible rule for selecting any particular method is that it enables you to find out what you want to know better than another. Follow your common sense and sensitivities about the appropriateness of each kind. You can use any and all techniques within your research project, whether a small selection that you use repeatedly throughout your research or a wider range, and mix and match them.

We identified some techniques in Chapter 6. Here are some more general categories, with ideas about how they could be used:

- logs and diaries;
- observation methods;
- questionnaires;

- interviews and surveys;
- case study;
- multimedia.

Logs and diaries

People keep diaries for a variety of reasons: to record their thoughts and feelings about the daily events of life, to remind them of future appointments, and to give them a record of these events when they are past. Research diaries are little different from ordinary diaries, except that they focus on issues to do with the research. You therefore need to think about how you are going to use what you write, and this will influence how you organise your diary.

Think about these possible uses for a diary:

- It may be used to make a time-line. Keeping a clear time-line is important. Aim to log relevant events with a date and make a note about the context where appropriate, and anything else you feel could be significant.
- It may be used to illustrate general points. Particularly important are 'thick' descriptions that show the complexities of a situation rather than 'thin' descriptions that present the situation as unproblematic.
- It may be used to chart the progress of your action research, including successful or unsuccessful action and the personal learning that emerges from your reflections on this.
- A way of interrogating your own thinking. When you reflect on something you have written, you may find yourself asking, 'Did I really think that at the time?'

Some writers make a difference between the terms 'log', 'diary' and 'journal'. It does not matter what you call it; what matters is that you keep one. Try to maintain your diary right through your research project. In the early stages, people often feel nervous about extensive writing, and short diary entries can be easier to manage. Whatever you write, it will provide you with documentary data that you can return to and reflect on. Try to establish good habits from the start. If you don't, you could seriously regret not keeping systematic entries.

Here is a diary entry from Jean, when she had just begun working in South Africa. The first seminar with the teachers had been a disaster, and here she was for the second seminar.

> Here I sit in Good Hope College, Khayelitsha. It is 10th May 2006. I think back to our first study seminar in January, and how despondent I was at my reception – veiled hostility, outburst because the administration stuff was not in place. Feeling of alienation – because I am a white woman? Then I sat on the plane home deciding whether to carry on, and beat myself up at home before deciding, which I had known all along. I would of course. This is too big to let go. And

now I have visited with the two universities and I understand the unquestioned epistemological hierarchies which are also layered in with the racial hierarchies, and those with forms of theory. So many unquestioned normative assumptions. So here I am today, in the foyer, waiting for it all to begin, not too ready to go, but willing to give it a try.

(Jean McNiff, personal diary, 10 May 2006)

Diaries kept by participants

We said in Chapter 8 that you could keep a diary yourself and invite your research participants to do so as well. You could ask their permission to use their diaries as data to show how you are influencing their thinking, and check that this is an educational process. This emphasises the need for good ethical conduct throughout. If you have permission to use other people's diaries then check with them that you have used their work in a way that is acceptable to them. This means submitting your reports to the scrutiny of the people concerned in order to get their approval before you go to print. You also need to establish whether anonymity needs to be maintained, or if the participant wishes to be acknowledged, which is more and more frequently the case in action research. Remember to thank them.

Also remember to:

- keep a small notebook with you all the time, to write quick notes that can be transferred to your main diary later;
- periodically review and summarise your diary; this is important for identifying connections and patterns in your data;
- try reading some of your diary entries to a critical friend and see what they think of it.

Observation methods

In a sense, all research begins with observation. You watch what is happening and systematically record your observations. John Elliott (1991) rightly speaks of the first phases of an action enquiry as including a reconnaissance phase, during which you take stock of what is happening. Be clear about what you are observing, however. In action research you aim to observe yourself, in company with others, to see whether you are exercising your educational influence in their thinking, and they in yours. It is a reciprocal relationship, learning with and from one another. You are at the centre of the action, so this involves considerable honesty.

For example, Jack tells how he experienced himself as a living contradiction because he was denying his own values in his practice when he observed his teaching through the lens of a video-recorder. The aim was to encourage young people to think and speak for themselves, but Jack found that he was doing all of the speaking. This was the beginning of his action enquiry. You can read Jack's story in the e-journal *Action Research Expeditions* at www. arexpeditions.montana.edu/articleviewer.php?AID=80. Perhaps you could consider accessing *Action Research Expeditions*, responding to any of the contributions that interest you and submitting your story for publication.

If you are a member of a team, your colleagues will probably be willing to observe you or allow you to observe them. Many examples of these processes are available from the 'passion' section of the website www.actionresearch. ca/, when you enter 'action research'. The examples show how Jacqueline Delong and others have been encouraging educators to undertake collaborative action research. Delong's doctoral thesis (2002) also shows that she was the first to set the example of observing and evaluating herself as a leader in a large district school board using a process of democratic evaluation in an attempt to create a culture of enquiry. She explains her commitments as follows:

> One of the basic tenets of my philosophy is that the development of a culture for improving learning rests upon supporting the knowledge-creating capacity in each individual in the system. Thus, I start with my own. This thesis sets out a claim to know my own learning in my educational inquiry, 'How can I improve my practice as a superintendent of schools?'
>
> Out of this philosophy emerges my belief that the professional development of each teacher rests in their own knowledge-creating capacities as they examine their own practice in helping their students to improve their learning. In creating my own educational theory and supporting teachers in creating theirs, we engage with and use insights from the theories of others in the process of improving student learning.
>
> The originality of the contribution of this thesis to the academic and professional knowledge-base of education is in the systematic way I transform my embodied educational values into educational standards of practice and judgement in the creation of my living educational theory. In the thesis I demonstrate how these values and standards can be used critically both to test the validity of my knowledge-claims and to be a powerful motivator in my living educational inquiry.
>
> The values and standards are defined in terms of valuing the other in my professional practice, building a culture of inquiry, reflection and scholarship and creating knowledge.
>
> (Delong 2002: retrieved 20 February 2009 from www.actionresearch. net/delong.shtml)

Observation methods include using schedules and tally sheets. You can use many publicly available observation schedules, such as the Flanders Interaction Analysis Categories (FIAC), but the observation schedule you design yourself may suit your purposes better. If you decide to design your own, you need to consider the following:

- What is the purpose of the observation? What do you want to find out?
- Which particular pieces of the action are you observing? Are all of the actions equally important?
- How will you use the data?
- Have you considered ethical issues throughout?

Here are some well-tried strategies for charting observation data.

Head counting

This is straightforward. You simply count the number of times a particular event happened, for example how many times a person speaks. It is virtually impossible to watch all the action at the same time in a particular situation, so be selective and break it down into time blocks over a designated period of time. Margaret Follows (1989) broke down her observations into time blocks that occurred daily for a specified period each morning and afternoon. During these times she observed whether the children who were engaged in each of eight activities came from one class, two classes or three classes. After five weeks she was able to produce the chart shown in Table 9.1.

Table 9.1   The class unit composition of pupils engaged in observed activities each week

	Week 1	Week 2	Week 3	Week 4	Week 5
From one class (%)	77	31	51	32	37
From two classes (%)	20	64	20	46	25
From three classes (%)	3	4	2	22	37
No. of activities	35	45	35	41	51

Interaction charting

The idea of interaction charting is to draw a graphic that communicates dynamically what is going on. Figure 9.1 shows how you could chart interactions among people. The small cross-lines indicate the number of times different people interact. The arrows show who speaks to whom.

Procedural analysis

This kind of exercise requires you to draw up an agenda, or time plan of a specific event, and then to plot the actions and interactions within the frame. McTaggart (1990) wanted to find out who spoke most in a staff meeting. He

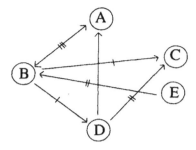

Figure 9.1 Sociometric analysis.

used a frame in which he listed the names of the people in the meeting along one axis and the amount of time they spoke along another. From this he was able to identify the number of contributions that individuals made in the meeting and the length of time they spoke. Because he participated in the meeting himself, he tape-recorded the meeting and used the tape to check his findings. Table 9.2 records the results of his observations.

Interaction process analysis

This kind of charting analysis may be used in a variety of ways. For example, the FIAC reported in Table 9.3 operates by way of a grid, and is used to capture the number and type of interpersonal interactions. This technique

Table 9.2 Participation analysis: staff meeting 1 March 1989

Participant talk time (%)	No. of contributions	Length of time	Total
Mr M	42	18.41	49.7
Head	36	9.29	25.2
Mrs S	14	2.25	6.4
Mr B	21	3.35	9.5
Mrs M	13	1.19	3.5
Mr A	6	1.10	3.5
Mrs B	6	0.13	0.5
Mrs A	1	0.02	0
Mrs R	6	0.23	1.0
Miss C	5	0.17	0.7
Mrs C	0	0.00	0
Total	150	36.14	100

Table 9.3 Record sheet to show conversation categories

Categories of behaviour	One-minute intervals						
Touches	||	||	—	—			|||	—
Nods	|||	|||||	||			—	|||	||
Initiates conversation	—	—			—	—					—
Listens	|||	|||	|||	|||||	||	|||	|||||
Is empathetic	||							|||	|||||		
Smiles			||	|||			|||||				

may be used to record sophisticated interactions, but is demanding in concentration. You need to be familiar with the categories of behaviour you have devised as indicators of the action you are watching. Table 9.3 shows the kind of schedule you could use if you wanted to see the types of interaction that take place in a conversation. You can use this kind of documenting system when watching live action and also videotaped action, to help you analyse the interactions and quality of relationships evident in the encounter.

Observation data such as these may be useful for tracking changes in a variety of situations over time; for example, in the relationships between yourself and a group of people, or among the people themselves. You could use the same observation schedule at regular intervals for six weeks. Observation schedules can be greatly enhanced when they are used in conjunction with audio and video records, or where they are used cooperatively by a group.

Questionnaires

First-time researchers often rush into producing questionnaires without sufficiently considering what is involved. This can be dangerous. Issuing a questionnaire is a political act because questionnaires are not neutral. They can influence their respondents and alert them to ideas they had not thought about before. If you send a questionnaire to parents asking if their children are being bullied at school, they may get the idea that bullying is occurring.

The responses from questionnaires can often be misleading. Moira Cluskey points out that respondents can be unreliable. 'If I ask my students today if they enjoy school I may get a 60% answer in the affirmative. If I ask the same question tomorrow the result may have dropped to 50%. This reduction may be caused by a variety of factors' (Cluskey 1996: 4).

Here is some common-sense advice about questionnaire construction and use. The basic advice is: do not use a questionnaire unless you have a good reason for doing so.

Some general guidelines

- Be clear about why you want the information. Is it essential to your project?
- If you already know the answers then do not use a questionnaire.
- Never ask questions if you can get the information elsewhere. If people have to answer too many questions, they will probably not return the questionnaire.
- If it is to be a postal survey, can you afford it? Remember you will probably have to send out reminders.
- If you want to ask a representative sample of people then you will need to read about sampling procedures, which is a specialised practice.
- Will you need to gain access to the people you wish to question? Have you the necessary permissions?
- If you are intending to send a questionnaire to colleagues at work, are you sure that this is the best way of getting your answers?

Constructing questionnaires

Collingwood (1939) said that there are no 'correct' answers. There are only 'right' answers that will keep the dialogue open. The same idea applies to questionnaires. There are no 'correct' questions or answers, but there are appropriate questions and answers that can move things forward. Always ask, 'Is this question appropriate? Is it going to give me the kind of feedback that will help me improve my thinking?'

Different kinds of questions exist, including closed and open questions, and these serve different purposes:

- *Closed questions* have a restricted format, such as ticking a particular box which contains a prespecified answer. The advantage of closed questions is that they require less space for answers and the answers are easier to tally. Their limitations are that you will not get back any answers that fall outside the range you have specified.
- *Open questions* allow the respondent to express a broader range of ideas. An open question is of the kind, 'What do you think about . . . ?' Open questions require more space for answers. You will also find these open questions to be more time-consuming to analyse because they can be diverse and rich in ideas. However, even an open question closes off possibilities because it sets boundaries for possible answers.

Questionnaire construction is a technical business. If you want to do it well you should first read a good text on questionnaire construction. Then you should try it out on a few friends to make sure your questions make sense. Pilot it again on a different audience, one that is familiar with the kind of situation you are exploring. Always show it to your tutor (if you have one) and to your critical friends. Aim to pilot the questionnaire several times. Remember: questionnaires can ruin the research context for you if they are not well constructed. *If you do decide to use a questionnaire then see the advice on procedures that follows.*

Guidelines for administering a questionnaire

- Decide what information you need to find out. Construct your questionnaire or use one that has already been piloted. Put the instructions for completing the questionnaire at the top of the paper.
- Be polite, and ask your participants to help. At the end of the questionnaire, thank your participants. Say that you will inform them of the results if they wish.
- Have a clear policy for dealing with confidentiality and share this with your respondents.
- Clearly word process and format your questionnaire. Leave enough space for your respondent to write their answers easily. Systematically number or otherwise annotate your items. Use good-quality paper. Pay attention to detail in content and appearance.
- If you photocopy the questionnaire, make sure that the copies are clean and legible.
- Pilot the questionnaire. Try it out on a few people and invite their critique. Analyse the responses to see if it is giving you the kind of data you are looking for.
- Run the questionnaire. Give your respondents a fixed time in which to return it. Write on the questionnaire itself when you would like it returned. If you want people to send it back to you, provide postage and envelopes.

Interviews

Interviews are used in a variety of research contexts and are used frequently within an action research design. Because action research always aims to be educational, interviews are likely to be informal discussions rather than formal interviews. Sometimes formal interviews are appropriate in order to establish some information or to evaluate an outcome, much in the same way as described for questionnaires. More often they aim to develop conversations that lead to enhanced insights for all participants.

Interviews have distinct advantages over questionnaires in that they provide richer data because you are able to probe further. Interviews range from fully structured to open, with variations between these extremes.

A fully structured interview is really the face-to-face delivery of a questionnaire. The interviewer must ask the questions exactly as they appear on the interview schedule. The aim is to provide the same questions, in the same order and style of delivery, to all interviewees.

An open interview has a starting point and an aim, but no set agenda of questions. The interviewer should be free to follow where the interviewee leads as long as it is within the general framework.

Choosing between open and closed interviews would depend on their purpose. If the interview is part of a formal evaluation, it would probably be more structured than if it were to establish what sort of situation existed prior to commencing the research.

Guidelines for conducting interviews

- Aim to document the interview unobtrusively. You can use some of the procedures for documenting data that are described in Chapter 10 if they are appropriate, such as the use of notebooks, audiotape- and videotape-recording. Always ask permission from the person you are interviewing whether they are comfortable if you do this.
- Be clear about the ethics of interviewing. Tell your interviewees what the interview is about or tell them that you are unable to do so.
- Do not mislead or deceive people in order to persuade them to share information.
- Be prepared to maintain complete confidentiality if this is requested. You must honour your commitment.
- Develop good listening skills. Active listening means controlling your body language, so that the person you are interviewing knows that you are interested and value what they say.
- Learn to give verbal and visual cues to encourage your interviewee to talk freely.
- Learn to sense when it is appropriate to feed back what the interviewee is saying, in order to help them maintain their flow. You could say, 'Now, as I understand it, you are saying that . . .'.
- Show that you empathise with your interviewee's position so that they feel confident to expand on what they are saying.
- Learn to accept silences and be silent yourself. Silences are important spaces in which people gather their thoughts or harness their courage.
- Practise using possible framing questions that help keep the conversation going. For example, *clarifying questions* to check something the speaker has just said: 'Can I check that, please?'; or *context-specific questions* which check that the interviewee: (1) is at ease with the question: 'Is it all right for us to talk about this?'; (2) understands the question: 'Can I ask you to put that question in your own words?'; or (3) is comfortable with your own performance: 'Have I said that correctly?'

The skills of interviewing develop over time and with practice. It is your responsibility to develop these skills and insights if you wish to conduct successful interviews.

Case study

Most projects in action research turn out to be case studies, in the sense that they are studies of singularities (an individual, 'I'), in company with other singularities (other people, you and your research participants). When those singularities enter into a cooperative or collaborative relationship, they become a collective (a group, 'we'). It is important not to think of 'we' as a homogenous group, or simply as a collection of individuals. What enables 'we' to refer to ourselves as 'we' is a shared purpose and commitment to certain values; for example, that we wish to work towards a more democratic social order. The aim is not to reach consensus, as this too often eliminates critique and slides into fundamentalism. Edward Said says: 'I take criticism so seriously that, even in the midst of a battle when one is unmistakably on one side against another, there should be criticism, because there must be critical consciousness if there are to be issues, problems, values, even lives to be fought for' (Said 1991: 28).

However, some sense of procedural agreement is important to enable people to work together in a non-violent way. Many case studies in action research show how these processes happen. For example, the doctoral enquiries of Eden Charles and Jocelyn Jones include such responses to some of the most difficult human experiences and offer hopeful ways of responding. Charles (2007) uses video-clips to communicate the relational energy and values of an African understanding of an Ubuntu way of being to respond to colonising influences in way that moves beyond the idea of decolonisation through his original ideas of reidentification and guiltless recognition. You can access his doctoral thesis at www.actionresearch.net/ edenphd.shtml. Jones (2008) uses narrative, historical sources and images in her enquiry 'Thinking with stories of suffering: towards a living theory of response-ability'. Her 'thinking with stories' includes responses to child abuse and dialogues with British and German prisoners of war from the Second World War. It is inspirational to read how Jocelyn responds to stories of suffering with responsibility and 'response-ability' and values that carry hope for the future of humanity (you can read her PhD thesis at www. actionresearch.net/jocelynjonesphd.shtml).

However, although most action research case studies involve you as the main action researcher, it is also often the case that you could do some analysis about what is going on in the social world that you feel needs interrogating. By asking 'What is my concern? Why am I concerned?' you would identify certain practices and attitudes that need specific interrogation, such as what is happening in your organisation. In this way you can examine organisational norms and orthodoxies, and produce, perhaps, a chapter that features as a case study of the situation in which you are located. Many masters and doctoral theses do this. For example, as a contextualising feature of her PhD research, Bernie Sullivan produces a chapter on how recent legislation is having a devastating impact on Traveller culture in Ireland (Sullivan 2006: you can read her thesis at www.jeanmcniff.com/bernieabstract.html).

Multimedia techniques

In the example just cited, it is possible to see how multimedia can bring scholarship to life as well as provide an authentic evidence base for claims to knowledge. This idea of a living form of scholarship is especially relevant to action research, as it is located within the increasingly popular movement of the new scholarship. The examples in this book bring to mind a children's pop-up book, where you open the book and objects and people on the page rise up from the page. The pictures that come to life in this way provide the evidence for your claims to knowledge. It is a lovely idea to think that your scholarship can also rise up off the page and enter people's consciousness and their lives, through the exercise of your educational influence in their learning, as they read your stories.

Managing the data

This section sets out some general principles for managing the data you collect, with some practical advice on matters arising.

First think about your working materials, along with aspects of categorisation, storage, retrieval and use of your data. Also consider your working situation, and how other people will be involved as you gather and use your data.

The section is therefore in two parts:

1   you and your data;
2   how to involve other people in the monitoring process.

You and your data

Think about the working materials and resources you need, and about where you are going to store your data, whether it is to be paper and artefact based, computer based, or a mix of both.

Your working materials and resources

Depending on what you decide, you will need some or all of the following:

- one or several working files;
- data boxes;
- a computer;
- an index box and cards, or a good filing system on your computer;
- a journal;

- key texts;
- your own workspace if possible;
- several small notebooks.

Your working files hold all your rough jottings and materials that you may need at a later stage. These are active files: you are constantly putting in and taking out material.

Your data boxes hold all of your paper-based pieces of stored data. Use several coloured or otherwise identifiable boxes such as box files or copy-paper boxes. Label each box with the categories for your data, such as 'conversations' or 'field notes'. You may change your categories as you proceed. For example, the general label 'conversations' may become 'conversations with colleagues' and 'conversations with participants', in which case you would sort the separate categories into their own files. Put your pieces of data into their appropriate boxes. These boxes begin to constitute your data archive.

Your computer may do the job for you. If you are using your computer to store everything, the same principles of well-organised filing and identification apply. Spend time keeping your computer tidy so that you can find things easily.

Index boxes and cards are ideal for keeping records of relevant books and articles (your computer can do this too). Wherever you store your information, make sure you keep an accurate record of the title of the book or article, author, publisher, place of publication and date, and always – *always* – note the page numbers from the article. If you find an important quotation, write it out and store it with its page number. Keep your references from the start. Remember that it can take ages to find a missing reference, particularly if the book is back in the library.

Your journal (or diary, or log) acts as a record of events, and also a record of your thinking about those events. You can use a notebook or a loose-leaf file or computer as your journal. This can also act as a piece of evidence, to show how your actions and thinking changed over time. Aim to write up your journal regularly. You don't need to do so every day, but you should set a pattern for yourself and stick with it – see detailed advice on diary keeping earlier in this chapter (p. 156).

Key texts will act as constant sources of reference. If you have access to a library, use its resources to help you locate texts. If you find some books are essential as key texts, buy them. Never deface library books. Regard your texts as good friends with whom you are having an ongoing scholarly conversation.

Your own workspace is important, if possible. Good lighting, space and ventilation are desirable. Good equipment is helpful but not essential. You may need to negotiate a space with your family or house mates, and they should not invade your space when you are occupying it. If you are sharing a space, arrange with others when you can each have access.

Small notebooks are handy. Important ideas hit us at any time. If you have a notebook with you whenever possible, you can jot down the idea. Leave your notebooks in key places in the home, at work, in your pocket. You never know when inspiration will strike. Get into the habit of writing things down, and this itself generates more ideas.

And, finally . . .

Yourself. The most important thing is your own sense of well-being. Sometimes the best thinking is done at unplanned times, and the best writing is done on the back of envelopes (or in small notebooks), on a bus or in the middle of the night. If you feel good about yourself then your work will be good. All of the equipment in the world cannot substitute for your own sense that you have something worthwhile to contribute. Be sure that you have, and enjoy your project.

Organising the data

Your data emerge as a result of monitoring your action as you work your way through your action research cycle. In this way, data begin to emerge as your records of plans and actions, and the steps you took to reflect upon and evaluate these as you created them. Try to be systematic in organising these records efficiently, whether you are working with paper or digital technologies. It does not matter which system you adopt, as long as you are consistent.

The organisation of data is rather like the organisation of memory, consisting of three parts – storage, (en)coding and retrieval:

- *Storage* refers to the system of organising data in a physical or virtual space.
- *(En)coding* refers to the process of sorting and labelling the data.
- *Retrieval* refers to the methods used to pull it out of the store and using it in a meaningful way.

Storage

It is not useful to place all the data willy-nilly into one large box or computer file and label it 'my archive'. You should aim to store your data in terms of the forms and sources in which it exists.

Data can take a variety of forms, which include:

- conversations;
- pictures and other visuals;
- notes;
- thoughts and ideas; and
- anything else that you consider to be important.

Sources for these types of data include:

- videotapes and audiotapes;
- children's and students' work;
- documents and archived materials;
- texts (including field notes, diaries, completed questionnaires and books);
- computers;
- record cards; and
- anything else that you consider to be important.

It is up to you to decide how to categorise and store your data and in terms of these categories. You may find that your categories change over time, and you should aim to re-sort your data when necessary.

Coding

Coding involves labelling and sorting.

Labelling

Each item of data should be labelled so that you know what it is. Your label should indicate:

- when it happened;
- where it happened;
- what it was about;
- who was involved; and
- anything else that you consider to be important.

Sorting

There are two main ways of sorting, which can also be cross-referenced:

1 types of data distinguished in terms of the *chronology* of the project; that is, data generated at different stages of an action research cycle or from different cycles that have occurred over time;
2 types of data about different *aspects* of the project, such as library research, reflective self-study, workplace contexts, a staff room context or conversations with critical friends.

You may find that different files or colour-coded boxes are helpful, or adopting a colour-coding system on your computer.

Sorting the data can provide an archive of case records that may be used as primary source material (Stenhouse 1978: 36). This case record is a comprehensive account of what you have done. A major criterion, as Stenhouse noted, is that the record should be accessible for critical scrutiny by others. Therefore, when you are preparing your data archive, remember that it is not only for your information but also for other people to see. You are familiar with your material; they are not. When you present your research report, you will have to lead people carefully through the records of your actions so always organise and present your work with this in mind.

Retrieval

You will need to retrieve your data and present it in order to provide evidence for the claims you make about the research. Many of these data can be large; for example, physical videotapes or diaries or portfolios of practice. Stenhouse (1978) recognised that many of the data in an archive were too bulky and detailed to present to others, and therefore he argued that the archive should have two aspects: the case data and the case records.

- The *case data* are all the materials you have assembled. These constitute your archive. When you write your report, you would refer to this archive, but you would produce it only if required. Some limited aspects may go into the report as appendices.
- The *case records* are what Stenhouse called 'a parsimonious condensation of the case data' or 'an edited primary source'. This means that, in the body of your report, you would insert extracts from your data to support a specific point. You would include other data that provide a context for your extract in your appendices.

Consequently, your data will appear in different forms in your final report:

- in the main body of the text, as extracts to support a specific point;
- in your appendices, as immediate contexts for the extracts, or as elaboration of the specific points you are making;
- in your archive, as the more general material from which you have extracted your data.

When planning the compilation and contents of your data archive, bear in mind the ethics of using data that involves other people (see Chapter 5). Have you cleared everything with your participants? Have you got their approval to use their real words? Are individual identities well hidden, or revealed and celebrated according to participants' wishes?

We now turn to using the data.

Using the data

You are going to use the data to generate evidence to back up any claims to knowledge and test their validity. This is important, if claims are not to be seen as opinion only. Consider some of the claims that you hear every day, such as:

- My clients are much happier with this product.
- Things have improved since the new computer system was put in.
- The situation is better under the new government.

These statements are not yet grounded in evidence, so you could be forgiven for being sceptical.

These issues are central to current debates about what counts as good-quality research, and who counts as a good-quality researcher. The most central debate is about validity and legitimacy in action research: here is a brief summary of the key points.

Demonstrating validity in action research

For some time, the practitioner research community has been regarded as something of a poor relation in the world of educational research. This is because it has not had the appropriate means to demonstrate its validity in relation to its methodologies and the kind of knowledge and knowledge claims made. Unfortunately, the quality of action research has until recently been judged by means of the criteria of traditional research; those criteria require research findings to be generalisable and replicable. These criteria are inappropriate for action research: a practitioner does not replicate their own practice from day to day, let alone someone else replicate it. Influential researchers such as Furlong and Oancea (2005) have recommended that the practitioner research community should task itself with finding new criteria and standards of judgement that the community itself would agree and act upon. Consequently, a good deal of effort has been expended over recent years to find those criteria and standards. One of the most influential ideas to emerge has been the idea of values as living criteria and standards of judgement (Whitehead 2004; Whitehead and McNiff 2006). It becomes possible for a researcher to identify pieces of data that show the realisation of values and to turn these into evidence. Consequently, because it is now possible to demonstrate the validity of action research, with much agreement from the practitioner research community, it is also possible for the practitioner research community to claim legitimacy for their research and for themselves as researchers. (These issues are expanded more fully in the next chapter.)

Knowledge claims should therefore be supported by evidence wherever possible, and the evidence should be used as the grounds for testing the validity of the claims. As an action researcher, you need to maintain and manage a vibrant data archive from which you can generate strong evidence, in relation to identified criteria and standards.

You can use various forms of evidence, whether in quantitative form, or in documentary or other appropriate form. You may wish to produce multimedia recordings to show the lived reality of your claims, or cross-reference your field notes and submit these as evidence. Whatever form your evidence takes, it must be there. These ideas continue in Chapter 10.

How to involve other people in the monitoring process

At the beginning of this chapter we said that monitoring the action is more complicated than simply collecting data about how you perform an aspect of your work. We suggested that it involved three distinct operations:

- collecting data about the action so that it provides the clearest possible description of what has happened;
- interpreting the data you have collected so that you can develop a tentative explanation of what has happened;
- evaluating what you have done so that you can plan further action.

Other people can help you make a disciplined and critical study of your practices in relation to each of these operations. Cooperation and collaboration are integral to action research because of its nature as an educational practice. The following two ideas, drawn from Pamela Lomax's six principles of action research (Lomax 1994b), are central:

- that action research is participatory and others are involved as co-researchers rather than informants, so that critical communities of people are formed;
- that action research is about sharing ideas, interpretations and conclusions with an 'educated' audience, who are able and willing to judge the authenticity and relevance of the work to a particular professional context.

In line with these principles, you need to develop relationships with others in which you:

- ask them to give critical feedback about your action;
- encourage them to share the educational experience of being an action researcher;
- persuade them to become co-researchers;
- are prepared to relinquish your ownership of the action if they are ready to take it over.

You will be most successful here if:

- you are open and avoid manipulating others;
- you are prepared to take risks and sometimes expose others to risk;

- you make your research transparent;
- you are clear about the ethical principles that govern collaboration.

Whom do you involve?

Start small and establish a working relationship with one or two work colleagues who are willing to provide critical but supportive friendship. These colleagues become critical friends, or critical colleagues. We authors use the term differently from some other writers (e.g. Bayne-Jardine and Holly 1994), who see a critical friend as an outsider process consultant. In our view, a critical friend is expected to act as a confidant/e or mentor and talk through the research at regular intervals, preferably from an insider perspective. Because critical friends are assumed to know the research context well, they can help you deal with the micro-politics of work. Sometimes they are chosen because their position in their organisation supports researchers in influencing processes of change. This is a perfectly acceptable situation, because researchers are often expected to negotiate the focus of their research with senior colleagues so that the work has organisational as well as personal benefit. The critical friend, regardless of status or role, is expected to help you achieve a critical perspective – what some philosophers call 'rendering the familiar strange' – even although this may challenge the normative assumptions underlying your work. Critique can be hard to achieve, especially when you and your critical friend share the same values and assumptions, but it is essential to maintain the integrity of what you are doing.

What part do they play in validating your research?

The idea of validation appeared earlier and will be dealt with in more detail in Chapter 11. When action research is carried out in an institution, it is common procedure to ask critical friends to join validation groups that have been set up to validate a colleague's action research. They can help in the following ways:

- as witnesses, confirming and verifying that the research had taken place in the way it was described;
- as helping the researcher give a good account of their research;
- as offering an evaluation ('critical partnership');
- as giving moral support for the researcher in terms of encouragement, positive feedback and sympathetic support.

(Lomax *et al.* 1996)

Who can act as a critical friend?

You should decide who will act as your critical friend/s. Decide on one or two special people drawn from your wider circle of personal and professional contacts. Make sure they will be supportive, but not so supportive that they do not provide critique. They may be drawn from anyone in your circle: managers, colleagues, students, family. They must be available to you when needed, so you need to negotiate with them how often you will meet, what you expect of them, and what they can expect from you.

Sometimes the critical friendship is seen as one of potential collusion. Collusion is obviously unfortunate, because some people may think your research was legitimised because you are a nice person, rather than because it is methodologically rigorous and has its own integrity. Your research should be judged on its own merits, so it is important to negotiate with your critical friends how you will assess the research and then make this public to anyone who wants to know. The critical friendship relationship should be educational for you and your friends. It is important to establish a trusting relationship in which you can establish the grounds for giving and receiving critique.

Summary

This chapter has set out ideas about collecting and managing the data. It has outlined the main different data-gathering techniques you may use. The ideas given are not exhaustive, and you are encouraged to find your own innovative ways of gathering data. Once you have begun to gather data, aim to keep them well organised so that you can find things when you come to generating evidence.

Checklist of reflective questions

Here is a checklist that may help ensure that you gather high-quality data and manage them in a way that will contribute to the success of your project:

- Are you clear about which kinds of data you intend to gather, and how you are going to gather them? It is important to identify those data-gathering techniques that are within your resources and that you will be able to manage.
- Select data-gathering techniques that you feel comfortable with. Do not feel pressured into using a particular technique because someone else says so. Stay in control of your own project.
- Keep things simple. It is useful to gather data from several sources, so that it can be triangulated (p. 179), but do not get too complicated and let your data or your data-gathering techniques run away with you.
- Develop your own ways of organising and managing your data. Have you already an idea about how you will build your data archive?

If you can be efficient in gathering and organising your data, you will do yourself a big favour when you need to sort it and find those pieces of data that will stand as evidence. It is to these issues that we now turn in the next chapter.

Chapter 10

Analysing and interpreting the data and generating evidence

Data and evidence are different things, although they are parts of the same realm of discourse, which is to do with making judgements, and both are essential in the rigorous processes of testing the validity of claims to knowledge. If you want your research and your findings to be taken seriously, and yourself as a researcher, you need to develop insights into these issues. This chapter tells you how to do so.

The chapter is organised as three sections:

- analysing and interpreting the data, and identifying criteria and standards of judgement;
- deciding what counts as evidence, and why;
- procedures for generating evidence from the data.

Analysing and interpreting the data, and identifying criteria and standards of judgement

Once you have sorted and categorised your data and compiled your data archive, you should begin analysing the data prior to interpreting it. Analysing is different from interpretation; analysing involves identifying trends and instances with a view to describing the action under consideration, whereas interpreting involves giving meaning to those actions, i.e. explaining why they are important.

Analysing the data

Analysing therefore involves looking at the data, taking account of your categories of analysis, and noting any emergent patterns within them. This is easily done when dealing with data to which quantitative analysis can be applied, such as questionnaires and surveys. You count the number of times a certain response or behaviour occurred. The questions you use to make such selections tend to be of the kind, 'How many?' or 'How often?' It is more problematic 'when dealing with data that defy quantification; for example, if you are looking for an enhanced sense of well-being among hospital patients, or if you believe that soft music in your supermarket will make the shoppers' experience more pleasant (and encourage them to buy more). Feelings and emotions cannot be quantified, so this means asking different forms of question, such as 'How well?' Both kinds of analysis are appropriate in action research.

When you analyse your data, you can produce descriptions that tell you what is going on. By sorting and searching through your data you can show what a situation is like at any time. You can show who is doing what, and what aspects are influencing others. However, we have said throughout that doing research goes further than offering descriptions that tell us what is going on. It is also about offering explanations that tell us why it is going on, and saying why the explanations are significant. This brings us to interpreting.

Interpreting the data

Interpreting actions means giving meaning to the data. Sometimes the meaning-making is straightforward. If someone says to you, 'Why are you going to bed so early?' you could say, 'I am going to bed early because I am tired.' Meanings can also be complex. How do you respond to the question, 'Why do you do the job you do?' or 'Why do you do voluntary work?' To find answers to these kinds of questions means thinking carefully about what gives meaning to your life. For most people, the answer lies in their values. If we understand values as the things we believe in and hold dear, then we can say that our values give meaning to our lives. This is the basis for how we can interpret actions.

Actions may be interpreted in relation to the values that inform them. For example, if you eat meat, you believe that it is acceptable to kill animals for food. This has implications for how you see yourself in relation to animals, and possibly to the environment. If you do not eat animals, you possibly feel that animals also have the right to live and not be eaten. Persons who eat animals, and those who do not, have different values perspectives about animals' rights and humans' responsibilities.

The idea of values informing practices can then transform into how we come to make judgements, specifically in terms of criteria and standards of judgement. Remember the example of a hotel (Chapter 1). You judge the quality of the hotel in terms of warmth and cleanliness. Warmth and cleanliness become criteria: you say, 'Is it warm? Is it clean?' This denotes a first choice prior to making a decision. Criteria are always identified and agreed in advance. However, different hotels have different standards: some high, some low. You now ask, 'How warm? How clean?' This denotes a second choice. Criteria and standards are key aspects of making judgements, in this case, judging the quality of the hotel and deciding whether you will stay there or go somewhere else. This is why it is so important to know what you are looking for and what you value, both in interpreting data and also in making life plans. When you interpret your data, you identify those pieces that show the transformation of what you are looking for and what you value into action. This is the basis of making judgements about the quality of your action research.

The ideas outlined so far are technical aspects of analysing and interpreting in relation to criteria and standards of judgement. In real life, many people have used these ideas to inform their action enquiries. They have been able to show how they can make judgements about the quality of their actions, by producing evidence that show how their actions were the realisation of their values to do with everyday living, such as the living out of fairness, or compassion, or entitlement (Cordery 2008; Moustakim 2008). They have also been able to show how they can make judgements about the quality of their research, by producing evidence that shows their understanding of epistemological issues and their appreciation of the need for methodological rigour. They have been able to articulate their values as their living criteria and standards of judgement in making judgements about the quality of their practices and their research.

Here are two examples that show these processes in action.

Mary Hartog studied her practice as a university tutor as she worked at improving her loving and life-affirming educational practice. Mary writes in the abstract to her PhD thesis:

> This thesis is a self-study of a tutor in higher education committed to practice improvement. It is presented as a study of a singularity and an example of first person education action research. It is epistemologically and methodologically distinct in that it is based on my values as an educator and ideas about what constitutes loving and life-affirming educational practice.
>
> The aim of this thesis is to present a storied account of my inquiry, in which I explore what it means to live my values in practice. Through descriptions and explanations of my practice, this thesis unveils a process of action and reflection, punctuated by moments when I deny or fail to live my values fully in practice, prompting the iterative question 'How do I improve my practice?'; the reflective process enabling me to better understand my practice and test out that understanding with others in the public domain.
>
> My claim to originality is embodied in the aesthetics of my teaching and learning relationships, as I respond to the sources of humanity and educative needs of my students, as I listen to their stories and find an ethic of care in my teaching and learning relationships that contain them in good company and that returns them to their stories as more complete human beings.

Evidence is drawn from life-story work, narrative accounting, student assignments, audio and video taped sessions of teaching and learning situations, the latter of which include edited CD-R files. These clips offer a glimpse of my embodied claims to know what the creation of loving and life-affirming educative relations involves.

(Hartog 2004: retrieved 21 February 2009 from www.actionresearch. net/hartog.shtml)

Simon Riding explains his educational influences in his own learning and in the learning of others as he seeks to live his values of relationship as fully as he can in a career trajectory that includes his transitions from being a classroom teacher through middle leadership and finally into senior school leadership. Here is the abstract from Simon's PhD thesis:

Within this text I propose and demonstrate an original relationally dynamic standard of judgement within my practice of Living Myself Through Others. I explore the ongoing nature of transition between living educational spaces upon myself and how this process of change is addressed as I move through different stages of my career and life. I argue that I am able to improve the quality of the living educational space because of the relationships and experiences that I have had, alongside the living core values that I hold. This thesis reflects on the potential impact of enabling teachers to engage as teacher-researchers within their own school and accounts for the process I went through in order to make this happen.

I further argue for the need to consider how practitioner accounts are assessed in order to ensure that the future of education is driven forward through the development of teachers as researchers influencing what educational knowledge is and how it is produced. The following text is a living educational theory action research enquiry that utilises autobiography as a way of accounting for one educator's transitions from being a classroom teacher, through middle leadership and finally into senior school leadership. I argue that I am the educator that I am because of the life I have led and the life that I am currently leading.

This thesis addresses the vastly important influence of relationships within education and explores how these relationships impact on my practice as an educator. The text incorporates and captures these relationships through enabling these others to speak through their own voice. This thesis explores how I was able to create the shared living educational space necessary to enable teacher-research to occur and flourish.

(Simon Riding 2008: retrieved 21 February 2009 from www. actionresearch.net/simonridingphd.shtml)

Deciding what counts as evidence, and why

Evidence, then, is to be found in the data, but it is more than data. It is those pieces of data that show what you believe is the realisation of your values in practice. The status of the data changes in the same way as your status changes when you are awarded your doctorate and change your title from 'Mr' or 'Ms' one second to 'Dr' the next, although you as a person stay the same.

First, however, you need to check that you are not imagining things, and that what you are looking at in the data really does count as the realisation of your values. This involves a process known as triangulation.

Triangulation

This is a process in which the data are looked at from a range of perspectives – usually at least three, if not more. Different authors have different ideas about which perspectives are in question: whether it refers to data gathered using at least three different methods, or data that relate to at least three different people or sets of people, or data that are viewed by at least three different agents. You should decide what interpretation is right for you.

Whatever you decide, the main point is that different people agree on what they are interpreting from a range of perspectives.

For example, if the issue is whether a researcher has encouraged independent thinking among other people, the data gathered could be:

- interviews with the persons in question, who would indicate whether or not they had developed their capacity for independent thinking;
- a videotape recording that showed those same people engaging in critical conversation that indicates they are thinking for themselves;
- a diary from two of the same people, with entries recording their original thoughts.

Once the data have been triangulated, therefore, you are in a good position to begin searching and analysing the data, interpreting them, and selecting those pieces that show the realisation of values.

Here are some of the places you could look for evidence as you work your way through the different steps of your project. Below we outline some of the questions you would ask, and indicate what kind of evidence you could look for.

What is my concern? What am I interested in researching?

Look for evidence in sources such as these:

- a journal in which you recorded your initial thinking;

- a tape-recorded conversation and transcript when you discussed the situation with your colleagues;
- a note of complaint to your manager, pointing out that a particular issue needed addressing; a letter from your manager in reply, suggesting that you do something about it first;
- other?

Why am I concerned? What values do I hold around this issue?

Look for evidence in sources such as these:

- an audio-/videotape-recorded conversation with colleagues and transcript, talking through the values you hold that make you want to do the research;
- a letter to a friend, saying that you want to get involved because . . .
- an informal written report, commenting on how much you have enjoyed reading a novel that spells out exactly what you are feeling in regard to your situation;
- other?

How can I show what the situation is like initially, and how it develops?

Look for evidence in sources such as these:

- a questionnaire to colleagues to get their reactions to the current situation;
- an invitation to students/workplace colleagues asking them to comment on their perception of the current situation (remember that this will involve your performance, which means that they may well critique you);
- a video-recording of current situation (again, be prepared to face up to reality when you view the video; view it alone first and then invite a trusted colleague to view it with you);
- other?

What can I do about it? What will I do about it?

Look for evidence in sources such as these:

- a written action plan about how you could engage with the issue;
- a journal to show how you gave it thought and imagined possible solutions;
- illustrations of your own, showing possible future scenarios once you

had interrogated your own thinking and begun to transform your practice;
- other?

What kind of evidence can I gather to show that what I am doing is influencing my own and other people's learning?

Look for evidence in sources such as these:

- a second questionnaire asking participants to comment on how the situation may have changed and if it is better;
- a video-recorded group discussion of how the situation may be better;
- letters from parents commenting on the difference in participants' attitudes at home;
- other?

How will I explain the nature of my influence?

Look for evidence in sources such as these:

- an audio/videotape-recorded conversation with validation group in which specific criteria and standards of judgement were discussed;
- a journal to show reflection on discussion;
- field notes from participants referring to group discussion when criteria and standards were discussed;
- other?

How can I be sure that any conclusions I come to are reasonably fair and accurate?

Look for evidence in sources such as these:

- an audio/videotape-recorded conversations and transcripts with validation group on viewing data from critical incidents;
- written feedback from validation group to say that they agree that you have done what you claim to have done – they are now validating your claim to knowledge; alternatively, suggesting other things you could have done or ways in which you could improve on what you have done;
- written feedback from participants to say that they agree with your report (further validation of your knowledge claim);
- other?

These are examples. You can probably find evidence in any or all data sources if you look. The secret is to know what you are looking for. The sources mentioned above are not exhaustive. Be imaginative, and find ways of selecting data that can generate quality evidence.

Procedures for generating evidence from the data

The above can be summarised to show the procedures involved in generating evidence from the data. The steps go like this.

1   You gather data using a variety of techniques (Chapter 9). You sort the data into categories.
2   You begin to articulate criteria that link to your research question, and that you believe will communicate the significant features of your practice. For example:

   • If your aim is to encourage greater participation in the workplace, a criterion (expectation) would be that people would work collaboratively.
   • If your aim is to encourage others' independent thinking, a criterion would be that all people would become engaged in their own thinking.

3   You generate evidence by searching your data archive and finding instances that relate to your criteria (and by definition to your research question, which is grounded in your values). For example:

   • Your January field notes tell how Mr A and Ms B did not participate very much in work-related social events. Your June field notes record how those two people organised a team-building exercise.
   • In a tape-recorded conversation with your study groups, Ms M's voice is not heard. In another recording, six weeks later, she is heard to challenge someone's opinion and voice her own.
   • A letter from now-employed Mr J thanks you for helping him develop his self-confidence, which has enabled him to get a new job.

4   From the data you extract specific pieces that you feel support or refute your beliefs:

   • 'Mr A and Ms B undertook to organise the team-building exercises' (field notes, 6.6.07).
   • 'I am not sure I agree with you. I think democracy should be by the people as much as for the people' (Ms B, tape-recorded conversation, 10.8.08).
   • 'I got the job mainly because I felt I could hold my own in the interview, thanks to your help' (extract from letter received from Mr J, 8.9.09).

These pieces of data can now stand as evidence because they relate to your research question, which in turn transforms into your knowledge claim, both of which are grounded in and informed by your values. The data do not change their form; their *status* is changed. The words and images remain words and images, but they now take on the status of evidence because they are the instances you feel are able to show the validity of your claims to knowledge.

Here is a story to illustrate these processes in action. It is based on a true story, reported on television, about a police officer and her encounter with two teenage boys.

Becoming swans

I am a police officer, engaged in my work-based continuing professional development (CPD) project. I am at the point where I have to submit my action research to my validation group, and I am writing a report to explain how I have succeeded, at least in this instance, to realise my values in practice. The story I tell has had significant influence in my own thinking, and possibly has implications for the professional learning of others in my police force, and indeed for police forces everywhere. The story concerns two young boys, two swans, and members of a team of professional staff at a swannery. Because the report is for my validation group, I am focusing here on issues of evidence generation, to show my awareness of the importance of these aspects for testing the validity of my claims that I have improved my practice through the realisation of at least some of my professional values.

I began my CPD programme with a deep contextualising concern. This was that my police force still had a policy of meeting targets. This took the form of number of arrests that would lead to custodial sentences, and it meant my fellow officers and I were not allowed to use our judgement when it came to dealing with minor offences. This went against colleagues' and my values of enabling young people in particular to become critical of their thinking and behaviours, and to explore their capacity for making wise judgements about what they were doing. Often, we felt, it would be better to take remedial action that would help the miscreant to confront their crime, and make amends on the spot, rather than face a court and perhaps go to prison, thus acquiring a criminal record for life.

We were all delighted therefore when our police force announced that they were changing their policy so that individual police officers could use their discretion about whether to charge offenders or take other action. This announcement coincided with my being allocated to investigate a case of two teenage boys who had allegedly been throwing stones at two swans. I immediately saw this as a potential project that I could use as part of my CPD programme.

Injuring swans in Britain is a serious offence. Swans are Crown property, and protected by law. When an accompanying officer and I interviewed the two boys, they admitted to their offence. Under previous policies, it would have meant automatically arresting the two boys. Instead, I was now able to arrange for them to do some community work at a swannery, and experience for themselves the delight of working with wild animals and birds.

I kept detailed records throughout the project, as was my usual practice as a police officer, and as I was required to do as part of my CPD programme; and I encouraged the boys to do so too, as part of compiling their schools-based learning portfolios. I also negotiated with and involved the swannery staff in the project, and they made video-recordings of the boys and themselves caring for cygnets and adult swans together. The boys began to show considerable care and mature behaviours in learning how to work with swans and members of staff, so that a rich data archive was compiled. Therefore, as part of my police report, which I negotiated also to use for my CPD project, I could show how I had addressed each of my research questions: 'What could I do? What did I do? How do I show the situation as it was and as it developed? How did I gather data?' In my case I gathered data collaboratively with others, with a common focus on keeping a record of progress of this experimental way of developing respect for others, including swans, and finding ways of living the kind of values that make life worthwhile for all.

I am now at the point where I have to submit my report to my senior offices, and also submit my CPD report to my work-based academic supervisor. I have been able to search my data archive for those special instances that in my view show the realisation of my values in practice. My notebook contains a record of my first encounter with the boys and the injured swans. I am submitting these entries as evidence of the situation as it was when I first began my 'experiment'. I am placing the record book itself in my data archive. I will photocopy the entire page that contains my notes at the time as an appendix to my report. With their written permission, I also have a videotape of the first introduction of the boys to the swannery staff, as the staff are tending to the needs of cygnets, and further extracts from videotapes show how the boys themselves begin learning the skills of animal welfare. I have field notes from the boys to show how they are delighting in their new-found skills and insights, and a member of staff has given me a copy of his official daily record that records a comment by one of the boys as, 'Looking after the swans is cool. One of the cygnets has begun to change colour. I am watching it turn into a swan. I feel a bit the same myself.'

For my validation meeting, I will extract from all the data those special pieces of data that I believe show the realisation of my values in practice. They include comments from diaries and written records, episodes from videotapes, and extracts from letters. I think of this process as extracting those pieces and filtering them through the stringent test of checking whether they really do show the transformation of my values into practice. In my imagination, this test takes the form of a dream-weaver I got when in Canada: those pieces that show the realisation of values flow through and emerge on the other side as evidence; any redundant or irrelevant pieces are caught in the strands of the net and stay on that side, to remain as data.

The pieces of data that manage to get through this stringent test emerge as my evidence. I can therefore build up an evidence base in which I can ground my claims that I have improved my practice, and made a significant contribution to new knowledge. In my case, I believe I am contributing to new thinking and new practices for a range of people: for myself, in that I am now more confident about my own practice; for the boys, in that they can now see ways of living and thinking that enable them to make their contribution in their own way, and stay true to themselves as human beings; for the swannery staff, in that they have found new ways of involving members of the community in their work, and how they can use their records as a publication to be disseminated world-wide; and to the professional formation of the police force, in that I am potentially influencing the development of new thinking and new practices, also with the potential for publication and influencing wider thinking and practice around the world.

Most especially, I am now able to articulate how I have generated my own living theory of being a police officer who is concerned with social well-being and is able to act in the direction of her humanitarian values. I have generated new knowledge about the processes involved in working with young people, and involving them in community life; and I have generated new theories about how this knowledge can inform future thinking and practices. I believe I am nearer to fulfilling my calling.

However (and we now step out of the story) ...
You are still at the point where you have only satisfied yourself that you have done what you say you have done, that is, you can demonstrate to yourself the validity of your knowledge claim, to your own satisfaction, by testing your knowledge against the criteria of your values, and you have

used your values to judge the quality of your work and your research. So it could be said that you are still at the point of claiming that this is your subjective opinion. What do you do about this, so that you can claim wider validity from the social and professional world, and thereby claim legitimacy for your actions, and further claim validity and legitimacy on behalf of, in this case, an innovative police force, to show that their new policy is well founded and well grounded in a coherent evidence base? This would be important if police forces actually took seriously the idea of initiating widespread CPD programmes using an action research approach. Projects such as the one told here could have far-reaching consequences for police forces around the world. These issues are discussed further in Chapter 12.

Summary

This chapter has discussed issues of generating evidence from the data. It has outlined ideas about analysing and interpreting the data, and offered detailed information about the steps involved. In considering what counts as evidence, and why, the chapter makes suggestions about the different sources of data where evidence may be found.

Checklist of reflective questions

This checklist may help you to extract evidence from your data, and offer a rationale for why you are doing so.

- Check that you are clear about the difference between data and evidence. Can you explain the difference to your reader? Do you show your understanding through your written reports?
- Are you clear about the difference between analysing and interpreting? Do you show that you do both, and do you explain to your reader what you are doing and why?
- Have you triangulated your data, so that your conclusions appear as tested against other people's critical feedback, and cannot be construed simply as your opinion?
- Check that you are aware of the different places in the data where you can look for evidence. Explain to your reader why you believe those pieces of data count as evidence.
- Explain that you now intend to subject your claims, grounded in authenticated data, to the critical scrutiny of a validation group.

Achieving wider social validity involves convening a validation group, who test the validity of researchers' claims in a more formalised setting, and with stringent tests. This becomes the focus of the next chapter.

Part V

Making claims to knowledge and validating them

When you say you have learned something, you are making a claim that you know something now that was not known before. This is your original claim to knowledge. If the knowledge is to be taken seriously, and not seen as opinion or conjecture, it has to be validated. This part therefore asks the question, 'How do I test the validity of my claims to knowledge?' This can, however, be problematic, because not all participants may agree about what counts as knowledge or who counts as a knower. The issue then transforms from validity to legitimacy.

The part deals with these issues, and contains Chapters 11 and 12:

- Chapter 11 deals with validating processes, that is, what is involved in making claims to knowledge and validating them.
- Chapter 12 is about legitimation processes, which are to do with presenting reports and legitimising them.

Chapter 11

Validation processes: making claims to knowledge and validating them

To return to basics, and to reinforce the understanding that doing action research is an integrated practice:

- Action research is about (1) taking action to improve something, and (2) doing research to explain and justify the processes of taking action. An implication is that you would explain and justify your efforts at improving the issue in question, and give an account of what you had done.
- The aim of research is to create new knowledge that can contribute to new theory. In action research, the knowledge is knowledge of practice. The theory is embedded in the practice, and the practice itself offers explanations for why it takes the form it does, i.e. you explain how you give meaning to your life through what you do and how you do it.

If we accept these basics as given then it becomes our responsibility, as action researchers, first to generate an evidence base for the knowledge claim, as explained in the previous chapter, and also to show the validity of the knowledge claim in relation to its evidence base, i.e. explain why it should be seen as honest and true, and therefore to be believed.

This chapter deals with these issues. It contains the following sections:

- What does making claims to knowledge mean?
- What processes are involved in validating?
- Who does the validating?

First, however, here is a note about the difference between validity and legitimacy, both of which are interrelated. This chapter deals with issues of validity; Chapter 11 deals with issues of legitimacy.

Validity and legitimacy

Think of the story of Galileo. Galileo had plenty of evidence to support his (radical) view that the earth travelled round the sun (a heliocentric view), which was contrary to the then dominant orthodoxy that the sun travelled round the earth (a geocentric view). He was called before the authorities, in the form of the elites in the Roman Catholic Church, to account for his views. Because his views were contrary to the dominant orthodoxy, he was required to recant his views, and was shown instruments of torture, as if they would be used on him. Galileo withdrew his claims, and all returned to normal, until his successors, who had learned from his work, also began to challenge orthodoxies. For Galileo, however, it was too late; he could demonstrate the validity of his knowledge claims by explaining their believability through his evidence base, but he was denied legitimacy through the existing power structures and the exercise of what Foucault (1979) calls 'disciplinary power'.

It can be much the same in contexts of practice-based action research, as noted in Chapter 2. Although much progress has been made to validate practitioners' knowledge claims about their knowledge of their own practices, these views are often still denied legitimacy. Validity has to do with showing the truthfulness of something; legitimacy has to do with the kind of power relations that sustain public opinion about what should count as the truth and who should be seen as a knower.

We now return to the main body of the text.

What does making claims to knowledge mean?

We said above that all research has the aim of advancing knowledge and generating theory. In doing your research, you are aiming to create new knowledge. In presenting your research to others, you are claiming that you have done this. In asking them to validate your new knowledge, you are asking them also to validate your assumptions about the knowledge-generating process, that is, how you believe you have come to know. These assumptions include the following.

The generation of new meanings

The social intent of your research was to improve your particular situation. Improvement would probably have occurred because you, working with other people, improved your understanding of what you were doing. You were working collaboratively, so you were clarifying for one another what this meant for you and your work. You were negotiating and construct-ing your own meanings out of your shared practices. In this way you were advancing your individual and collective knowing.

Making tacit implicit knowledge explicit

People have a deep reservoir of tacit knowledge (or personal or intuitive knowledge). This knowledge is usually hidden, even to the person who has this knowledge, and often cannot be articulated. It is manifested in differ-ent ways, for example, knowing that you are cold and putting on another jumper, or knowing what someone is going to say before they say it. Many researchers draw on the idea of tacit knowledge as the basis of good practice (for example Nonaka and Takeuchi 1995; Sternberg and Horvath 1999). They explain how organisations may be improved by encouraging people first to share their tacit knowledge about their work, and then go through processes of making this knowledge more and more explicit. Practitioners are encour-aged first to share their values, and then to find ways in which they can live out these values.

You are claiming that you have done this in your research. You articulated your values, and you possibly identified a situation in which these values were being denied in some way. You decided to take action to improve the situation, first by improving your understanding of how you were positioned in that situation. You began to make your tacit knowledge explicit. You and others worked collaboratively to raise your collective tacit knowledge about your shared values to a conscious level. You offered reasons for your actions. You are able to show how you tried to exercise your educational influence in your own and other people's learning, so that you all became more reflec-tive and aware of your positioning in social situations, in order also to take action to improve those situations by influencing others. You are now able to demonstrate how your actions are underpinned by a moral commitment, and how you are aiming to help other people also to understand the need for moral accountability. You are aiming to transform practice into praxis at an individual and collective level.

Contributing to the wider body of knowledge

You are claiming that you have generated new knowledge out of the pro-cesses of shared story-telling, and you are explaining how story-telling is a form of research that is validated in terms of its own criteria (McNiff 2007). These criteria are different from traditional ones, which are inappropriate for the new scholarships of action research (see Chapter 12), as the aim is to understand rather than predict, to liberate rather than control. People do research on themselves, not on others; they do research with others in order to understand and improve their social practices. People offer stories of their own improved understanding as outcomes. They share those stories, not competitively but collaboratively. This shared learning can lead to the construction of collective knowledge.

Traditional forms of scholarship believe that a self-contained body of knowledge exists in books and artefacts. If people go away and leave the books behind, the knowledge continues to exist in the books. New forms of scholarship believe that knowledge is always being created, and exists in people and the stories they tell. These stories may appear in book form, but these books are books that tell experience, not only facts. People tell their stories to other people, and those other people re-story the originals into their own stories (Connelly and Clandinin 1990). The accumulation of individual stories constitutes a knowledge base that is always in transformation. What is known today can transform into a new form tomorrow.

These shared stories represent the present best thinking of a community of independent thinkers, each willing to submit their claim to knowledge to the critique of others, to ensure that their claim is robust and legitimate. Sometimes researchers working in traditional ways criticise action researchers for not maintaining standards of rigorous scholarship. On the contrary, action research represents a new form of scholarship that both respects and frequently incorporates traditional standards, within a desire to create new standards to test new forms of practices that focus on demonstrating originality of mind and critical engagement. It demands intellectual independence as well as honesty and responsibility. Validation methods involve ensuring that claims to knowledge are tested and approved by the most rigorous standards.

Formative and summative assessment

You are claiming that you can show the processes of ongoing evaluation throughout your project, in terms of how your reflections on your current learning have led to new improved learning.

Your research question was, 'How do I improve . . . ?' Your research project shows the processes you went through to improve, possibly by working your way through several cycles. Each cycle comprised periods of action, followed by periods of reflection (perhaps these happened almost simultaneously), followed by new actions informed by new insights that emerged from your reflections. Your research processes probably took the form of identification of an issue, imagination of a solution, implementation of the solution, gathering of evidence, evaluation of the solution, articulation of the significance of the research, and modification of practice. Although you might present these stages as straightforward sequences of events, you explain that the realities were not so neat, and the research process probably involved a lot of re-evaluation and criss-crossing.

You might present your project as constituting only one cycle of action and reflection, or it could constitute several cycles. Turning your project into several cycles can make it easier to handle, because one cycle contains the beginnings of the next within itself. Any provisional answers you come to in one cycle will contain a new question for the next. For example, Geoff Mead's (2001) PhD thesis shows how questions can develop during the course of the enquiry (see www.actionresearch.net/mead.shtml). The question 'How can I improve my practice so as to help my pupils to philosophise?' that Mary Roche (2000) asked for her masters dissertation work transformed into a new issue: 'Towards a living theory of caring pedagogy: interrogating my practice to nurture a critical, emancipatory and just community of enquiry' for her PhD thesis (both are available at www.jeanmcniff.com/maryabstract.html and www.jeanmcniff.com/MaryRoche/index.html respectively).

In presenting each cycle you would have made intermediate claims in the form of progress reports, and you would have presented evidence in support of your claims. These reports were your formative (ongoing) evaluation, to check whether you were on the right lines in relation to your original research question. At the end of each cycle, you would have offered a summative (concluding) evaluation statement, to show that you had addressed your research question, at least in part. If your project took the form of several cycles, you would have aimed to produce ongoing progress reports (formative evaluation statements) at strategic times during the research. Your summative evaluation of each cycle then became the starting point of the next. You explain that, although you have broken the process down into separate parts to explain it in an analytical way, the whole thing was seamless and transformational. You also explain that, although the process of doing the research might appear chaotic, there was in fact a deep underlying order to the work, and this order began to emerge during the synthesising process of making the claim to knowledge available for public scrutiny.

Making validity claims

In presenting your work you are making all these validity claims about your new knowledge and about the processes that have led to this new knowledge. The knowledge has not been 'given' or 'discovered'; it has been created. You explain how your knowledge creation processes are transformations of embodied knowledge into explicit knowledge, which you are now able to stand over and claim as your original contribution to wider thinking and wider practices. You are now asking for your validity claims to be legitimised by the community of action researchers.

What processes are involved in validating?

Earlier in this chapter we looked at the differences between validating and legitimising. Both are complex processes. Let's first consider the idea of establishing validity, which is the focus of this chapter. We discuss issues to do with establishing legitimacy in Chapter 12.

Establishing validity is not just about making a claim and producing evidence to back it up, though this is an important first step. You also need to get other people to agree on the validity of your claim, because, unless other people agree with you, your claim could be construed as your own opinion and your research rendered invalid. When you say you have done something (your claim) you need to have available as evidence those pieces of data that you understand as in relation to your criteria and that show your criteria in action (see Chapter 1 for issues about criteria). Other people consider your claim, in relation to your evidence, and they then agree that you are justified in making your claim or they recommend that you think again or make adjustments, either to your practice or to your report (for example, include more evidence or evidence of a different nature).

Furthermore, there are two main forms of validation, and different groups of people who do the validating.

Two forms of validation

The two forms of validation are *personal validation*, which is a form of self-validation, and *social validation*, by which other people consider the validity of your claim to knowledge.

Personal validation, or self-validation

The first form of validation is personal validation. This is when you check your findings, in the form of your knowledge claims, against your own values. We saw this kind of validation at work in the story in Chapter 10 in 'Procedures for generating evidence from the data'. Your values can take a range of forms: they can be ontological values (how you understand yourself, especially in relation with others); epistemological values (what you hold valuable about knowledge and knowledge-creation processes); social values (how you see other people in relation with yourself and with one another); political values (how you think power may be used in promoting specific human interests); and thousands of other kinds of values, which you can identify for yourself. These values give meaning to your life and are embodied in and realised through your practices. You can make judgements about the quality of your practices by assessing the extent to which you bring those values to life in and through what you do. If you are satisfied that you really have managed to live those values in practice, you can claim personal validity for your research findings, to do with how you believe you are now living a good life in relation to your values.

However, this kind of self-validation may appear to others as bordering on self-congratulation rather than self-critique. This can be especially worrying in reports that mention disconfirming data and evidence, yet do not say what action was taken to address what the data were saying to the researcher. This appears too much as sweeping under the carpet those things that you would rather not see; and experienced readers will start asking questions about the validity of the research in general and whether you are to be trusted. Therefore, to avoid suspicion, you need to subject your claims, even though they match up to your values, to the critical scrutiny of others. This then turns into a process of social validation.

Social validation

Social validation is when others test the validity of what you are saying in light of your evidence. This means also considering the validity of the evidence itself, and coming to a decision about whether or not it, and you, are to be believed. This is a form of reaching what Habermas (1976) calls intersubjective agreement. Habermas says that people talk with one another, negotiating what they are prepared to agree; so it is not a case of group-think, but dialogical interaction with a view to reaching agreement. He also says that this is a process of rigorous assessment, in which people set themselves clear procedures and criteria to guide their judgements. He identifies four criteria: comprehensibility, truthfulness, authenticity and appropriateness, as follows:

- *Comprehensibility*. Is the claim comprehensible? Does it make sense to the reader?
- *Truthfulness*. Is the researcher telling the truth? Do they provide a firm evidence base against which to test the validity of the claim?
- *Authenticity*. Does the researcher demonstrate their authenticity by showing, over time and through interaction, that they have committed to living as fully as possible the values they espouse?
- *Appropriateness*. Does the researcher show that they are aware of the normative background of the claim, i.e. do they show that they understand how historical, cultural and other forces form a taken-for-granted context for the claim?

These criteria act both as social criteria, and also as communicative criteria, in considering how it is possible to make judgements about the capacity of the researcher to communicate their findings clearly to an interested audience.

Who does the validating?

This question is always contested, because it involves philosophical questions about the validity of certain kinds of knowledge, and the validity of validation/verification procedures themselves. There are no universal answers to these questions; they always need to be negotiated, and this can be done only in a context in which all participants honour the capacity of others to come to reasonable judgements.

Here are some of the participants involved in validation procedures:

Yourself

You are the only participant in processes of personal validation. You make judgements about the validity of your own research claims, by explaining how they show the realisation of the values that inspired the research, and you then make these public: i.e. you show how you make the implicit explicit. Many researchers have shown how they personally identify the criteria and standards by which they wish their research to be judged: many examples are cited in this book, for example Jocelyn Jones (2008), Karen Riding (2008) and Simon Riding (2008).

Peer validation

You then subject your subjective opinions to the critical evaluation of others, in the form of your peers. You invite them to demonstrate their own criticality by considering whether you are showing criticality and originality of thinking in relation to the negotiated criteria of comprehensibility, truthfulness, authenticity and appropriateness. Your peers could comprise your colleagues, managers (up-liner validation), and clients, customers, employees or students (client validation).

Academic validation

You also need to establish academic validity; this is important for all contexts, and is especially important if you are studying on an award-bearing course. For your research to be taken seriously as research, and not just personal or professional development, you need to show how you have gone through rigorous academically legitimised processes about how knowledge is created and tested. This is because the Academy (higher education) is still regarded as the highest body for what counts as valid, or true, knowledge. However, the forms of academic validation have changed significantly over recent years with the introduction and legitimation of procedures that enable practitioner researchers to identify their own criteria and standards of judgement, as well as through the legitimation of multimedia forms of evidence.

Public validation

Your ultimate validation group will be the general public, who show that they find your work useful by reading it and using your ideas to inform their own lives. The processes of securing validity and legitimacy are reported in an article in *Time* by Grossman (2009: 53), who explains how some authors, who could not get their work published by mainstream publishers, decided to self-publish, and their books went on to become best-sellers (see, for example, Genova 2009). Although practitioners' reports have not always received the validity and legitimacy they deserve, much pressure from the practitioner research community has enabled those reports now to be taken seriously, even to the extent that monies previously allocated only to recognised research universities are now being allocated to traditional teaching-led universities (*THE* 2009).

We now outline how these people come together in contexts of formal evaluation meetings. These usually take the form of a validation group, which also has specific procedures.

Your validation group

In formal contexts, when you are presenting your work to a group of peers for their critical feedback, you would convene a validation group. The job of the group is to consider your knowledge claims and give critical feedback that will enable you to feel confident about the validity of your knowledge claims and your research in general, and to proceed with your research or perhaps to reconsider certain elements and go back and take appropriate action.

Your validation group should comprise individuals whose opinions and capacity for making critical and balanced judgements you trust. It is important to include individuals who are sympathetic to the research, but who are able and prepared to give critical feedback. There can be a real dilemma here in protecting the emergent thinking of the researcher while also giving the critique that will move forward the researcher's thinking (Lomax 1994b). There is no point in inviting people who are hostile or indifferent to your research to be in your validation group. You do, however, need to establish a group that is prepared to be critical in order to avoid possible challenges of collusion.

It is helpful, though not always possible, to identify the people you wish to be in your validation group from the start of your project, and invite them to take part. The size of the group should be conducive to the work to be done. The group should not normally number more than ten, and would usually comprise four or five members. Explain their responsibilities (see 'Guidelines' below), and that they are making a commitment for the duration. Ideally you should have much the same group throughout, so that they will be able to comment on your progress by comparing and contrasting events such as critical incidents, and make judgements about the development of your professional learning. Give your group a list of dates for meetings: once every two months, perhaps. The intervals depend on your circumstances and the willingness and availability of your group. It is much easier for people to meet together if they are working in the same organisation. If people have to travel, organising meetings is more difficult and calls for careful forward planning.

The final validation meeting would aim to look at the overall report (summative evaluation), together with the data archive from which you have selected your evidence, when the group would agree (or not) that the claim to knowledge is valid, so that this knowledge may be put into the public domain and acted on by others.

On formal award-bearing programmes, members of validation groups should be given specific guidance about the form the meeting should take and the criteria to be used. At the end of this chapter is an example of guidelines that apply to these formal meetings. In other less formal contexts, how you conduct the validating sessions is up to you. You may appoint a neutral chairperson, or conduct the session yourself, or invite another member of the group to do so. At the meetings you should aim to fulfil the basic principles of:

- producing a progress report that may be transformed or incorporated into your final report, and that specifies what you have achieved and what you still need to do;
- organising the evidence into an easily comprehended form that shows work in progress and aims to test the validity of the knowledge claim;
- offering your own critical analysis of what you have achieved so far, with perhaps specific questions about how you can develop certain aspects.

In validation meetings, be realistic about your expectations. Do not expect everyone to agree with you automatically. The point of a validation meeting is that people will debate with you, and perhaps challenge what you are saying when you claim validity for your work. If everyone agrees with you, you could take this as a licence to continue in the way you are already working, but if someone disagrees with you, you should take their feedback seriously and consider alternatives. If no one agrees with you, you would need to reconsider all round, and present your research later in a way that shows you have taken their responses into account. Cases have been reported when a researcher decided to go it alone, despite critical feedback: stories such as those of John Nash (Nasar 1998; see also Chapter 5) and Richard Feynman (2001) show that brilliant people went their own ways, but these stories are exceptions rather than the norm. Common-sense advice for you is to listen carefully and act on the feedback with due regard for other people's opinions, but always to exercise your own originality of thinking and capacity for creativity in your own way.

Example

A good example of how a validation group encouraged a researcher to re-think his position is the case of Martin Forrest (1983), in his MEd dissertation on 'The Teacher as Researcher'. He studied his own practice as an in-service supporter in helping primary schoolteachers to improve the quality of pupils' learning about the use of historical artefacts. In the first validation meeting, he asked the group to respond to the questions:

- How can we know that an improvement has taken place in the classroom? What criteria do we use to judge whether an innovation has led to an improvement in the quality of learning?
- In the context of my work as an INSET tutor, how effective am I in my role as a disseminator and supporter of innovation? What evidence is there to support my claim to be helping teachers to improve the quality of their children's learning?

In his first validation meeting, and following the presentation of his report, Forrest was asked to strengthen the evidence in relation to his claim that he had been effective in helping the teachers to improve the quality of the children's learning. The validation group wished to see stronger evidence that he had done so. Forrest went away and worked on the issue. During a second validation meeting several months later, he produced evidence, including videotapes, which showed a teacher who initially did not believe that her pupils could think creatively and independently. Forrest showed her a videotape of a class of similar-aged children being taught by another teacher and doing what she did not believe was possible with her pupils. The teacher in question therefore tried out some of the strategies that Forrest recommended, and found that her pupils were indeed capable of doing the things she had not initially thought them capable of doing. The evidence provided by Forrest convinced his validation group that he had sufficient evidence to justify his claims. You can read Forrest's account of the validation group meeting at www.jackwhitehead.com/writeup/alval.pdf.

Guidelines for a validation group

Here are some guidelines for a validation group, which you can adapt as appropriate for your context. This example draws on the work of Pamela Lomax when she was Professor of Educational Research at Kingston University.

Example

Guidelines for a validation meeting
The following are guidelines for researchers and assessors. Both parties should read them carefully.

Purpose of the meeting
The purpose of the meeting is for the researcher to present their report, focusing on the claim(s) to knowledge they are making. They should

present accompanying evidence and explain why the claim(s) should be accepted. The validation group should be prepared to listen carefully.

Composition of the validation group

The validation group should comprise (ideally):

- the researcher's supervisor;
- critical friend(s);
- interested parties such as a manager or principal;
- independent person from elsewhere in the institution;
- any other interested parties.

The validation meeting can also be used as an opportunity to involve others on similar professional development programmes, or supervisors, to help them build capacity in learning and supervisory practices.

Preparation for the meeting

The researcher should prepare a brief progress report and send it to members of the validation group at least one week in advance of the meeting. The report could address issues raised in the original research proposal, as follows:

- What was my concern?
- What was my research question?
- Why was I concerned?
- What did I do about my concern?
- What are the outcomes?
- What are my provisional knowledge claims?
- What are my provisional conclusions about (1) the validity of my claims to knowledge and (2) the significance of what I am doing?
- What do I think could be improved?
- Where do I go from here?

The report should be accompanied by a statement about which criteria and standards the researcher has used in making judgements about the quality of the report. Specifically they should say how they judge the quality of the practice and the research.

Organising the meeting

The date of the validation meeting should be negotiated in consultation with the supervisor and other key stakeholders, and the date, time and place should be posted on a noticeboard in the institution.

Conduct of the meeting

The meeting should last about one hour. The researcher should document what is said carefully, or invite a critical friend to do so. Audio- or videotape-recording can be useful. An account of the validation meeting should go into the subsequent report (dissertation or thesis), together with any multimedia recordings and analyses of these.

Assessment

The *researcher* should present their report, outlining the methodological steps that have led to the present claim to knowledge, supported by clear evidence. They should also specify how they have made judgements about the quality of their practice and their research. First they should explain how the claim may be tested in relation to their personal values. Second, they should show how they have fulfilled the criteria identified by Habermas (1976: 2–3) as follows:

Comprehensibility. The researcher and their account can be understood.
Truthfulness. The researcher produces authentic evidence in relation to the claim.
Authenticity. The researcher shows how, over time and interaction, they have committed to living their values as fully as possible.
Appropriateness. The researcher shows their awareness of the normative background of the writing and the research.

They should also address the criteria of ironic validity (Lather 1991) and reflexive and dialectical critique (Winter 1989) by offering reflections on their account, and indicating how their understanding has developed through the research process.

The *assessors* should listen carefully, and offer responses in relation to the identified criteria. General agreement should be reached that the nominated criteria have been met. Suggestions should be made to the researcher about future progress and/or modification of the research plan.

Summing up

At the end of the validation meeting the validation record should be completed and signed by the group. The supervisor should ensure that the researcher has a copy to include in the report, and that a copy goes into the administrative file for future reference.

Summary

This chapter has outlined issues to do with the validation of claims to knowledge. It has discussed ideas about (1) what making a claim to knowledge means; (2) the processes involved in validating, including ideas about personal and public forms of validation; and (3) who is involved in validation procedures. It has set out the kinds of criteria used to test the validity of knowledge claims, such as the criteria of comprehensibility, truthfulness, authenticity and appropriateness (Habermas 1976); reflexive and dialectical critique (Winter 1989); and ironic validity (Lather 1991).

Checklist of reflective questions

Here is a list of questions that should help you to demonstrate the validity of your knowledge claims.

- Are you confident about what making a claim to knowledge means, and what validation of those claims involves? Can you explain these to other people?
- Are you clear about which claims to knowledge you are making in your action research? Are you confident that you have tested the validity of those claims against the criteria of your own values?
- Have you thought carefully about how you will demonstrate that you are fulfilling the criteria of comprehensibility, truthfulness, authenticity and appropriateness? Do you show your capacity for reflexive and dialectical critique, and for ironic validity?
- Have you fully prepared for your validation group meeting? Do you know what to expect? Are you confident that you will be given permission to proceed with your research? Yes, of course you are, but why do you feel you have reason to feel confident? It is important that you explain this to yourself first, because your validation group may ask you the same question.

If you can show that you have fulfilled all these issues, you should expect your knowledge claim to be validated by your peers. However, this is not the end of ensuring that your research may enter the public domain. We have said throughout that validity is a prerequisite for legitimation: now that your work is pronounced valid, how do you ensure its legitimation by others? This is the focus of the next chapter.

Chapter 12

Legitimation processes: presenting reports and legitimising them

This chapter deals with how you present your reports and the kinds of standards used to assess their quality. The focus of the enquiry therefore changes, from validating claims to knowledge (accepting that they are truthful), to validating the report through to assessing its quality (accepting the report as a valid research document). It is worth emphasising that if you wish to have your research and its report legit-imised, i.e. accepted in the public domain, you need to develop certain capacities. The first capacity was dealt with in Chapters 10 and 11, to do with how you demonstrate the validity of claims to knowledge, which entered into your broader understanding of what constitutes a good-quality report. The second capacity is to demonstrate your understanding of how to negotiate assessment procedures, in relation to producing what is expected in the form of a report. It also involves the skills of negotiating, when you ask for your report to be judged according to certain criteria and standards. These are issues to do with the politics of knowledge, as well as the politics of how knowledge is used and managed for specific purposes.

The chapter is organised to deal with these matters, and is in three sections:

- current debates;
- criteria and standards for judging the quality of action research reports;
- establishing the legitimacy of action research and its reports.

Current debates

We explained in Chapter 2 why it was important for practitioners to see themselves both as high-quality practitioners and also as high-quality researchers. This involves:

- showing (producing evidence) that you have improved your practices in ways that meet the criteria for good-quality practice, often to do with enabling yourself and others to realise your potentials for critical engagement and originality of thinking and action;
- showing (producing evidence) that you have conducted your research in ways that meet the criteria for good-quality research, often to do with how you have improved practices, and offering explanations for how these now constitute new theories and contribute to the wider body of knowledge.

This is where it becomes problematic, because, although considerable gains have been made in recent years, new practices are emerging that threaten the integrity of action research. Here are some of the gains, and the potential losses.

Gains

Gains have been made in the legitimation by the Academy of action research. The Academy is considered by many as the highest body for establishing what counts as valid knowledge and who counts as a valid knower. 'The Academy' is not an abstract entity, but a real-life, widespread institution comprising real-life people. These people have different views and opinions, and are subject to processes of changing their minds in the same way that other citizens do in other workplaces. Some members of the Academy are delighted to be identified as working practitioners, whereas others are still resistant to the idea that they should be seen as practitioners working in a workplace. However, many now accept this identity as a norm. This acceptance is intensified given current moves to position higher education institutions as businesses first and knowledge-creating institutions second; and also to look to higher education as the site for accrediting work-based learning as a means of encouraging social and economic regeneration. This has presented considerable challenges for many traditional academics, not only to reidentify themselves as practitioners, but also to welcome 'ordinary' people into their midst. Increasingly, however, the knowledge of practitioners is respected, and there is greater openness to considering new forms of knowledge and new forms of establishing its validity, as evidenced by the large numbers of validated masters and doctoral degrees in many universities. These accounts have been further facilitated by the legitimation of newer forms of representation, such as e-books, e-journals, websites and blogs: see www.actionresearch.net and www.jeanmcniff.com for examples of such forms of representation and communication. In 2001 Catherine Snow called for a coherent knowledge base that would synthesise the new knowledge emerging from the community of educational practitioner–researchers. It is unlikely that even she could have foreseen the explosion that has since occurred in the formation of such a knowledge base and the interest it has generated.

However, although gains have been made, losses have also been incurred. Here are some of them.

Losses

In the scramble to turn higher education institutions, and even mainstream education institutions such as schools, into businesses, within an over-all concentration on markets and their mechanisms, action research has become dangerously technologised into an instrumental form that focuses on targets and behavioural outcomes. This danger was forecast by Herbert Marcuse in 1964 when, although he was not speaking about action research, he spoke about the dangers of persons becoming subservient to their own technologies. In some places, influential textbooks reinforce the messages communicated by market-oriented governments, so action research has been taken over as a new technical form of activity that requires practition-ers to produce 'results'. The quality of their practices and research is assessed accordingly. For example, the UK Best Practice Research Scholarships were allocated on the basis that practitioners seeking research funding would qualify if they achieve the targets they identified as research outcomes. If they did not achieve the targets, the quality of research was deemed suspect. Overcoming these difficulties requires the engagement of all members of the action research community in critical dialogue about how they understand the educational nature of action research, and their engagement in dissemi-nation exercises that will influence international thinking about what counts as validity in action research, and how this is to be achieved and legitimised.

This is where you come in.

Your responsibility is to develop your knowledge about these issues, especially in relation to the criteria and standards used to judge good-quality practice, research and reporting. You need to understand the origins of these criteria and standards, their nature and their uses, so that you too can con-duct high-quality action research and produce a high-quality report that will enable other people to see the high quality of your work, in relation to its originality, rigour and significance. So let's look at these issues of criteria and standards in more detail.

Which criteria? Which standards?

First we need to remind ourselves that there are different forms of research and scholarship. In this book we are speaking about what has come to be known as the new scholarship (Boyer 1990; Schön 1995), which is where action research is located. We have throughout contrasted the new scholarship, largely to do with personal forms of enquiry, with traditional scholarship, largely to do with social scientific enquiry. We have also made the case that traditional scholarship and new scholarship forms are judged by different criteria and different standards, as follows.

Traditional scholarship criteria and standards of judgement

Although things are changing, the situation remains for many that:

- Work is often judged on the technical quality of the report rather than the quality of the practice that the report describes. The set pattern of report writing can be considered more important than accounts of real-life practice.
- Although the generic criteria for report writing maintain that the report should demonstrate originality of mind and critical judgement, these criteria can be variously interpreted. In traditional scholarship, 'critical judgement' would take the form of, say, documentary analysis of a literature review, whereas in new scholarship approaches, researchers would use the literature to ground and test the validity of their own emergent living theories.
- The predetermined criteria of examiners tend to be considered more important than the negotiated criteria of practitioners. Therefore, the work may be judged in terms quite different from those that the practitioner intended.
- Reports are sometimes judged by examiners who hold different values from the researcher. Examiners might expect to read of an improvement in the external situation. When concrete 'results' are not reported, the work might be considered inadequate. Researchers, however, might consider that showing an improvement in the quality of their own learning is sufficient.

These dilemmas are reported in a range of publications, including Lomax (1994a).

New scholarship criteria and standards of judgement

- New scholarship criteria emphasise the quality of the researcher's learning as much as situational outcomes. In fact, if the research does not go as planned, and if the researcher can show that they have learnt through dealing with the situation, this is often considered sufficient.

- The report shows the process of personal professional learning. This may be expressed through demonstrating how the researcher took stock of a particular situation, reflected on what they might do, and took appropriate action in order to make a claim that they had improved their practice.
- The criteria of the researcher are expressed in terms of the values they hold. Values transform into living practices. The research focuses on the extent to which these values were lived out. Reasons are given why they were realised, or not.
- Values also come to act as living criteria and standards of judgement.
- Reports are judged by the degree of demonstration of originality, creativity of mind and critical judgement. This refers to how researchers use existing theories in the literature to help move forward their own thinking in enabling them to create their own living theories of education.

So, how do you articulate and achieve these criteria at every step through your project, and by what standards – and whose standards – do you judge its quality as you proceed? Here are some ideas about how you could do this.

Criteria and standards for judging the quality of action research

It can be useful to identify criteria and standards of judgement for every step of your project, so here is a simple strategy to help you do so. The strategy has been adapted from an original idea by Pamela Lomax, which appeared in the first and second editions of this book.

Think of your action research as a series of steps, something like the action plan outlined in Chapter 6. Give each step a title, such as 'identify a research issue' or 'taking action'. For each step, identify the criteria for that step, i.e. what you would expect to see happen, and also how you would judge the quality of what you have done in that step, i.e. the standards of judgement you would use. For each step say which values are transformed into standards of judgement. This will enable you to show how you understand your work as a process of theorising.

Here are some ideas about how you might begin, which include the kinds of criteria you could identify that are going to help you decide whether or not the action has been successful. Remember that you can adapt everything here for your own use, and also set your own values-based criteria for judging the quality of your research. You could use this strategy to show how you make considered judgements about any aspect of your action research.

Here are some steps: you can think of many others.

Step 1
Identify a research issue and a research question; give reasons for the concern.

Research questions: What is my concern? Why am I concerned?

Intention for the research: what do you hope to do?

You signal your intent to do the following:

- The action research addresses an issue you have identified in your practice with a view to making changes.
- This is focused into a question of the kind, 'How do I improve my practice?'
- As well as seeking answers to this question you will be exploring the underlying meaning of the question itself.
- You explain why your concern is professionally relevant and sufficiently important to warrant your personal engagement and commitment.

Criteria: what would you expect to see in the action research and in the report?

You would expect to see the following:

- a clearly formulated research issue;
- a well-articulated research question;
- a coherent rationale for undertaking the research;
- an outline of what the significance of doing this research might be for your own and other people's learning and practices.

Standards of judgement used

You judge the quality of your action research in terms of the following:

- Do you show that you are able to identify an area of concern?
- Do you demonstrate the capacity to stay focused and concentrate?
- Can you offer a cogent rationalisation for your research?
- Are you already aware of the potential significance of your work for your own learning and the learning of others?

You judge the quality of your action research in relation to how you live your values of focused concern, clear communication of your research intent, rationalisation, and understanding of underlying significance.

Step 2
Action planning

Research questions: What can I do about the situation? What will I do?

Intention for the research: how do you plan to do your research?

You signal your intent to do the following:

- Translate the initial intention into a manageable plan. Start small, keep focused and see how it develops.
- Aim to establish a clear link between why you want to act and what you do then (this is your link between your values and your actions). Try to develop strategies that will help you to reflect critically.
- Learn to step back from the action and ask critical questions, such as, 'Why am I doing this? What do I hope to achieve?'

Criteria: what would you expect to see happening in the action research?

You would expect to see the following:

- Formulation of a clear plan of action that includes possible strategies for addressing your research question.
- Willingness to modify this plan as the research progresses. Detailed records of how your intentions become clearer as you proceed.
- Identification of where your practice possibly contradicts your espoused values and how you might resolve these dilemmas.

Standards of judgement used

You judge the quality of your action research in terms of the following:

- A link between values, reflection and action is established.
- The research process has been made transparent.
- Values are lived in practice.

You judge the quality of your action research in relation to how you live your values of theory–practice integration, transparency in research, the living out of values.

Step 3
Involving others

Research question: How do I involve others so that my research is collaborative?

Intention for the research: how do you hope to involve others collaboratively?

You signal your intent to do the following:

- Work to involve colleagues as co-researchers rather than research subjects.
- Encourage colleagues to share your educational experience by doing their own research.
- Involve a colleague such as your critical friend and ask for critical feedback.
- Be prepared to relinquish your ownership of the action when colleagues are ready to take it over.
- Be open. The integrity of action research depends on not manipulating others.
- Be ready to take risks and possibly expose others to risk.
- Establish clear ethical principles to guide your research.

Criteria: what would you expect to see in the action and in the report?

You would expect to see the following:

- Your research role is made transparent.
- Your collaborative intent is realised.
- Ethical principles are developed and put into practice.
- You demonstrate a readiness to take risks and make yourself vulnerable.

Standards of judgement used

You judge the quality of your action research in terms of the following:

- You are committed to involving others in a democratic way.
- You are committed to inclusional and relational practices.
- You show respect for others.
- You show openness to critique.

You judge the quality of your action research in relation to your values of honesty, openness, democracy, inclusion and relationship, respect, and capacity for critical reflection.

Step 4
Taking action, and gathering data to show the situation as it is and as it changes over time

Research question: What will I do? How will I keep track of what I do?

Intention for the research: what action do you intend to take, and how will you gather data to show its influence?

You signal your intent to do the following:

- You take action in the direction of your educational values.
- You monitor the action systematically. You collect a range of data, using as many data-gathering techniques as appropriate.
- You sort and store the data carefully to use for further reflection.
- You interrogate, analyse and interpret the data regularly, and begin to identify emerging patterns and themes.

Criteria: what would you expect to see in the action research and in the report?

You would expect to see the following:

- Comprehensive data are collected from different sources.
- Patterns begin to emerge, and any contradictions are acknowledged.
- Your analysis is exposed to critique.
- You consider which alternatives may be viable.

Standards of judgement used

You judge the quality of your action research in terms of the following:

- You acknowledge the existence of different kinds of data from a range of sources.
- You appreciate patterns and trends, and show an understanding for contradictions in the data.
- You are willing to change your mind.
- You demonstrate critique, inventiveness and originality.

> You judge the quality of your research in relation to your values of willingness to take purposeful action, capacity for exercising critical judgement, capacity for inventiveness and originality.

Step 5
Evaluation

Research question: How will I ensure that any judgements I come to are reasonably fair and accurate?

Intention for the research: you intend to show how you have exercised responsibility in testing the validity of your knowledge claims

Your signal your intent to do the following:

- Indicate the criteria and standards used to make judgements about the quality of the action and the quality of the research.
- Gather data and produce an evidence base against which to test the validity of the claims.
- Show how you have developed professionally, and can articulate the significance of your action and your learning.
- Pay attention to disconfirming data and evidence, and take appropriate action.

Criteria: what would you expect to see in the action research and in the report?

You would expect to see the following:

- the exercise of considered judgement in arriving at conclusions about the quality of the action and the research;
- a clear articulation of the methods used to establish validity of knowledge claims;
- strategic data gathering and generation of evidence;
- attention paid to disconfirming data and evidence;

Standards of judgement used

You judge the quality of your action research in terms of the following:

- You demonstrate methodological rigour and epistemological responsibility.
- You articulate the methods used to gather data and generate evidence.
- You show integrity in how you demonstrate originality.
- You demonstrate the authenticity of your claims.
- You use your findings as part of critical professional debates.

You judge the quality of your action research in relation to how you live your values of a respect for rigour and responsibility, the combination of integrity and originality, a concern to demonstrate truthfulness and authenticity, and a desire to bring your learning into critical professional debates.

Step 6
Modification of practice

Research question: How do I modify my ideas and practices in light of my evaluation?

Intention for the research: what do you hope to do?

You signal your intent to do the following:

- Show how you have reflected on and learned through the processes of doing the research.
- Explain how you appreciate that research is not always a smooth process, but requires inventiveness and creativity.
- Show how you have transformed negative aspects into new productive forms of enquiry.
- Explain how you will manage the research process in the future.

Criteria: what would you expect to see in the action research and in the report?

You would expect to see the following:

- awareness that you could have done the research differently, and possibly with different outcomes;
- a willingness to take action in new directions;
- a desire to explain your educational influences in your own and other people's learning;
- insights into how future cycles of action reflection could be managed.

Standards of judgement used

You would judge the quality of your action research in terms of the following:

- awareness of the need for creative responses and transformational thinking;

- openness to new beginnings and opportunities;
- acceptance of responsibility and a desire to demonstrate authenticity;
- insights into future potentials, and a desire to make them come true.

You judge the quality of your action research in relation to how you live your values of openness to new possibilities, understanding that the future is in the now, creative capacities for original thinking, and willingness to engage with the unknown.

Step 7
Making public

Research question: How do I disseminate my findings?

Intention for the research: what do you hope to do?

You signal your intent to do the following:

- Produce a high-quality report that demonstrates its capacity for originality, rigour and significance.
- Seek to exercise your educational influence through the high-quality content, form and presentation of your report.
- Make your work public to a wide audience, so that they can learn with and from you.
- Seek to contribute to new thinking and new practices about the need to do action research, and how this might best be done.

Criteria: what would you expect to see in the action research and the report?

You would expect to see the following:

- Awareness of the need to produce a high-quality report that demonstrates originality and rigour, and articulates the significance of the work for your own and others' learning.
- Relevant content, communicated clearly, concisely, and with authority. Appropriate form of writing and organisation of ideas.
- Care and attention to detail in form and presentation of language used.
- Responsibility in reporting: unambiguous messages that demonstrate critical and dialectical reflexivity.
- Desire to influence new directions in thinking and actions.

Standards of judgement

You would judge the quality of your action research in terms of the following:

- awareness of the need for clear communication;
- relevant content, appropriate form of communication;
- potential to influence new learning, thinking and action;
- promotion of critical and dialectical reflexivity;
- responsibility and accountability in writing and communication.

You judge the quality of your action research in relation to how you live your values of clear communication, desire for educational influence, promotion of critical and dialectical reflexivity, responsibility and accountability in writing and communication.

These ideas can act as starting points to get you going as you evaluate the quality of your action research. You may adapt and adopt them as you wish. You can also create many more items, as appropriate for your needs. Work with others in critiquing your ideas, and aim to develop them collaboratively.

Establishing the legitimacy of action research and its reports

In any field of human action there are those who speak and who are listened to, and those who do not speak and who are not listened to. This situation is contrary to the values of social justice and the entitlement of all to speak for themselves. In situations such as these, it is important to try to establish three things as preliminaries for social and cultural change:

1 What has happened in the past that has led to this situation?
2 What is happening now that is perpetuating the situation?
3 What can you do to change it?

You can do nothing about (1). You can do something about (2) by improving your understanding of (1). You can (3) decide to improve your understanding and take action in your own learning and in your efforts to influence the learning of others. This means that you are ready to engage with issues relating to who is already speaking, who else should speak, and why, and who agrees that they have the authority to make those kinds of decisions. These are problematic and political issues, and involve understanding the nature of power and how power is and can be used for social and cultural renewal and regeneration.

This section is organised to address these issues, and is in three parts:

1　understanding the origins of power;
2　understanding the nature of power;
3　understanding the uses of power.

Understanding the origins of power

Power is not a 'thing'; it is within the relationships among people. Foucault (1980) speaks about the 'capillary action' of power, as it is drawn along the threads of relationships, and comes to rest in some people and groups and not in others. Some people regard themselves as in power, and they go to elaborate lengths to persuade others that this is the case. Often their systems of persuasion have the desired effect; other people agree with the script, and agree to speak it, not asking whether it can be changed, or even questioning whether it should be changed, or how it came into being in the first place. The general assumption is that this is the way things are because this is the way things are. People already in power continue to make the rules that will keep them in power. They become the gatekeepers of what counts as power and who should be powerful, and of the rule-making procedures for deciding these things. They use many overt strategies to control the thinking of others, including intimidation, marginalisation and flattery, and many subtle strategies such as controlling public discourses that inform and perpetuate existing cultural norms. The general public becomes obedient and many are persuaded not only to conform, but also to believe that it is their duty to conform. They forget their potentials to see other better ways. This is one of the most pernicious forms of mind control and social engineering in societies: critique is systematically factored out of private and public conversations, and uniformity, complacency and acceptance settle in. It is the case in many professional education contexts, too, where people are persuaded, by whatever means, to toe the institutional party line and not speak out if they disagree.

Key authors who give penetrating insights into these ideas are Arendt (1958), who says that the first responsibility of people is to think and to take their place in the world; Chomsky (2002), who speaks of the need for people to build up their intellectual defences so that they are aware of how power works, and how they are caught up in webs of power; Said (1991, 1994), who speaks of the way discourses are created to provide a basis for social practices that objectify the other, and for the need for intellectuals to challenge such practices; and Foucault (1980), who links power and knowledge and reveals how power works and is exercised to maintain existing power relations. Many others have the same messages, and you should extend your reading and thinking so that you get to grips with the issues and position yourself as someone who understands issues of power and is therefore better equipped to exercise their own power responsibly and with universal intent (Polanyi 1958).

Understanding the nature of power

The situation outlined above applies to you and your research project as much as it does to international affairs, especially if you are in a formal academic context. Although massive shifts are taking place in the knowledge base of educational enquiry, there are still deeply contested issues about who should know, and who should be regarded as a legitimate knower. Many people in institutions of higher education still do not regard practitioners as legitimate knowledge creators, nor do they regard practitioner-based enquiry as a valid form of theory generation. The increasing number of validated dissertations and theses are challenging the traditional knowledge base, and showing practitioner research to be legitimate, especially in terms of how it relates to and has relevance for social and institutional reform. We have also made the point in this book that many practitioners collude in their own subjugation by going along with the story that professional development is about developing good practices, but not about generating good theory. Many practitioners say, 'Don't tell me about theory; leave that for the academics.' In this they do themselves or others little service. We all can, and we all do, generate our living theories about how the world works many times during our waking days. Too often, however, we do not take the time to make our implicit living theories explicit, or to explain the significance of what we are doing. Too often practitioners, and their supervisors, do not believe practitioners are capable of the highest quality academic enquiry, and remain content simply to produce reports that focus on descriptions of practice only ('I did this, I did that'), without moving the discourses into explanations ('I did this because . . .' and 'I did this in order to . . .'). Too often people are willing to compromise standards in report writing for speed of production or desire to get jobs done, ignoring the fact that demonstrating validity actually is a prerequisite for achieving legitimacy. This is a key insight when it comes to understanding the potential uses of power.

Understanding the uses of power

Immediate implications for you are that you need to decide for yourself whether or not you are going to go along with popular discourses, or whether you are going to write your own script. Writing your own script will require you to produce a high-quality report that will communicate how you have conducted high-quality research. There are no two ways about this. Validity is a prerequisite for legitimacy.

This entails a range of tasks. First you need to check in advance what is necessary for your work to be approved. If you are part of an established award-bearing course, it is likely that precedents have now been established and you have nothing to worry about. If you are in a new scenario, especially if you are involved in doctoral work, you do need to check. Before you submit your work at any point in the validation processes, find out about your audience and their expectations. Clarify which criteria and standards of judgement are going to be used in assessing your report. Check whether or not you have any say in negotiating these criteria. If not, there is little you can do, other than play by the established rules and wait until you are in a position to work towards negotiating what counts as the rules. If you are able to negotiate, you will be able to negotiate your own criteria. This will probably also apply to the form of representation of your report, in which case it is up to you to justify why you have chosen to present your work as a conventional written report, or by another means, such as a multimedia presentation (see www.actionresearch.net for a range of examples, and also the examples in this book). Newer criteria are being used (such as those outlined in this book) that emphasise processes of learning as much as behavioural outcomes. When you read your report, ask yourself: Does the work show the processes of learning involved? Does it show the development of critical and dialectical reflection? Does it constitute an original contribution that demonstrates creativity of mind and critical engagement? If you are in a situation that allows negotiation, give your examiners guidance about what they should look for in your work, and explain how the work should be validated.

Remember that some of these ideas would not be acceptable to many people working in educational and organisational settings. The values we authors hold in writing them include a commitment to our understanding that people can think, speak and act for themselves, that we all capable of generating an infinity of knowledge and acting on it. We believe that each and every person is entitled to make their contribution to public debates and should be listened to respectfully. We celebrate diversity in ways of knowing, and we do not privilege certain forms of knowledge because of the power structures that support them. Our work, and the work of those in networks we support, shows how these values are being realised in practice (see www.actionresearch.net and www.jeanmcniff.com). You can do the same.

Be aware of your own potential as a practitioner, provider and supporter, if you are so positioned, by speaking for yourself and showing how your contribution has improved the quality of educational experience for yourself and others, and encourage other people to do the same. Always be ready to offer justification for your work and the values that inform your work, and explain how you demonstrate your intellectual and social responsibility in accounting for yourself. Be open to other people's ideas, and respond carefully to suggestions about how you can strengthen your contribution. This was the case for Terri Austin and Kevin Eames. Terri was asked by her examiners, following her viva voce, to make minor amendments to her PhD doctoral thesis 'Treasures in the snow: What do I know and how do I know it through my educational inquiry into my practice of community?' You can read her response at www.actionresearch.net/austin.shtml. Kevin responded to his examiners in the afterword to his thesis, which he titled 'How do I, as a teacher and educational action-researcher, describe and explain the nature of my professional knowledge?' (Eames 1995: 414–42). You can read his entire thesis at www.actionresearch.net/kevin.shtml

Remember that you do not require other people to accept your values; they are free to make their own choices. Be aware (and perhaps caution other people) that, if you do decide to commit to investigating your practice as the first step in a long process of social change, things may become uncomfortable. You could be going against established norms and creating new ones, and this can be a risky business. However, the risks are worthwhile in terms of the contribution you can make to human flourishing.

Perhaps the most practical advice at this stage is to be aware of the risks, and balance out your options. If you choose to fight battles, be selective about what kind of battle it is, and make sure you have powerful allies, such as a tutor who will support you and other sympathetic colleagues who will lend comfort when the going gets rough. Try to engage people in conversation. Do not set out to score points. Be wise; also be courageous. Stand up for what you believe in. People will admire you for your integrity even if they disagree with your ideas. You know who you are and what you can do. Make sure your voice is heard in the world.

Summary

This chapter has dealt with demonstrating the validity of your knowledge claims and explaining how that validity may transform into legitimacy. It has discussed the politics of criteria and standards, and offered ideas about how to articulate these at each step of an action enquiry. Issues of power and privilege have been considered in legitimation processes, and ideas suggested about why you should be confident about the legitimacy of your contribution to the field in the form of your original claim to knowledge.

Checklist of reflective questions

This checklist should help you to feel confident about demonstrating the validity of your knowledge claims, and securing their legitimacy.

- Do you feel confident about how to demonstrate the validity of your knowledge claims? Are you clear about which criteria and standards of

judgement are appropriate for action research, and how these differ from the criteria and standards of judgement of traditional forms of research?
- Are you confident about how you can make judgements about every step of your action enquiry?
- Have you insights into how validity is linked with issues of truth, whereas legitimacy is linked with issues of power? Do you appreciate the nature of power, and how it comes to be located in certain places and not in others?
- Are you aware of how powerfully you are positioned? Are you aware of how you can use your power, and for what purposes? Are you resolved to do so?

If this is the case, then you should now go on to the next chapter, which offers advice about how to write your report.

Part VI

Disseminating your knowledge

A key component of doing research is to make it public, throughout the project, not only at the end. The question now becomes, 'How do I disseminate my knowledge?' Making your work public is important for several reasons. First, you can articulate the significance of your work for your own and other people's learning, so that it is clear what they can learn with and from you. Second, making your claims public is a political act that enables you to claim your place as a legitimate researcher who has something of importance to contribute to others' learning.

The two chapters in this part deal with these issues.

Chapter 13 deals with how you write your project.

Chapter 14 discusses how you can disseminate your findings, so that you can further make your contribution to the learning of others in your field and beyond.

Chapter 13

Writing your report

So, if the key to legitimacy is validity, and if the key to validity is high-quality research, scholarship and communication, then how do you produce a report of sufficient quality that it will gain you entry to and acceptance in the public domain?

This chapter tells you how to do this and focuses on three aspects of report writing:

- different ways of communicating using different forms of representation;
- writing reports for different purposes;
- how to write a structured report.

You can also find detailed advice in McNiff and Whitehead's (2009) *Doing and Writing Action Research*.

Different ways of communicating using different forms of representation

Traditional and new forms of enquiry create and communicate different kinds of knowledge in different ways, so they usually use different forms of representation.

Traditional forms of enquiry tend to use traditional ways of thinking. The aim is to show how processes of enquiry lead to certain conclusions, and how linear forms of thinking and reporting can show the processes of establishing causal relationships: 'If I do this, that will happen'. New forms of enquiry tend to use non-traditional ways of thinking. The aim is to show how dynamic processes of enquiry can lead to improved practices; perhaps the best way is to use creative ways of thinking and non-linear forms of reporting that show the processes of 'I wonder what would happen if . . .'. Non-linear ways of thinking and reporting can be represented using a variety of forms and media, including writing, story-telling, dialogue, visual narratives, and other forms of physical representation such as dance or performance, and a combination of all these forms. Different ways of knowing may be communicated using different forms of representation; we can show how our embodied values become real using a variety of forms. Here are some of them.

Writing

Writing is still the primary form for presenting reports. If you share the views of Derrida (1997), all forms of communication become a form of writing, because, in his view, writing involves making one's mark on a surface, whether that surface is a piece of paper, a computer screen, a stage or a radio wave. The idea of 'making one's mark' can be extended metaphorically, to say that, if you make your mark through writing, you also make your mark in the world.

Writing takes many forms and has many purposes, the most common of which are as follows.

Communicating the processes of thinking

Writing can be a valuable way of showing the processes of thinking. Some writers explain how the experience of writing can be a form of thinking and knowledge creation.

> In writing I tap my tacit knowledge. I externalise my thoughts-at-competence through my action-at-performance. My writing becomes both symbolic expression of thought (this is what I mean) and the critical reflection on that thought (do I really mean this?). My writing is both reflection on action (what I have written) and reflection in action (what I am writing). The very act of making external, through the process of writing, what is internal, in the process of thinking, allows me to formulate explicit theories about the practices I engage in intuitively.
>
> (McNiff 1990: 56)

Representing dialogue

Many researchers use a dialectical/dialogical way of representing meaning by making public their authentic conversations that show the processes of the creation of their living theories of practice. These conversations show how people talk about the dilemmas and contradictions in their work, and how they were successful, or not, in finding ways through. Some dialogical accounts (for example Larter 1997) explain that the outcomes of the research are located more in the emergent understandings that are inspired through engaging in those conversations. Shobbrook (1997) uses letters to communicate the processes of how her reflections led her to new insightful actions. An entire section of Dadds and Hart's *Doing Practitioner Research Differently* (2001) explains how conversational approaches can lead to new insights and new practices. Mary Roche's (2007) PhD thesis records the many conversations she had with very young children as she encouraged them to think critically; many of these conversations were video-recorded, and may be seen at www.jeanmcniff.com/MaryRoche/index.html

Drama

Some researchers use drama to communicate their meanings. The research story unfolds through the experiences of the persons involved. Using this form, it is possible to communicate both the action of the research as well as a critical commentary on the process. Kay Johnson (1998) explains how she uses drama for action research with students with severe, profound and multiple learning difficulties (see http://educ.queensu.ca/~ar/sstep2/johnson.htm). An excellent example can be found in Jack Whitehead's reconstruction of the meeting with a Senate Working Party on a Matter of Academic Freedom. You can see the reconstruction at www.youtube.com/watch?v=MBTLfyjkFh0 and you can read Jack's critical commentary on the same event at www.jackwhitehead.com/aerictr08/jwictr08key.htm (see also p. 151).

Diaries

Many researchers use extracts from their diaries to communicate the insights generated through the research process. Diary entries are often used as valuable pieces of data. Extensive and systematic use of diaries can show the process itself. In her thesis 'Creating an uncompromised place to belong: Why do I find myself in networks?', Madeline Church writes in the abstract:

> Through this research I am developing new ways of knowing about what we are doing as reflective practitioners, and by what standards we can invite others to judge our work. I am, through my practice, making space for us to flourish, as individuals and communities. In this way I use the energy released by my response to bullying in the service of transformation.
>
> (Church 2004: ii)

You can access Madeline's thesis at www.actionresearch.net/church.shtml and see how she uses diary writing as a technique for recording her thoughts.

Story

The work of Jean Clandinin and Michael Connelly set a strong base for story-telling as a valid form of enquiry, and this consolidated in a new research genre called narrative inquiry (Clandinin and Connelly 2004). Story can be used in a variety of forms for representing ideas and meanings.

Remember that there are different forms of story. Todorov (1999) explains that some stories take a linear format, whereas others adopt a transformational approach. This is well represented in the postmodern novel, in which the beginning, middle and end of traditional story have been suspended. Barry (2002) gives a good account of what is special about postmodern stories.

It is important in action research not to be lulled into a false sense of security that persuades you simply to tell descriptive stories. This relegates action research to a form of professional learning, but does not grant it the status of theory generation. You thus maintain your status as a practitioner, but are not allowed to identify yourself as a practitioner–researcher. Beware those textbooks that tell you to 'simply tell your story'. The entire project of Foucault shows how the minimalist form of 'just telling our stories' places people in subordinate positions (see Foucault 1980). In his (2001) view, Foucault says that is a moral duty to exercise what he calls *parrhesia*, one's capacity to speak the truth, despite the hazards involved. This means that stories need to be explanatory stories, that explain and contain the story-teller's own living theory within itself (see McNiff 2007, who explores the idea of how one's story can be one's living educational theory).

Two good examples of research as story-telling are Dadds and Hart's (2001) *Doing Practitioner Research Differently*, and Winter and Munn-Giddings's (2001) *A Handbook for Action Research in Health and Social Care*. Authors use many ways of story-telling to communicate their truths. Joe Geraci (2001, in Dadds and Hart) uses story to explain how an outsider can 'get inside' the experience of another person's autism. Philip Ingram (2001, in Winter and Munn-Giddings) takes the sensitive subject of a close relative suffering from Alzheimer's disease and uses story to communicate the emotions the experience evokes. The experience of the reader is probably more profound through reading these stories than through a conventional form of reportage.

Jacqueline Delong, while she was superintendent of education in Ontario, supported the practices and publications of hundreds of teacher action researchers through the series *Passion in Professional Practice* (menu item 'passion' in the 'enter action research' section at www.actionresearch.ca/); and the free-access online journal *Ontario Action Researcher* (at www.nipissingu.ca/oar/reports_and_documents.htm) publishes practitioners' accounts of how they have improved their practices.

A further account for online access is Jane Spiro's (2008) PhD thesis 'How I have arrived at a notion of knowledge transformation, through understanding the story of myself as creative writer, creative educator, creative manager, and educational researcher'. In the epilogue to her thesis Jane uses story as a story-tribute to the supervision of Jack Whitehead, available at www.jackwhitehead.com/janespiropdfphd/storyepilogue.pdf.   Similarly, Moira Laidlaw (1996) explicitly uses stories in her PhD thesis, in the form of fictional narratives, stories and poetic communications. Her thesis is entitled 'How can I create my own living educational theory as I offer you an account of my educational development?' You can access the abstract to her thesis at www.actionresearch.net/moira2.shtml, where she says:

> By showing how my own fictional narratives can be used to express ontological understandings in a claim to educational knowledge, and by using insights from Coleridge's 'The Ancient Mariner' to illuminate my own educational values, I intend to make a contribution to action research methodology. By describing and explaining my own educational development in the creation of my own 'living educational theory', I intend to make a contribution to educational knowledge.

If you go to www.actionresearch.net/mastermod.shtml all the practitioners' personal professional accounts use story in report writings, in the sense of autobiographies about their own learning.

Poetry

Similarly, poetry can be used to communicate the experiences of doing research and the understandings that emerge. It can show how embodied values emerge as lived realities. Perhaps the best example is Jane Spiro's PhD thesis, cited above, in which Jane uses all of the resources of a creative writer to communicate the experience of doing and learning from her action research; see also McNiff (1993: 110–115).

Multimedia representations

We have spoken throughout about the power of multimedia representations, as living forms of storied communications. The examples cited throughout this book show these realities.

We now turn to how reports can be put to use.

Writing reports for different purposes

This section offers general guidelines on how to write research reports. There are many different kinds of report, and different ways of writing them. In this section we consider two kinds:

1 a general report, which tells the explanatory story of doing your action research;
2 a report written specifically for academic accreditation.

Both forms are widely used, and you can mix and match them to suit your own purposes.

Whatever form of report you write, you will have to observe certain conventions and practices, some of which are as follows:

- *Write for a reader, not for yourself.* This advice is often ignored in report writing. It is your responsibility, as author, to ensure that your reader can read your text with ease. Too many writers assume that their reader will automatically understand what they are writing about, which is not often the case. The only thing your readers know about you is what they see on the page. Make sure that you lead them through your text so they know what you are aiming to say and what they are supposed to understand. Provide multiple signposts, such as 'Let me explain what I mean by this . . . ' or 'To repeat, the main issue is that . . .'.
- *Write in a clear and concise way.* Produce a text that is attractive and fluent, which speaks with authority and with no pretentiousness.
- *Ensure that you produce an explanatory text, not only a descriptive text.* This means that the entire text will stand as an explanation for what you are doing and why you are doing it.
- *Make sure that the content and form are appropriate for an action research report.* The content deals with how you were trying to improve your learning in order to improve your practice, and how you tried to exercise your educational influences in other people's learning so they also could improve their practices. The form is an autobiographical form through which you offer an account for what you are doing and why you are doing it.

Here are some guidelines for writing different kinds of report, but please remember that you can mix and match, or adapt to your own purposes.

A general report that tells the explanatory story of doing your action research

Your report is about what you know about your practice, and how you have come to know it. It is an explanation for how and why you consider your practice to count as good-quality practice, and why you feel justified in holding this view. This explanation is communicated both in what you write (the content) and the way in which you write it (the form). A useful framework to adopt would be to engage with the questions below. By doing so, you would fulfil the criteria for both content and form. The questions are not exhaustive, and you can add more if you wish. Here is a basic framework.

- What did I wish to investigate when I undertook this piece of study?
- Why did I wish to investigate it?
- How did I gather data to show what the situation was like at the time?

- What did I think I could do about it?
- What did I decide to do about it?
- How did I gather data and generate evidence to show what happened when I decided to take action?
- What did I learn?
- How can I account for my learning?
- How do I evaluate the quality of my influence in other people's learning, and in my own? Was my influence educational, or was it otherwise?
- How do I show how I bring this learning into my new educational practices?
- How has doing the project extended me as a professional?
- How do I communicate the significance of what I have done, for my own learning and for the learning of others in my context and in wider contexts?
- How do I show that I have taken care to check that any conclusions I come to are reasonably fair and accurate?
- How have I modified my present practice in light of past learning?

Presenting your report

You can use the questions above as section headings for your report, if you wish. You can make up other headings of your own. The main point is to communicate that this was an ongoing action enquiry, in which you were creating new knowledge through studying your practice, and then testing the validity of the new knowledge by presenting it for the critical evaluation of others. You could organise your writing by considering the following points.

What did I wish to investigate when I undertook this study?

Contextualise the study. Explain who you were at the time, what the context was, what prompted your research question. Was it a problem? Why? Was it a demonstration of good practice? How? Have you given a description of your practice so that any reader will understand what inspired you to investigate the issue in question?

Why did I wish to investigate it?

Give a brief statement of your own professional values base. If the situation inspired you to begin taking action to influence change, what was it about the situation that needed changing? Was something happening that went against what you believe in? Perhaps the situation was so excellent that you wished to explain why this was the case. This would mean communicating your processes of evaluation, and producing reasons and purposes for what was happening.

Throughout this section, try to relate your research issue to the values you hold as a professional, and show what relevance doing the research has had for your professional life. If you are giving an account of the changes you made in your practice, make sure you explain why you felt you were justified in doing so. Always discuss the steps you took to show that you checked with others to test where your perceptions of the situation were accurate. Why could you not tolerate the ambiguity? Why did you not leave well alone? By considering these issues, you will show how you believed you were justified in taking action, that it was not just interference, and that you were acting in the interests of a specific value such as social justice. These kinds of issues contribute to your explanation for why you did what you did, and are an important part of your overall explanatory framework.

How can I gather data to show what the situation was like at the time?

Was there a problem? If so, how would your reader understand what the problem was like? Was it an excellent situation? What picture of the context can you paint? Produce some kind of evidence, using any of the ways outlined in Chapter 12, to show why you felt you wanted to investigate or evaluate it. The main point here is to show your reader what the situation was like and what was happening that inspired you to take action. This would involve explaining how you monitored the situation and what kind of data you gathered.

What did I think I could do about it?

Spell out what you felt your options were, and any possible solutions. Explain that you consulted with others (if you did) in helping you to decide what to do. There could have been a range of options for you to choose from. Explain why you decided on one course of action to begin with, and also say how you may have developed a different action plan if your first option proved unproductive.

What did I decide to do about it?

What course of action did you take? Was it straightforward? Did you stick to only one option, or did you try out several in quick succession? Did you change your mind? Why? What happened?

This section gives an account of your action. Remember that your reader has no idea what you did. Tell the story in a direct way. Say the obvious. Often researchers imagine that the reader will anticipate the most obvious things, because they are so obvious. This is not so. State the obvious, even if it seems excessive to do so.

It can help to tell the story into a tape recorder, or to talk it through with someone else and ask them to tape-record it or make notes as you go along. They will probably say, 'What happened when . . .?' They will check on pieces you may have left out or that are unclear. Telling someone the story can act as your first draft; when you write it down, imagine that you are telling the story again to another person.

How did I gather data and generate evidence to show what happened when I decided to take action?

Here you need to produce ongoing sets of data, which by now you should also be turning into evidence by showing the relationship of the data to identified criteria. You will try to establish what influence you may have had on the research situation.

Explain what data-gathering techniques you used. Why did you choose them and not others? What significant features of the data did you select as representative of what you were hoping to achieve? Why these features and not others? Can your reader clearly see your evidence, as well as a statement from you about which criteria you chose to help you make judgements about your practice? Were these criteria linked with your values, as set out earlier in your report?

By this stage you should be producing evidence generated from your data. This could be in the form of field notes, videotape-recordings, transcripts and selections from any other aspect of your data. Put this evidence in the main body of your text. Do not aim to include long pieces of evidence. Short, concise extracts are needed. Place all raw data in the appendices or in your archive as appropriate. Here, include only those excerpts from the raw data that will act as evidence to show an improvement in your practice, and possibly in the practices of other people.

What did I learn?

A common error in report writing is to concentrate on the descriptions, but not to document the learning. It is quite easy to write a description of the action. It is difficult to write about your own learning. For example, suppose you tried a different method for chairing meetings. You would describe what you did: you invited Mr J to chair rather than yourself. What did you learn? Perhaps you learned that people need help to be a successful chairperson. Perhaps you feel frustrated when people do not do the job as well as you can. Perhaps you have come to appreciate that people have to practise in order to learn, and it is your job to provide opportunities for that learning to take place. Or suppose you praised someone publicly. You may have learned that people shine when praised, that perhaps you do not praise often enough, that there is a relationship between productivity and people's sense of well-being. This kind of reflection on personal learning is at the heart of accounts of good practice. To document these processes during your action research, look again at the form of diary keeping in Chapter 9.

How can I account for my learning?

You can use a variety of techniques for communicating your learning. As you write the description of what you did, you could also weave in an explanation for what you did in terms of your learning, so that descriptions and explanations appear as integrated (as they should). You may choose to write a short reflection after the description. You could use different type fonts to differentiate the descriptions and explanations. You may write the descriptive account under one section heading, and then take a new section to offer explanations in terms of your own reflection and learning. At this point, always aim to include evidence of your own learning, extracts from your data related to the criteria of your values, that you have learned something of value. For example, you could include a diary entry from earlier in your study, and then a current entry, to show the differences in your own thinking. Or you could include a one-minute extract from a videotape to show how you behaved earlier, and then a second extract to show how your behaviour has changed. This behavioural evidence would have to be backed up by a commentary that stated specifically how you had become aware of changes in your own behaviour and why that may have happened.

To repeat: producing evidence of one's own professional learning is perhaps one of the trickiest aspects of written reports, but it is crucial. It also marks the difference between a report that will pass on adequate merit and a report whose merit is outstanding.

How do I evaluate the quality of my influence in other people's learning, and in my own? Was my influence educational, or was it otherwise?

When you speak about your educational influence, you are referring to the extent to which you have influenced people so that they will realise more fully the potentials of their own learning. This implies that you need to evaluate whether or not you have helped people to grow, mentally, physically and spiritually, and to appreciate how they come to grow. You can do this by finding evidence within the written or visual accounts of other people to show that you have helped them to learn for themselves. This evidence exists throughout your data. In your field notes you may find a note saying how one person appears to have become more confident because you have started spending quality time talking with them about their work; in your tape-recordings someone will have said that they understand their work schedule better because you worked with them in a considerate manner. These pieces of evidence, particularly when triangulated, make up a powerful scenario of your educational influence in the learning of other people, to the extent that the quality of their lives has been improved through your influence in their learning.

How do I show how I bring this learning into my new educational practices?

You are testing how your systematic reflection and learning about your practice is helping you to understand where you still need to change things. You understand what you are doing well, and you see areas where you still need to adjust. Other issues may also have arisen.

Although you may feel one aspect of your practice is now satisfactory, this may have revealed other aspects that need attention. The external situation may also have changed, which now prompts you to change what you thought was satisfactory. It never stops!

How has doing the project extended me as a professional?

Significant features of a professional include care and responsibility to others, expert subject knowledge and personal accountability. By studying your practice, and producing ongoing evaluations, you are demonstrating that you are showing care and responsibility for the welfare of others. You are constantly weighing your decisions in light of what you know and what you still need to know, and you are holding yourself accountable for your actions.

How do I communicate the significance of what I have done, for my own learning and for the learning of others in my context and in wider contexts?

Your action research has considerable potential for influencing new learning. By reading your report, and working with you during the period of the research, other people will be able to see how doing the project has influenced learning. This could be your own learning, in that you have learned to do things better. It could also be the learning of other people, such as your peers and colleagues, or the wider community that contextualises your work: perhaps your managers, the parents of children, or the patients you work with. It could also be the social formation of which you are a part, or other social formations. You could say that you are contributing to education: the education of yourself, of others, and of social formations (see Whitehead and McNiff 2006 for an extended development of this idea).

How do I show that I have taken care to check that any conclusions I come to are reasonably fair and accurate?

What validation procedures did you put in place to support and test your claim that you were influencing the situation? What changes did you record, in yourself and in the situation? Who were your validators? Why did you choose them? Did they bring a critical perspective to the process or could there be any collusion? Where are the records of the validation processes? Did you tape-record the meetings, and can these recordings be accessed? Did you ask people to observe you in action, and keep records of their observations? Did you keep your own records? Are you clear that you formulated your criteria in terms of the values that inspire your work, and can you show that you have fulfilled those criteria by producing evidence? How did people validate your evidence? How can you ensure that anyone reading your report believes this to be an authentic account, and not a piece of fiction?

These are stringent conditions for ensuring that your validation procedures are rigorous and trustworthy. They ensure that your action research meet the highest standards of rigour, and should be taken seriously. These are still important considerations in what counts as knowledge and who is considered a legitimate knower.

How have I modified my present practice in light of past learning?

What influence has your study had on your practice? Did you begin doing things differently? Did you decide to continue with the research perhaps from a different perspective? Has your research influenced your workplace in any way? Can you show that others have adopted new practices because of your influence? Are policies changing because of your findings? Can you show that your work has influenced your own personal development and the professional development of others, and led to changes in wider institutional structures and processes? If so, you can say that your living theories have transformed into living theories of professional development and organisational change.

Now let's look at how you could write a formal report.

A report written specifically for academic accreditation

This section sets out how to write a more formal report that is appropriate for some kind of accreditation, such as a work-based report, a report for a foundation or first degree, a masters dissertation or a PhD thesis. To gain accreditation, you would have to fulfil the nominated criteria of the accrediting institution. Institutions tend to set their own criteria, but all would share a common view that the criteria below are important. Be aware that these criteria differ according to different levels of accreditation: for example, at master's level you are expected to make a claim to knowledge, whereas as doctoral level you are expected to make a claim to original knowledge. Also, you would not be expected to produce work of publishable standard in a work-based report, although this may and does happen. However, despite these variations, all formal reports should broadly observe the following criteria (adapted from the University of Bath 2008).

- The work contains a claim to knowledge and makes a contribution to knowledge of the field.
- The work demonstrates an ability to undertake an educational study or enquiry in an appropriately critical, original and balanced fashion in a particular subject.
- The work demonstrates an understanding of the context of the research.
- The work shows improvement in the practice described or explains what may have constrained improvement.
- The work is written in an appropriate form.
- The work contains material of peer-reviewed publishable merit.

- The work is error free and technically accurate with a full bibliography and references.

Below is the conventional structure for a formal report written for an award-bearing programme, including a masters dissertation. Although you do not have to stick to it, this structure is widely accepted in academic contexts, and you won't go far wrong if you do. You can also use the material in the previous section to inform your writing, and you could use roughly the same form. However you write your report, make sure you address the stipulated assessment criteria. Many people studying for MPhil and PhD degrees also use the basic structure below, although it is unlikely that a completed action research PhD thesis would be presented in quite this linear way. We have found that all the researchers we have supervised have created their own unique forms of presentation that accord with what Dadds and Hart (2001) have called 'methodological inventiveness':

> Perhaps the most important insight for both of us has been awareness that, for some practitioner researchers, creating their own unique way through their research may be as important as their self-chosen research focus. We had understood for many years that *substantive choice* was fundamental to the motivation and effectiveness of practitioner research (Dadds 1995); that *what* practitioners chose to research was important to their sense of engagement and purpose. But we had understood far less well that *how* practitioners chose to research, and their sense of control over this, could be equally important to their motivation, their sense of identity within the research and their research outcomes.
>
> (Dadds and Hart 2001: 166, emphasis in original)

Remember also that, although the guidelines below act as broad outlines, you are encouraged to create your own structure, provided you address all the elements mentioned here. You may also find that aspects identified below as belonging to one chapter may go more usefully into another. There are no hard and fast rules about this. Regard the advice as outlining the jobs that need to be done. Where and how you do the jobs is up to you. Just make sure that they are done properly.

The parts of a structured report are:

- title page;
- abstract;
- contents, including content of appendices;
- list of illustrations, figures and tables;
- acknowledgements;
- introduction;
- body of text, organised as chapters or sections;
- references;
- appendices.

Here is a guide to what goes into the chapters.

What goes into the chapters

Abstract

Job to be done: let the reader see at a glance what the research is about, and its importance.

Your abstract consists of about 250–400 words. It is always written in the present tense. It outlines the structure, purposes, methods and overall significance of the work. Most importantly, it says what the claim to knowledge is. It enables another researcher to assess whether the report contains material that is relevant to their interests. It is not the place for descriptions of practice, or for extracts from data or the literature. The abstract should always be succinct, rather like the preview you would read in a television magazine. Your abstract is important, because an examiner would check that your report does what you say it will do in the abstract.

Introduction

Job to be done: give an overview of what you have done in the research, why you have done it, and what its potential significance might be.

Your introduction indicates what the report is about, its main findings and their significance. Here you explain why you wanted to do the research in terms of your educational values, and how doing the research enabled you to live in the direction of these values. You outline the main findings in terms of the evidence you have generated, and speak briefly about their significance for your own professional learning, as well as the learning of others, and the possible potentials for the development of organisational and social formations. In doing so, you are outlining your claim to knowledge and its significance for local and wider contexts. In general, the introduction offers an orientation guide to your reader, so that they know what they are going to encounter. It gives an overview of chapters and their contents. It may also refer to the literature that you have identified as informing your conceptual frameworks. It is particularly helpful if you set out your research question, and then show how that question is systematically addressed throughout (but may not be answered), and how the whole study represents whatever claim to knowledge you make.

Chapter 1: Background to the research

Job to be done: focus the reader's attention on the issue you were addressing, and why.

This chapter could also be called 'Focus of the research'. You should choose the chapter heading that is most appropriate for you. The chapter gives reasons for why you have undertaken your research, and outlines the background against which the research has been undertaken. This background is similar to the contexts (Chapter 2), but different in that it identifies the conceptual frameworks you are using in which to locate your research. A reminder that 'conceptual frameworks' is a commonly used term that refers to issues in the literature, such as social justice, democracy, gender issues, mixed-heritage issues, and theories of change management. You may identify three or four major conceptual frameworks (possibly more) and refer to their associated literature. These issues then become part of the explanatory frameworks of your report.

You should spell out the values that inspired you to do the research (perhaps refer back to your introduction), and show how these values can also be located in your conceptual frameworks, and how you are showing the development of your own understanding of these issues through doing your research. At this point you must state your research question, probably in terms of 'How do I . . .?'; for example, 'How do I ensure equal participation by all in staff meetings?' The point of this chapter is to focus the reader's attention on why you wished to do the research and how you set about doing it. You will show how your research question was informed by your values, and how the research process then became a systematic enquiry into how you could address the question, so that eventually you could make a claim that you had addressed it. It does not matter if you cannot claim that the situation may have improved because of your research. The situation may have been influenced by unforeseen circumstances. What is important is that you show your emergent understanding of your own learning, and how you have used that learning to help other people to learn.

Chapter 2: Contexts

Job to be done: provide background information on why the research needed to be done, and its potential implications.

Here you give an outline of the contexts that inform your work. You should give information about your personal and situational contexts (who you are and where you are located), and any research and policy contexts that are relevant (what research has been undertaken in this area, and what policy recommendations exist in relation to the area). You may have other relevant personal and professional contexts which may inform your work: for example, if you are deaf, or a member of a religious congregation, or a politician.

You may find that there is slippage between policy recommendations and real-life practice. You should not give a life history or detailed analysis, but you should include sufficient background information to help your reader understand why the research was important, and its potential relevance to future personal and organisational development.

Chapter 3: Methodology

Job to be done: provide an outline of the research design, justify your choice of design including your chosen method of enquiry, and demonstrate awareness of the need for good ethical practice.

In this chapter you give an explanation for your overall research design, which includes your choice of form of enquiry. You outline the overall plan in terms of who was involved as participants and validators, and why/ where the research took place, how long it lasted, the main issues addressed, and some of the practicalities of the research that helped or hindered it. You identify and discuss the research methods used, carefully explaining the modes of data collection and analysis, the identification of criteria for judging the validity of claims and justification for their selection, how evidence was generated in relation to the criteria, and how the evidence was organised in support of your claim to knowledge. You give reasons for choosing practitioner research rather than another form of research, and also for choosing one particular approach to action research rather than another. At the same time, you show that you are consistently questioning your own assumptions. This involves demonstrating your knowledge of the different epistemological and methodological assumptions within research traditions. Because you are explaining how other people were central to your methodology, you have to outline what ethical considerations informed their involvement in your research. Describe how you distributed your ethics statements, and gained permission to do the research. You would put copies of your ethics statements and blank copies of your letters of permission into the appendices.

When you write your methodology chapter, bear in mind that what people know of your research is what you tell them. They cannot be expected to understand how you conducted your research unless you tell them. Be clear and state the obvious.

Chapter 4: Your project

Job to be done: tell the story of the research in a clear, systematic and coherent way.

In this chapter you tell the story of your research. Explain what actions you took, what happened, and how you monitored progress and gathered data. Present the data you have gathered and show how you have generated evidence. It is important always to be clear about the difference between descriptions of data (what happened) and explanations of data (your interpretations, what you think was the significance of what happened). These are interdependent, but if you are clear it will help your presentation.

Descriptions of data constitute an account of the progress of the research at various stages. It is useful to include here a chronological table of relevant events, graphic representations of different research cycles, and summary tables. Make sure these match the action plans you outlined in your 'Chapter 3'. If they deviated (which is often the case), explain why.

Interpretations of data constitute a summary of your principal results and claims. You need to show how the claims are supported by the data, and begin to show how the data will generate, or have already generated, evidence. This means you must establish criteria by which you wish your claim to knowledge to be judged, and show how these criteria, related to your values, act consistently as the signposts that guide your work.

Chapter 5: Significance of your research

Job to be done: show the significance of the research and its potential implications.

Discuss the significance of your research in terms of the following:

- How has it contributed to your own personal professional learning? Are you doing things differently? Better? In what way?
- How has it contributed to the professional learning of others in your workplace? Have other people been influenced by your research? Are they doing things differently? Could this collective change to practice be seen as organisational change?
- Can it make a contribution to the wider body of knowledge? In generating your own living theory of practice by studying your practice, and then making your account public, can you say that you are contributing to educational theory?

Taking all of these points into consideration, can you show how your research could inform future research programmes and generate useful knowledge?

Chapter 6: Modification of practice

Job to be done: explain how your research has enabled you to improve your practice, and generate your living theory of practice.

In this chapter you refer back to your introduction, where you set out your research aims and ambitions, in terms of trying to realise your values in your practice. You explain whether or not you are justified in making your claim that you have improved what you are doing, and say that you know how and why you have improved it. In offering this account of practice, you are also saying that you have generated your own living theory of practice. In this way, you are contributing to the wider body of theory, as well as making your contribution to the field. You let your reader know that you are aware that you still need to develop your ideas, and that what seems to be the end of this research programme is actually the beginning of a new one.

Conclusion

Job to be done: round off the report well, and remind your reader of some of the key points they have read.

You conclude the work nicely, and point out some of the key issues you have addressed during the report. You say that you have enjoyed doing the project, and now cannot wait to get onto the next one.

References

Make sure that all of your references and citations are included in your references section. Reports have been rejected in the past if they fail to observe technical conventions. Make sure you adopt the appropriate institutional style, such as the Harvard system. Your tutor will give guidance about what is appropriate. Also study the way that journals and books reference texts, and check in the library how other people have set out their work. These form important precedents.

Appendices

This is where your raw data are presented. Appendices should be organised carefully, and labelled accurately. In the appendices you can also indicate where your larger data archive is to be found, and what its contents are.

Presenting your report

The following guidelines apply to most formal report writing:

- Text should be word-processed or typed using double or one and a half line spacing.
- Margins should be 3 cm on the inside and 2 cm at each of the remaining three.
- Pages in the main body of the text should be numbered consecutively using arabic numerals. The introduction should be numbered separately using roman numerals. Appendices should be numbered consecutively using arabic numerals, and the numbers should begin at (1) at the beginning of the Appendices.
- All material must be labelled clearly. Tables and figures should have full titles. Cross-referencing must reference pages accurately.

- All quotations must be correctly referenced, including date of publication and page on which the quotation appears in the original.
- Citations and references must follow the approved institutional style such as the Harvard system. No footnotes should be used.
- Appendices should not include raw data. Appendices should be for derived data (e.g. tables and figures not included in the main body of the text), examples of archived materials (e.g. blank copies of questionnaires) or summaries of key meetings (e.g. validation meetings). Use your archive for raw data and also for bulky original data, such as videotape- and audiotape-recordings. List archived material in your first Appendix.

Checklist for writing the report

The following checklist will help you to evaluate both the content and the organisation of your report.

- Have you organised your report in such a way that the reader has easy access to the main themes and arguments? Does an explanatory statement or abstract appear at the beginning? Does the report have section headings and subheadings? Are there concluding statements/ summaries?
- Have you explained your reasons for doing the research and set out your overall aims? Is a research question evident throughout? Have you addressed it consistently? Can you show how you have generated your own living theory of practice from studying your practice?
- Is the context of the research well described? Have you shown:
  - its importance for your workplace or institution?

  - a link with your values position?
  - links with other work and research?
  - how your research may inform future policy?

- Have you shown how you developed a coherent action plan? Have you explained why you chose an action research methodology for conducting the research?
- Have you described what interventions you made, and what actions you took to try to contribute to improving the situation? Have you explained why you did this?
- Have you described the particular techniques you used to monitor your research and gather data? Have you explained why you made those choices, and who else was involved?
- Have you made the process of the study explicit? Have you explained how the data were generated and analysed? Have you explained the significance of the data, and shown how the data may be turned into evidence by testing them against identified criteria?
- Have you described your validation procedures? Have you shown how

formative evaluation played a part in possible action research cycles? Have you presented and discussed the outcomes of the final validation meeting? Was the authenticity, accuracy and relevance of your research agreed?

- Have you explained the implications of the study for personal and professional practice in relation to:

  - a better understanding of your own practice?
  - how your work could contribute to organisational change?
  - how the work could contribute to the development of educational theory?

- Have you taken care in presenting your references? Have you proofread the work at least three times?
- Have you booked a holiday to celebrate your finished project?

Summary

This chapter has discussed different ways of writing an action research report. It has outlined some of the techniques used in report writing, what the content of a report should be, and what form it should take. It is emphasised that there is no single way of writing a report, and you should use your creative capacities in producing an original account that is yours and yours alone. However, you do need to address commonly agreed criteria, to establish the high quality of the epistemological and methodological rigour of your report.

Checklist of reflective questions

This checklist will help you write a high-quality report.

- Are you reasonably clear about what goes into an action research report, and what form it will take? Do you appreciate that you need to discuss the different steps in an action enquiry, and explain the relationship between them?
- Have you a clear overview of how you can produce a report that will capture and hold your reader's attention?
- When you write your report, keep in mind the agreed generic criteria. Also show your knowledge of the literatures, and explain how you can test the validity of your claims against the ideas of other people.
- As you write your report, make sure it is attractive to your reader, clean and uncluttered, and written in a dynamic and interesting way.

If you are reasonably confident that you have addressed all these issues you can now consider how you can disseminate your work. This is the focus of the next chapter.

Chapter 14

Disseminating your research and getting published

In Chapters 11 and 12 we looked at the relationship between validity and legitimacy, and said that validity is a prerequisite of legitimacy. Legitimacy is to do with getting your work accepted in the public domain, so this means learning how to negotiate ways and means of getting it accepted.

The chapter deals with these issues. It discusses how you can share your work, and what is significant about your work that it deserves to be shared. It also discusses how you can get published. The chapter is organised into three parts:

- disseminating your work;
- what is special about your work?;
- getting published.

Disseminating your work

The purpose of sharing your work is so that people can learn from it and adopt or adapt your ideas to their own situations, in terms of its subject matter as well as the enquiry processes involved. Here are some of the people you could share your work with and the places where you may do so.

Whom do I share my work with?

People in your workplace

The most obvious people to share your research with are your work colleagues. They already know that you are doing research, and you have kept them informed, because you wanted to work collaboratively, and wanted to avoid being seen as doing something 'unusual'. Some people may already perceive the value of what you are doing and want to learn from it themselves, and may even wish to begin their own action research.

Check with your manager or principal about how to make your research available to others in your workplace. You could make your final report available, or ask for time at a staff meeting, or circulate a memo. Perhaps ask your manager to say publicly that your work is available, so that professional learning is seen as normal practice. With the current international emphasis on the accreditation of workplace learning, you could find yourself in a position of academic leadership. Action researchers often set precedents for collaborative learning in their workplaces, especially if their research is relevant to improving the quality of workplace life. Networks of colleagues within the same organisation can work collaboratively on individual as well as group projects.

For example, Madeline Church (2004), whose work was cited in Chapter 13, helped to form a networked community in which she was network coordinator, action researcher, activist and evaluator. She showed how her approach to this work was rooted in the values of compassion, love and fairness, and was inspired by art. She held herself to account in relation to these values, as living standards by which she judged her self and her actions in the world. Madeline says:

> This finds expression in research that helps us to design more appropriate criteria for the evaluation of international social change networks. Through this process I inquire with others into the nature of networks, and their potential for supporting us in lightly-held communities which liberate us to be dynamic, diverse and creative individuals working together for common purpose. I tentatively conclude that networks have the potential to increase my and our capacity for love.
>
> (Church 2004: ii)

Such research communities can build an atmosphere of workplace collegiality for everyone's benefit, and managers often support their development with funding or remitted time.

For example, in the work undertaken at York St John University, a focus developed on raising research capacity and awareness. The symposia for the British Educational Research Association 2009 annual meeting 'Institutional research: How do we influence processes of epistemological transformation through the creation of academic practitioners' living educational theories of practice?' and 'Academic practitioner–researchers: shifting the epistemological centre in higher education' are collective efforts that show how collaborative work among higher education staff can contribute to the well-being of the wider community (Carter 2009; Wickham 2009). Karen Llewellyn (2009) also writes about the research-informed teaching project that involved multiple subprojects. She explains how a paradigm shift from learning to discovery related to the university context and how enquiry-based learning (EBL) engaged both staff and students in a shared enterprise of enquiry and research.

People outside your workplace

Aim to let other people outside your workplace know about your research: perhaps CEOs, regional and branch managers, or continuing professional development organisers may be interested. Send them a copy of your report, and say you would be happy to talk with them about your work. Chris Glavey (2008), working in Northern Ireland, explains how he let other people in his organisation know about his efforts to involve young people in the organisational planning and running of their schools. His work is having significant influence in wider thinking: see www.jeanmcniff.com/theses/glavey.html.

Often organisations have wider networks, particularly if there are special interest groups. Professional development centres can act as meeting places. Aim to join these groups. Most have newsletters and e-mail networks. They also organise conferences and host discussion groups. You stand a better chance of meeting influential people here than in large organisations. Start small, and see how it develops. Following a personal initiative of Jean and Paul Fields, Director of the Centre, to develop a network in Ireland, Kilkenny Education Centre has become a focus for action research in Ireland. Similarly, the MOFET Institute in Israel supports practitioners' enquiries throughout the country (Kozminsky *et al.* 2009); and in China, the Experimental Centre for English Languages Teaching located at the Ningxia Teachers University has been influential in encouraging practitioner enquiry throughout the country (see www.actionresearch.net/moira.shtml).

If there is no existing network, learn how to start one. Begin by organising a social evening (negotiate the use of facilities from a sympathetic manager somewhere). Produce a newsletter and get others to contribute. This will mean chasing people for material, so be aware and be good humoured. Learn how to start an electronic discussion forum (see, for example, the British Educational Research Association Practitioner Research network, which you can access at http://groups.tlrp.org/). This can be productive although often demanding to manage. If you are not brilliant at technology yourself, find someone who is and let them know how valuable they are as a provider as well as a discussant. Public electronic lists such as JISCmail are valuable for bringing and keeping people together, and a great source of collaborative learning. At a face-to-face level, find opportunities to share your work with a wider community in local or regional centres, or head offices. Make contact with managers, and ask them about opportunities to present your work.

Now think about where to share your work.

Where to share your work

Make your work public in as many venues as possible. Go to conferences and meetings, which is one of the best ways of gaining further legitimacy and credibility. It also raises your profile as a researcher, and gives added prestige to your organisation. Many institutions depend on funding from publications, so would probably support you financially if you were presenting a paper.

Exposure at conferences can help you do the following.

Meet other people

Social occasions at conferences can be the best time to meet researchers from other institutions and contexts. These contacts can be enormously valuable, both for learning about what other people are doing, and for inspiring new ideas for yourself.

Keep up to date

Listening to top people in the field helps you keep up to date with new ideas, as well as get a feeling for developments within a particular field.

Generate new ideas

The buzz around conferences tends to spark off new ideas. Take your notebook everywhere. Write down keywords or points from lectures and do not attempt to keep a record of the entire presentation. Your notes can lead to new lines of thought. Many researchers write papers in skeleton form at conferences, getting inspiration from others. However, remember it is not permissible to use other people's ideas without referencing them. *Never* tape-record a presentation without the speaker's permission, and don't get cross if it is denied.

Learn how to write papers

Writing papers can be one of the best exercises for focusing the mind and clarifying what is important in your research. Don't expect to write the paper in one go. Good papers take about ten drafts, often more, to final completion. The discipline of the refining and editing process forces you to synthesise to give sense to the whole. It also ensures that you write for an audience, not only for yourself.

Learn how to present papers

Presenting papers is part of bringing coherence to and making sense of your work. It requires you to organise your material for other people. Responding to questions forces you to address issues you may not have thought about, and helps you to see the value of your work for other people. Watch good presenters. See how they relate to an audience, respond to questions, use technology, and generally conduct themselves. Model yourself on the best.

Raise your own profile

There is always a group of people who regularly attend conferences. You would become known in a short time, especially if you give a paper. The intellectual stimulation and fellowship of these contacts can boost your own morale, as well as provide the support and conversational community that all researchers need.

Present your paper

Most organisations ask you to send in a proposal or abstract, which is usually peer reviewed. Getting a paper accepted is often far from easy. The rigorous process does show, however, that your peers value work like yours. Your abstract often goes into the conference programme, so regard it as part of writing the paper, and write a good one. Other people know you first by what you write.

Make the presentation

Rehearse beforehand. Present your paper with care. Never read the paper to an audience; this can be boring and frustrating for them. Summarise the key points, and write them down as prompts for yourself, in large lettering, on one or two sheets of paper or index cards so you can speak spontaneously and keep on track. Put these key points on PowerPoint slides or other visuals to support your presentation. Put them in order beforehand and number them. Mark up your presentation copy to remind yourself when you are going to use them. Be prepared to invest time and effort at this stage. You will thank yourself when you come to present the paper.

Produce your talk as a handout, paper or PowerPoint frames for distribution. Decide whether to give this out at the beginning or the end, and let your audience know. You want them to listen to you, not divert their attention to taking notes. Be careful if you hand out copies of your paper in advance. The audience may have read it before you finish talking. Or you may want to refer to it as part of the talk. Lively and engaging presenters who are enthusiastic about what they have to say always capture people's attention.

Stay relaxed and businesslike. Your audience is knowledgeable, so don't talk down or up to them, and they are generally interested in what you have to say. They would not have taken time to come to your presentation if they weren't, so don't expect hostility or be defensive. Tell it as it is, don't put on airs and graces, and be honest and engaging. Always do your best, which is a great deal.

Use multimedia technology

Make sure you are confident around any technology you are using, and make sure it works. Set up well in advance. Avoid fumbling with your computer while talking through ideas. If the technology fails, stay cheerful and focused. People will still listen to what you have to say.

Deal with questions

At the beginning of your presentation, let your audience know if and when they can ask questions or interrupt, whether during the talk or at the end. If someone asks a question while you are speaking, answer the question briefly, but don't lose track of what you are saying, and don't be intimidated into thinking that you should answer the question if it is irrelevant or inappropriate. This is your presentation so retain ownership of it.

Acknowledge all questions, and aim to answer as many as possible. If you don't know the answer, say so. People respect honesty. Give concise answers to questions, and don't wander off the point. Stay courteous and friendly throughout. People tend to value the opinions of those they respect, so present your work as something of value and be enthusiastic about it yourself, and others will warm to you and your subject matter.

Set up Internet-based e-seminars

These can be a particularly powerful form of communicating with a network of like-minded people. E-seminars enable participants to share and develop ideas in a live forum. A good example is the British Educational Research Association practitioner–researcher e-discussion, being led by Jack Whitehead at time of writing. You can access the archives of this discussion by clicking http://groups.tlrp.org/, getting your username and password and accessing the practitioner–researcher e-discussions. On 11 February 2009, Jack posted the following, which has direct relevance for part 2 of this chapter ('What is special about your work?'):

> I've been asked to lead the BERA Practitioner-researcher e-seminar on an episte-mological transformation in educational knowledge, from the 16-22 February on the new BERA web-site. . . . I'll be sending in my introductory comments on 13th February for posting on the new BERA web-site to begin the week so do please let me have your suggestions for improving the introductory comments. Don't hesitate to be 'robustly critical'. . .

An Epistemological Transformation in Educational Knowledge

A few words of introduction

The introductory ideas for this e-seminar are on pages 28–29 of Issue 105 of *Research Intelligence* (November 2008) on an epistemological transformation in educational knowledge. You can access Issue 105 at www.bera.ac.uk/blog/category/publications/ri/

My focus on the standards of judgment used in the Academy to legitimate the educational knowledge in educational theories relates to a mistake made by some academics about the nature of educational theory. This mistake has had serious consequences for programmes of professional development. It led many academics to believe that the practical principles used by educators to explain their educational influences in learning were 'at best pragmatic maxims having a first crude and superficial justification in practice that in any rationally developed theory would be replaced by principles with more fundamental, theoretical justification' (Hirst 1983: 18).

The mistake in replacing the explanatory principles of educators by the principles from the disciplines of education, is still within the habitus of higher education. The mistake has a 2,500-year history and can be traced back to the language and logic of Aristotle. It is a mistake that is both difficult to recognise and to rectify. I hope that this e-seminar will help by making explicit the energy-flowing and values-laden practical principles that educators use to explain their educational influences in learning. I am thinking of explanations that draw insights from the theories of the disciplines of education, without being reduced to the conceptual frameworks of any individual theory or any combination of such theories.

I use the term 'living educational theories' to distinguish these explanations from explanations derived from theories in the traditional disciplines of education.

I am hoping that this seminar will serve to widen the influence of living educational theories in an epistemological transformation of educational knowledge. I believe that it will draw attention to the educational knowledge created by practitioner-researchers who see themselves as creators of a body of professional knowledge (Saunders 2009, p. 10).

I also believe that it will highlight forms of educational enquiry that are owned by professionals in doing the job better and perhaps go beyond the provision of a tool-kit (Pollard 2009, p. 10) in asking, researching and answering questions of the kind, 'How do I improve what I am doing?'

References

The references used in this extract are in the main references section of the book. Saunders (2009) and Pollard (2009) are both contained in Hofkins (2009).

This message was posted on 11 February 2009, and subsequently generated a lively debate. You can access and read the practitioner–researcher SIG archives after getting your username and password from http://groups. tlrp.org/. You can also participate in the annual practitioner–researcher e-seminars on JISCmail, convened by Jack, by joining the seminar from the 'What's New' section of www.actionresearch.net.

It often pays to remind yourself how and why your work is special, so that you are convinced of the rightness of disseminating it, and re-energise yourself about the need to do so. Some ideas, which relate to the above posting, are as follows.

What is special about your work?

Your action research report is special because it explains two important things:

1   how it is possible to improve one's learning as the means to improving a social situation;
2   how your living theory makes an original contribution to new knowledge and new theory.

How it is possible to improve one's learning as the means to improving a social situation

As noted throughout, action research is part of a new paradigm that deals with how to contribute to sustainable forms of living and new social orders. Doing so involves changing how we think, which has implications for what is regarded as a legitimate form of theory (see next section and the posting above).

Currently, many writers assume that it is enough to talk about a situation and make recommendations about how it can be improved. Libraries are full of these kinds of texts. Popular authors explain what you need to do to influence wider thinking. For example, many critical theorists such as Agger (2006) explain the importance of understanding the social, political, economic and other forces acting on people that bring them to their current situations. However, critical theorists do not move into action theories, or explain what actions are necessary to improve the situation. Today we have plenty of action theories, but we are still stuck in a propositional form of logic that prevents those action theories actually transforming into action. You may have a mission statement on your office wall, but to transform that mission statement into real-world action involves your conscious intent, and the realisation of your capacity to take action. So the theory has to become live in the life of the person who espouses the theory. It needs to move from the propositional form of action theory into the lived form of living theories.

The reason for this situation is that the dominant form of logic is propositional, as is the dominant form of theory. By logic we mean the way we think. Propositional forms of logic mean that people can position themselves outside a situation and see it as an external object of enquiry. They speak about a situation 'out there' but they do not necessarily step into the situation and engage with it. It is possible to talk about one's own learning as an external object, but to show how that learning can influence other people's learning involves actively engaging with it.

To contribute to improving a social situation therefore means first engaging with one's own learning, and then bringing that learning into a social situation. This means talking with people, and showing your awareness of your own learning and how you might influence them. We have said throughout that a 'social situation' refers to groups of people in a particular context with a particular intent. Therefore, contributing to improving a social situation means trying to influence people's thinking, for them to bring that new thinking to bear on their possible new actions.

This brings us to the second point, about the most appropriate kind of theory for moving into a new living paradigm. This is called 'living theory' in the literatures.

How your living theory makes an original contribution to new knowledge and new theory

This section deals with matters relating to different forms of theory. It explains the differences between traditional forms of theory and living forms of theory.

Traditional forms of theory

Traditional forms of theory conform to Richard Pring's (2000) definition of a theory:

> Theory would seem to have the following features. It refers to a set of propositions which are stated with sufficient generality yet precision that they explain the behaviour of a range of phenomena and predict which would happen in the future. An understanding of these propositions includes an understanding of what would refute them.
>
> (Pring 2000: 124–5)

In much empirical research a theory is expressed in terms of a set of determinate relationships between a set of variables to see which verifiable patterns or regularities can be explained. This means that researchers test whether one aspect of a situation, the dependent variable, is affected by another aspect, the independent variable. They aim to establish a cause and effect relationship between the variables. They come to conclusions about these relationships (which constitute their findings) and make statements about them, and those statements then come to be regarded as theory, which goes into the public domain and is regarded as true for all time. The theory is pronounced a good theory provided it can be applied to circumstances similar to the situation in which the original experiments were carried out, so the criteria of replicability and generalisability are held to be the hallmarks of a good theory.

This experimental procedure has come to be known as 'the scientific method'. Philosophers of science such as Medawar and Popper have pointed out that there is no such thing as 'the' scientific method, but the terminology has stuck. It is widely believed that this is the 'correct' way of generating 'correct' forms of theory.

Two basic assumptions underpin the idea that only traditional forms of theory are legitimate; and both are equally dangerous for human flourishing. The first is that there is one correct way to do research. This way is predetermined and linear, and produces concrete results that may be applied to all similar circumstances. The second is that there is one correct way of thinking. This way leads to certain answers, which are there to be found, and are unproblematic (Berlin 1998). These assumptions are far from the realities of human experience. As well as being full of joy and fulfilment, human experience is also full of anomalies, dilemmas without resolution, tradeoffs, compromise and irremediable disappointment. Human experience is spontaneous, creative, unpredictable, uncontrollable, and frequently incomprehensible. Traditional forms of scholarship and theory may be sufficient to predict and control certain forms of behaviour, but they are inadequate for understanding and explaining how people give meaning to their lives as they live with the muddle. New forms of theory are needed.

Living forms of theory

Action research is one route to new forms of thinking and new forms of theory. When people study their own practice, they produce descriptions (what they did) and explanations (why they did it) of their practice. They act and reflect, and act in new ways as their reflections suggest. When they think about what they are doing, they are theorising their practice. In the same way that you can say, 'I have a theory about cats' or 'I have a theory about why people do such and such', you can also say, 'I have a theory about what I am doing'. If your work is in management education, you could say, 'I have created my own theory about management' or even 'I have created my own theory of management'. You can create your own personal theory about any aspect of your work, regardless of where that work is located. This theory is a part of you. Because you are a living person, you are changing every day; and because you are reflecting consciously on what you are doing, and making adjustments as you go, your theory is also developing with you. Your theory is part of your thinking and living, which is continually transforming. So your theory, as part of your own thinking, is living.

You are constantly creating, re-creating and living your own theories. If your living theory constitutes an explanation for how you help people to grow in ways that are right for them, you can say that you are creating your own living educational theory.

Jack Whitehead explains his ideas about living educational theories, a term he created, as follows: 'In living educational theories the explanatory principles are embodied values that have been transformed in the course of their emergence in practice into communicable standards of practice and judgement. In living theories the explanations are not derived from sets of interconnected propositions as in traditional theories. In living educational theories the explanations are produced by practitioner–researchers in enquiries that are focused on living values more fully in the practice of enquiries of the kind, "How do I improve what I am doing?"' You can find these ideas expressed throughout Jack's writings, especially at www.actionresearch.net.

Problematics arise when it is a question of forms of validation. In traditional approaches, theory is held as constituted of verbal statements that are arrived at through analysis of the relationships between variables. The theory is tested when the relationships are demonstrated to conform to accepted norms. It is validated when norms are maintained. In new scholarship approaches, theory is held to be constituted of verbal and non-verbal statements that are arrived at through reflective dialogue about the nature of lived experience. It is tested when the experience can be demonstrated as the grounds for learning and growth, and as nurturing further learning and growth. It is validated when the processes of learning and growth are agreed to have been nurtured.

The validity of living theories is therefore tested against other people's experience. To have your living theory authenticated as valid, you have to produce evidence that shows how and why you have influenced other people's learning in the way you hoped. Although the theory exists within you, and is part of you, it is also part of other people, because they contribute to your life and you to theirs. Your living theory is manifested in your relationship with other people, and it develops as your relationships develop.

These ideas about the nature of theory and theory generation are exciting and provide opportunities for engaged scholarly debate. However, such debates will probably never be conclusive, because debates themselves develop the field and generate new forms. Perhaps this is the nub: action research, as part of the new scholarship, is about resisting closure, a commitment to re-creation. It is this very commitment to open-endedness that is antipathetic to traditional ways. Traditionalists are secure with certainty and are often threatened by uncertainty, so they attempt to retain certainty about certainty. In many ways it is about how we view life, whether life is a forward-looking, living-on-the-brink experience, or a journey towards the end. Each one of us must make our own decisions about this.

We now turn to how you can get your action research published.

Getting published

Getting published is not always easy but it can be done. Like learning how to drive a car, or dancing the salsa, everyone has to start somewhere. Getting your writing published is no different. The key to publishing is a small amount of talent and a lot of hard work. The talent comes naturally. The work comes from the belief that you have something worth saying, and the determination and tenacity to say it. Books such as Jack Cranfield's (2007) *How to Get from Where You Are to Where You Want to Be* contain stories of determination and tenacity. Decide if you want to get published and then do it. Be single-minded. Don't let anything stop you.

Key points for getting published

Here are some key points for getting published.

Submitting papers

The first rule of getting published is to know what you want to say, why you want to say it, and whom you want to say it to. This last aspect is key. It means knowing who you are writing for and then writing for them.

Writing for a market means getting to know your readers and what they like reading. To get to know your readers, make yourself familiar with what other people are writing for them. This knowledge comes through reading journals, books and other publications, and then writing in a way that is appropriate for those publications. This involves doing your homework prior to submitting your piece. Get a feel for the style of a particular journal. Read the 'Notes to contributors' and write accordingly. Also submit your material in exactly the way that editors request. If you don't, your material may be rejected out of hand.

Be prepared to edit your work. Most papers and proposals are sent out to reviewers. Reviewers' comments are often sent to authors, and you should pay close attention to what they say. Even if you don't rework the paper entirely in light of their feedback, you should consider modifying it.

Also be prepared to shorten the paper. This can be painful, but you have to be firm. Anything you cut at this stage can be used in a later paper, so effort and bright ideas are not wasted.

Writing books

Target the market. Look at the books in your field. Who publishes them? Get a feel for the style and appearance of the books. Make a short-list of publishers who may be interested. Their addresses appear in their books. Do your homework carefully and thoroughly. The effort will pay off in the long run.

Once you have a good idea for your book, organise the idea as a proposal and send it to the publisher. Aim to produce three or four sides of A4 paper using the following headings (most publishers have guidelines for new authors on their websites):

- rationale for the book;
- about the author (you);
- contents;
- possible market, and possible outlets such as your own networks and professional organisations;
- why your book is needed;
- competition – what other books similar to yours are available and why people should read your book;
- timeline for writing the book and likely delivery date.

Include some sample writing. This could be one or two chapters, or extracts from several chapters. The editor needs to see what your writing is like. If you think this is a tall order, remember that editors are bombarded with proposals. It is a competitive business, and budgets are limited. You have to sell your work to the publisher, as they will have to sell it to purchasers. Your book is something special, so tell people how special it is and why they must read it.

People who get their work published tend to be compulsive writers. They have to be, because books are seldom written in one go, and involve substantial amounts of editing and redrafting. This can take months, even years. Allow plenty of time, but get on with it. Someone else may get the ideas out before you.

Also allow plenty of time for the book to appear. When it leaves you, you will see it only twice again, once at copy-edited stage, and again for proofreading. After that you can expect to wait months before it appears as a book.

But when it does, there is nothing quite so thrilling as hearing the thump of a book on the mat or seeing your name in print. All that hard work has been worthwhile, from when you began your project to now that it is there in the public domain. All the effort and time were for something. You have produced a work of value and have made a productive contribution to the world, and you can feel affirmed when others acknowledge that they have found value in your ideas and your influence is felt in their lives.

Well done! Now for the next project.

Summary

This chapter has set out some ideas about how you can disseminate your research and get it published. It speaks about whom you can share your work with, and where you may do so. It also discusses the potential contribution your work can make to the field, especially in relation to reconceptualising theory, from its traditional propositional form, to a new living form. Living forms of theory have the capacity to make considerable contributions to the development of sustainable social and cultural orders.

Checklist of reflective questions

- Are you clear about the importance of sharing and disseminating your work? Too often people do not appreciate the significance of what they are doing. You should develop a keen awareness, perhaps by talking with other people, of how much people can learn from you and what you can contribute to your own and others' education.
- Be confident in attending conferences and seminars, and otherwise engaging in public life. Many opportunities exist for presentation of your work. With the digital age, the opportunities for disseminating your ideas are bounded only by your imagination or level of energy. Believe that you can do it, and you will.
- Now that you have come to the end of this book, why not think about writing your own? You have a special story to tell, and only you can tell it in the way it should be told. Have faith in your capacity to do it, and then do it. Nothing in the world can hold you back if you believe in yourself.

Thank you for reading our book. Please let us know when we can read yours.

References

Adams, G. (2008) 'How do I improve my practice as a mathematics educator as I encourage my learners to become independent learners and take responsibility for their own learning?', paper presented at the Self-study for Teacher Education Practices Special Interest Group symposium 'Action Research: A Framework for Supporting Innovative Teaching Approaches for Diverse Student Audiences' at the American Educational Research Association Annual Meeting, New York, March. Retrieved 17 February 2009 from www.jeanmcniff.com/khayelitsha/gerrie_AERA_2008.htm.

Adler-Collins, J. K. (2007) 'Developing an inclusional pedagogy of the unique: how do I clarify, live and explain my educational influences in my learning as I pedagogise my healing nurse curriculum in a Japanese University?', PhD thesis, University of Bath. Retrieved 20 June 2008 from www.actionresearch.net/jekan.shtml.

Agger, B. (2006) *Critical Social Theories*, 2nd edn. Boulder, CO, Paradigm Publishers.

Alford, C. F. (2001) *Whistleblowers: Broken Lives and Organizational Power*. Ithaca, NY, Cornell University Press.

Arendt, H. (1958) *The Human Condition*. Chicago, University of Chicago.

Arendt, H. (1977) *Eichmann in Jerusalem*. London, Penguin.

Aston, S. (2008) 'How do I contribute to student teachers' critical development? A practitioner's personal account of a move towards a more critical and emancipatory pedagogy through design and technology', paper presented at the Collaborative Action Research Network Conference 'Cultural Kaleidoscopes: Exploring Ethics, Contexts and Conceptions', Liverpool Hope University, November.

Bakhtin, M. (1981) (ed. M. Holquist) In *The Dialogic Imagination*. Austin, University of Texas Press.

Barnes, P. (2008) 'How do I improve my leadership as a head of department in order to enhance teaching and learning?', MA dissertation, St Mary's University College, Twickenham.

Barry, P. (2002) *Beginning Theory: An Introduction to Literary and Cultural Theory*, 2nd edn. Manchester, Manchester University Press.

Bayne-Jardine, C. and Holly, P. (1994) *Developing Quality Schools*. London, Falmer.

Belenky, M., Clinchy, B., Goldberger, B. and Tarule, J. (1986) *Women's Ways of Knowing*. New York, Basic Books.

Bell, J. (2005) *Doing Your Research Project*, 4th edn. Buckingham, Open University Press.

Berlin, I. (1969) *Four Essays on Liberty*. London, Oxford University Press.

Berlin, I. (1998) *The Proper Study of Mankind: An Anthology of Essays*. London, Pimlico.

Blayi, S. (2008) 'A managerial approach towards improving my school's overall results', MA dissertation, St Mary's University College, Twickenham.

Bosher, M. (2001) 'How can I, as an educator and professional development manager working with teachers, support and enhance the learning and achievement of pupils in a Whole School Improvement Process?', PhD thesis, University of Bath. Retrieved 16 February 2009 from www.actionresearch.net/bosher.shtml.

Boyer, E. (1990) *Scholarship Reconsidered: Priorities of the Professoriate*. San Francisco, Jossey-Bass.

Brown, J. S. and Duguid, P. (2002) *The Social Life of Information*. Boston, Harvard Business School Press.

Buber, M. (1970) *I and Thou*. Edinburgh, T. & T. Clark.

Bullough, R. V. and Pinnegar, S. (2004) 'Guidelines for quality in autobiographical forms of self-study', *Educational Researcher* 30(2): 13–21.

Cahill, M. (2007) 'My living educational theory of inclusional practice', PhD thesis, University of Limerick. Retrieved 20 June 2008 from www.jeanmcniff.com/margaretcahill/index.html.

Calderisi, R. (2007) *The Trouble with Africa*. New Haven, Yale University Press.

Callahan, R. (1962) *Education and the Cult of Efficiency*. Chicago, University of Chicago.

Carpenter, J. (2009) 'Building reflective relationships for and through the creation of educational knowledge', paper presented at the symposium 'Academic Practitioner–Researchers: Shifting the Epistemological Centre in Higher Education', British Educational Research Association annual meeting, Manchester, September.

Carr, W. and Kemmis, S. (1986) *Becoming Critical*. London, Falmer.

Charles, E. (2007) 'How can I bring Ubuntu as a living standard of judgement into the academy? Moving beyond decolonisation through societal reidentification and guiltless recognition', PhD thesis, University of Bath. Retrieved 19 February 2009 from www.actionresearch.net/edenphd.shtml.

Chomsky, N. (1986) *Knowledge of Language: Its Nature, Origin and Use*. New York, Praeger.

Chomsky, N. (2000) *Chomsky on MisEducation* (ed. D. Macedo). Lanham, MD, Rowman & Littlefield.

Chomsky, N. (2002) (eds P. R. Mitchell and J. Schoeffel) *Understanding Power: The Indispensable Chomsky*. New York, The New Press.

Church, M. (2004) 'Creating an uncompromised place to belong: why do I find myself in networks?', PhD thesis, University of Bath. Retrieved 2 June 2009 from www.actionresearch.net/church.shtml.

Clandinin, J. (ed.) (2007) *A Handbook of Narrative Inquiry: Mapping a Methodology*. Thousand Oaks, CA, Sage.

Clandinin, J. and Connelly, M. (2004) *Narrative Inquiry: Experience and Story in Qualitative Research*. San Francisco, Jossey-Bass.

Cluskey, M. (1996) 'The paradigms of educational research and how they relate to my practice', *Action Researcher* 19(5): 2–14.

Cohen, L., Manion, L. and Morrison, K. (2000) *Research Methods in Education*, 5th edn. London, RoutledgeFalmer.

Collingwood, R. (1939) *An Autobiography*. Oxford, Oxford University Press.

Connelly, M. and Clandinin, D.J. (1990) 'Stories of experience and narrative inquiry', *Educational Researcher* 19(5): 2–14.

Cordery, M. (2008) Academic Paper: Module 7, MA PVP programme, St Mary's University College, Twickenham.

Costello, P. (2003) *Action Research*. London, Continuum.

Cranfield, J. (2007) *How to Get from Where You Are to Where You Want to Be*. London, HarperElement.

Dadds, M. (1995) *Passionate Enquiry and School Development: A Story About Teacher Action Research*. London, Falmer.

Dadds, M. and Hart, S. (2001) *Doing Practitioner Research Differently*. London, RoutledgeFalmer.

Delong, J. (2002) 'How can I improve my practice as a superintendent of schools and create my own living educational theory?', PhD thesis, University of Bath. Retrieved 20 February 2009 from www.actionresearch.net/delong.shtm.

Derrida, J. (1997) *Of Grammatology*. Baltimore, Johns Hopkins University Press.

Dewey, J. (1938) *Experience and Education*. New York, Macmillan.

Eames, K. (1995) 'How do I, as a teacher and educational action researcher, describe and explain the nature of my professional knowledge?', PhD thesis, University of Bath. Retrieved 20 February 2009 from www.actionresearch.net/kevin.shtml.

Elliott, J. (1991) *Action Research for Educational Change*. Milton Keynes, Open University Press.

Farren, M. (2005) 'How can I create a pedagogy of the unique through a web of betweenness?', PhD Thesis, University of Bath. Retrieved 20 June 2008 from www.actionresearch.net/farren.shtml.

Feynman, R. (2001) *The Pleasure of Finding Things Out*. London, Penguin.

Finnegan, J. (2000) 'How do I create my own educational theory in my educative relations as an action researcher and as a teacher?', PhD thesis, University of Bath. Retrieved 22 February 2009 from www.actionresearch.net/fin.shtml.

Follows, M. (1989) 'The development of co-operative teaching in a semi-open-plan infant school', in P. Lomax (ed.) *The Management of Change*. Clevedon, Multi-Lingual Matters.

Formby, C. (2007) Educational Enquiry Masters Unit, 'How do I sustain a loving, receptively responsive educational relationship with my pupils which will motivate them in their learning and encourage me in my teaching?', University of Bath. Retrieved 22 February 2009 from www.jackwhitehead.com/tuesdayma/formbyEE300907.htm.

Formby, C. (2008) Educational Enquiry Masters Unit, 'How am I integrating my educational theorizing with the educational responsibility I express in my educational relationships with the children in my class and in my school and wider society?', University of Bath. Retrieved 22 February 2009 from www.jackwhitehead.com/tuesdayma/cfee3April08.htm.

Forrest, M. (1983) 'The teacher as researcher; the use of historical artefacts in primary schools', MEd dissertation, University of Bath. Retrieved 22 February 2009 from www.jackwhitehead.com/writeup/alval.pdf.

Foucault, M. (1979) *Discipline and Punish: The Birth of the Prison*. New York, Vintage Books.

Foucault, M. (1980) (ed. G. Gordon) *Power/Knowledge: Selected Interviews and Other Writings 1972–1977*. New York, Pantheon Books.

Foucault, M. (2001) *Fearless Speech*. Los Angeles, Semiotext(e).

Frankl, V. (1959) *Man's Search for Meaning*. Boston, MA, Beacon.

Furlong, J. (2004) 'BERA at 30. Have we come of age?', *British Educational Research Journal* 30(3): 343–58.

Furlong, J. and Oancea, A. (2005) *Assessing Quality in Applied and Practice-Based Educational Research: A Framework for Discussion*. Oxford, Oxford University Department of Educational Studies.

Gardner, H. (1983) *Frames of Mind: The Theory of Multiple Intelligences*. New York, Basic Books.

Genova, A. (2009) *Still Alice*. New York, Pocket Books.

Geraci, J. (2001) 'Towards an understanding of autism: an outsider's attempt to get inside', in M. Dadds and S. Hart (eds) *Doing Practitioner Research Differently*. London, RoutledgeFalmer.

Glavey, C. (2008) 'Helping eagles fly: a living theory approach to student and young adult leadership development', PhD thesis, University of Glamorgan. Retrieved 20 February 2009 from www.jeanmcniff.com/theses/glavey.html.

Glenn, M. (2006) 'Working with collaborative projects: my living theory of a holistic educational practice', PhD thesis, University of Limerick. Retrieved 19 February from www.jeanmcniff.com/glennabstract.html.

Grayling, A. C. (2003) *What is Good?* London, Weidenfeld & Nicolson.

Griffiths, M. (1990) 'Action research: grass roots practice or management tool?', in P. Lomax (ed.) *Managing Staff Development in Schools: An Action Research Approach*. Clevedon, Multi-Lingual Matters.

Grossman, L. (2009) 'Books unbound', in *Time*, 2 February 2009, pp. 53–5.

Gungqisa, N. (2008) 'How do I encourage my learners to be more self-disciplined?', MA dissertation, St Mary's University College, Twickenham.

Habermas, J. (1976) *Communication and the Evolution of Society*. Boston, Beacon.

Hartog, M. (2004) 'A self study of a higher education tutor: How can I improve my practice?', PhD thesis, University of Bath. Retrieved 21 February 2009 from www.actionresearch.net/hartog.shtml.

Hirst, P. (ed.) (1983) *Educational Theory and its Foundation Disciplines*. London, Routledge & Kegan Paul.

Hofkins, D. (2009) 'Eight letters starts with P', in *Teaching*, GTC Magazine, Spring.

Holley, E. (1997) 'How do I as a teacher-researcher contribute to the development of a living educational theory through an exploration of my values in my professional practice?', MPhil thesis, University of Bath. Retrieved 20 February 2009 from www.actionresearch.net/holley.shtml.

Hopkins, D. (1993) *A Teacher's Guide to Classroom Research*, 2nd edn. Buckingham, Open University Press.

Horton, M. and Freire, P. (1990) *We Make the Road by Walking: Conversations on Education and Social Change* (eds B. Bell, J. Gaventa and J. Peters). Philadelphia, Temple University Press.

Husserl, E. (1931) *Ideas: Pure Phenomenology*. London, Allen and Unwin.

Hymer, B. (2007) 'How do I understand and communicate my values and beliefs in my work as an educator in the field of giftedness?', EdDPsych thesis, University of Newcastle. Retrieved 19 February 2009 from www.actionresearch.net/hymer.shtml.

Hymer, B., Whitehead, J. and Huxtable, M. (2009) *Gifts, Talents and Education: A Living Theory Approach*. Chichester, Wiley-Blackwell.

Ingle-Möller, R. (2009) 'Action Research: a new look at you as a professional!', paper presented at the International Conference on Environmental Enrichment, Torquay, June.

Ingram. P. (2001) 'Pauline and Alzheimer's: "reflections" on caring', in R. Winter and C. Munn-Giddings (eds) *A Handbook for Action Research in Health Care*. London, Routledge.

Jackson, D. (2008) 'How do I learn to inspire and support my primary education students' creativity in design and technology? Finding the courage to move from craft to creativity in primary design and technology', paper presented at the Collaborative Action Research Network Conference 'Cultural Kaleidoscopes: Exploring Ethics, Contexts and Conceptions', Liverpool Hope University, November.

Johnson, K. (1998) 'How can I use drama with severe, profound and multiple learning difficulties?', paper presented at the Second International Conference on Self-Study of Teacher Education Practices, Herstmonceux Castle, August. Retrieved from www.educ.queensu.ca/~ar/sstep2/johnson.htm

Jones, J. (2008) 'Thinking with stories of suffering: towards a living theory of response-ability', PhD thesis, University of Bath. Retrieved 19 February 2009 from www.actionresearch.net/jocelynjonesphd.shtml.

Kemmis, S. and McTaggart, R. (1982) *The Action Research Planner*. Goolong, Deakin University Press.

Koshy, V. (2005) *Action Research for Improving Practice*. London, Paul Chapman.

Kozminsky, L., Golan, M. and Guberman, A. (2009) 'Nurturing teacher educators as researchers – The MOFET Institute experience', paper presented at the European Conference on Educational Research 'Theory and Evidence in European Educational Research', European Educational Research Association, Vienna, September.

Krashen, S. (2003) *Explorations in Language Acquisition and Use*. Portsmouth: Heinemann.

Laidlaw, M. (1996) 'How can I create my own living educational theory as I offer you an account of my educational development?', PhD thesis, University of Bath. Retrieved 20 June 2008 from www.actionresearch.net/moira2.shtml

Larter, A. (1997) 'An action research approach to classroom discussion in the examination years', MPhil thesis, University of Bath. Available at www.actionresearch.net/andy.shtml.

Lather, P. (1991) *Getting Smart: Feminism Research and Pedagogy with/in the Postmodern*. London, Routledge.

Lewin, K. (1946) 'Action research and minority problems', *Journal of Social Issues* 2: n.p.

Llewellyn, K. (2009) 'How does a teaching quality enhancement project contribute to pedagogic change?', paper presented at the European Conference on Educational Research 'Theory and Evidence in European Educational Research', European Educational Research Association, Vienna, September.

Lohr, E. (2006) 'Love at work: what is my lived experience of love and how may I become an instrument of love's purpose?', PhD thesis, University of Bath. Retrieved 19 February 2009 from www.actionresearch.net/lohr.shtml.

Lomax, P. (1994a) 'Standards, criteria and the problematic of action research', *Educational Action Research* 2(1): 113–25.

Lomax, P. (1994b) 'Action research for managing change: an action research study', in N. Bennett, R. Glatter and R. Levacic (eds) *Improving Educational Management through Research and Consultancy*. London, Paul Chapman/Open University Press.

Lomax, P., Woodward, C. and Parker, Z. (1996) 'Critical friends: collaborative working and strategies for effecting quality', in P. Lomax (ed.) *Quality Management in Education*. London, Routledge.

Lovelock, J. (2009) *The Vanishing Face of Gaia: A Final Warning: Enjoy It While You Can.* Santa Barbara, Allen Lane.

McCormack, C. (2002) 'Action research in the home', in J. McNiff (ed.) *Action Research: Principles and Practice*, 2nd edn. London, RoutledgeFalmer.

McDonagh, C. (2007) 'My living theory of learning to teach for social justice: how do I enable primary school children with specific learning disability (dyslexia) and myself as their teacher to realise our learning potentials?', PhD thesis, University of Limerick. Retrieved 20 February 2009 from www.jeanmcniff.com/mcdonaghabstract.html.

McNiff, J. (1990) 'Writing and the creation of educational knowledge', in P. Lomax (ed.) *Managing Staff Development in Schools: An Action Research Approach*. Clevedon, Multi-Lingual Matters.

McNiff, J. (1993) *Teaching as Learning: An Action Research Approach*. London, Routledge.

McNiff, J. with J. Whitehead (2002) *Action Research: Principles and Practice*, 2nd edn. London, Routledge.

McNiff, J. (2007) 'My story is my living educational theory', in D. J. Clandinin (ed.) *Handbook of Narrative Inquiry: Mapping a Methodology*. Thousand Oaks, CA, Sage.

McNiff, J. (2008a) Action research, transformational influences. Lecture series at the University of Limerick, May. Retrieved 22 February 2009 from www.jeanmcniff. com/papers/limerick/UL_paper_final.htm

McNiff, J. (2008b) 'Learning with and from people in townships and universities: how do I exercise my transformational influence for generative systemic transformation?', paper presented at the American Educational Research Association Annual Meeting as part of the Symposium 'Communicating and Testing the Validity of Claims to Transformational Systemic Influence for Civic Responsibility', New York, March.

McNiff, J. (in preparation) *Action Research in South Africa*. Poole, September Books.

McNiff, J. and Whitehead, J. (2009) *Doing and Writing Action Research*. London, Sage.

McTaggart, R. (1990) 'Involving a whole staff in developing a maths curriculum', in P. Lomax (ed.) *Managing Staff Development in Schools: An Action Research Approach.* Clevedon, Multi-Lingual Matters.

Majake, T. (2008) 'Creating a dialogical classroom through a dialectical approach', paper presented at the American Educational Research Association Annual Meeting, New York, March. Retrieved 20 June 2008 from www.jeanmcniff.com/khayelitsha/tsepo_AERA_2008.htm

Marcuse, H. (1964) *One-Dimensional Man*. Boston, MA, Beacon.

Marlin, R. (2002) *Propaganda and the Ethics of Persuasion*. Peterborough, ON, Broadview Press.

Mead, G. (2001) 'Unlatching the gate: realising my scholarship of living inquiry', PhD thesis, University of Bath. Retrieved 8 June from www.actionresearch.net/mead.shtml.

Mellor, N. (1998) 'Notes from a method', *Educational Action Research* 6(3): 453–70.

Moustakim, R. (2008) 'Working for Social Justice', MA dissertation, St Mary's University College, Twickenham.

Mpondwana, M. (2008) 'How do I encourage good relationships in my community?' MA dissertation, St Mary's University College, Twickenham.

Murdoch, I. (2001) *The Sovereignty of Good*. London, Routledge

Naidoo, M. (2005) *I Am Because We Are (A Never Ending Story): The Emergence of a Liv-*

ing Theory of Inclusional and Responsive Practice. Retrieved 17 February 2009 from www.actionresearch.net/naidoo.shtml.

Nasar, S. (1998) *A Beautiful Mind*. New York, Touchstone.

Ngugi wa Thiong'o (1993) *Moving the Centre: The Struggle for Cultural Freedoms*. Oxford, James Currey.

Nonaka, I. and Takeuchi, H. (1995) *The Knowledge-Creating Company: How Japanese Companies Create the Dynamics of Innovation*. Oxford, Oxford University Press.

Nongwane, A. (2008) 'How do I involve parents in their children's education?', MA dissertation, St Mary's University College.

O'Donoghue, J. (1997) *Anam Cara: A Book of Celtic Wisdom*. London, Bantam Press.

O'Neill, R. (2002) 'Where shall we put the computer?', in J. McNiff (ed.) *Action Research: Principles and Practice*. London, Routledge, pp. 126–8.

O'Neill, R. (2008) 'ICT as political action', PhD thesis, University of Glamorgan. Retrieved 20 February 2009 from www.ictaspoliticalaction.com.

Pearson, J. (2008) 'How do I continue to improve my practice as I encourage others to become critical of their learning experiences?', paper presented at the symposium 'Developing an epistemology of academic enquiry for a new scholarship of educational knowledge': Collaborative Action Research Network conference, Liverpool, November.

Polanyi, M. (1958) *Personal Knowledge*. London, Routledge & Kegan Paul.

Popper, K. (1963) *Conjectures and Refutations: The Growth of Scientific Knowledge*. London, Routledge & Kegan Paul.

Popper, K. (1972) *Objective Knowledge: An Evolutionary Approach*. Oxford, Oxford University Press.

Pring, R. (2000) *Philosophy of Educational Research*. London, Continuum.

Rawls, J. (1972) *A Theory of Justice*. Oxford, Oxford University Press.

Raz, J. (2003) *The Practice of Value*. Oxford, Oxford University Press.

Riding, K. (2008) 'How do I come to understand my shared living educational standards of judgement in the life I lead with others? Creating the space for inter-generational student-led research', PhD thesis, University of Bath. Retrieved 22 February 2009 from www.actionresearch.net/karenridingphd.shtml

Riding, S. (2008) 'How do I contribute to the education of myself and others through improving the quality of living educational space? The story of living myself through others as a practitioner-researcher', PhD thesis, University of Bath. Retrieved 21 February 2009 from www.actionresearch.net/simonridingphd.shtml.

Roche, M. (2000) 'How can I improve my practice so as to help my pupils to philosophise?', MA dissertation, University of Limerick. Retrieved 23 February 2009 from www.jeanmcniff.com/reports.html

Roche, M. (2007) 'Towards a living theory of caring pedagogy: interrogating my practice to nurture a critical, emancipatory and just community of enquiry', PhD thesis, University of Limerick. Retrieved 20 February 2009 from www.jeanmcniff.com/MaryRoche/index.html.

Said, E. (1991) *The World, the Text and the Critic*. London, Vintage.

Said, E. (1994) *Representations of the Intellectual: The 1993 Reith Lectures*. London, Vintage.

Said, E. (1997) *Beginnings: Intention and Method*. London, Granta.

Schön, D. (1995) 'Knowing-in-action: the new scholarship requires a new epistemology', *Change*, November–December: 27–34.

Shobbrook, H. (1997) 'My living theory grounded in my life: how can I enable my communication through correspondence to be seen as educational and worthy of presentation in its original form?', MA dissertation, University of Bath. Retrieved 23 February 2009 from www.actionresearch.net/hilary.shtml.

Sinclair, A. (2008) 'Developing my living theory of symbiotic practice', paper presented at the symposium 'Developing an epistemology of academic enquiry for a new scholarship of educational knowledge': Collaborative Action Research Network conference, Liverpool, November.

Skuse, A. (2007) Educational Enquiry Masters Unit, 'How have my experiences of Year 2 SATs influenced my perceptions of assessment in teaching and learning?', University of Bath. Retrieved 22 February 2009 from www.jackwhitehead.com/tuesdayma/amyskuseeeoct07.htm.

Snow, C. (2001) 'Knowing what we know: children, teachers, researchers', *Educational Researcher* 30(7): 3–9. Presidential Address to the American Educational Research Association Annual Meeting, Seattle.

Spiro, J. (2008) 'How I have arrived at a notion of knowledge transformation, through understanding the story of myself as creative writer, creative educator, creative manager, and educational researcher', PhD thesis, University of Bath. Retrieved 20 February 2009 from www.actionresearch.net/janespirophd.shtml.

Sowell, T. (1987) *A Conflict of Visions: Ideological Origins of Political Struggles.* New York, Morrow.

Stenhouse, L. (1978) 'Case study and case records: towards a contemporary history of education', *British Educational Research Journal* 4(2): 21–39.

Stenhouse, L. (1983) 'Research is systematic enquiry made public', *British Educational Research Journal*, 9(1): 11–20.

Sternberg, R. and Horvath, J. (1999) *Tacit Knowledge in Professional Practice: Researcher and Practitioner Perspectives.* Mahwah, NJ, Lawrence Erlbaum Associates.

Suderman-Gladwell, G. (2001) 'The ethics of personal subjective narrative research', MA dissertation, Brock University. Retrieved 17 February 2009 from www.action-research.net/values.gsgma.PDF.

Sullivan, B. (2006) 'A living theory of a practice of social justice: realising the right of traveller children to educational equality', PhD thesis, University of Limerick. Retrieved 20 February 2009 from www.jeanmcniff.com/bernieabstract.html.

Times Higher Education (2009) 'Leader', 5–11 March, p. 23.

Todorov, T. (1999) *Facing the Extreme: Moral Life in the Concentration Camps.* London, Weidenfeld & Nicolson.

Training and Development Agency Website (2009) 'Professional standards for teachers'. Retrieved 16 February 2009 from www.tda.gov.uk/teachers/professional-standards.aspx.

University of Bath (2008) *Guidelines for Examiners.* Bath, University of Bath.

Walsh, D. (2004) 'How do I improve my leadership as a team leader in Vocational Education?', MA dissertation, University of Bath. Retrieved 2 June 2009 from www.actionresearch.net/walsh.shtml.

Walton, J. (2008) 'Ways of knowing: can I find a way of knowing that satisfies my search for meaning?', PhD thesis, University of Bath. Retrieved 23 February 2009 from www.actionresearch.net/walton.shtml.

Whitehead, A. N. (1967) *The Aims of Education and Other Essays.* New York, The Free Press.

Whitehead, Jack (1989) 'Creating a living educational theory from questions of the kind, "How do I improve my practice?" ', *Cambridge Journal of Education* 19(1): 137–52.

Whitehead, Jack (1993) *The Growth of Educational Knowledge: Creating Your Own Living Educational Theories*. Original publication Bournemouth, Hyde. Retrieved 20 February 2009 from www.actionresearch.net/writings/jwgek93.htm.

Whitehead, Jack (1999) 'Educative relations in a new era', *Pedagogy, Culture & Society*, 7(1): 73–90.

Whitehead, Jack (2004) 'What counts as evidence in the self-studies of teacher education practices?' in J. J. Loughran, M. L. Hamilton, V. K. LaBoskey and T. Russell (eds) *International Handbook of Self-Study of Teaching and Teacher Education Practices*. Dordrecht, Kluwer Academic Publishers.

Whitehead, Jack (2008) 'Combining voices in living educational theories that are freely given in teacher research': a keynote presentation to the International Conference on 'Combining Voices in Teacher Research', New York, March. Retrieved 19 June 2008 from www.jackwhitehead.com/aerictr08/jwictr08key.htm. Streaming video available from mms://wms.bath.ac.uk/live/education/JackWhitehead_030408/jackkeynoteictr280308large.wmv.

Whitehead, Jack and McNiff, J. (2006) *Action Research: Living Theory*. London, Sage.

Whitehead, Joan (2003) 'The future of teaching and teaching in the future: a vision of the future of the profession of teaching – making the possible probable'. Keynote address to the Standing Committee for the Education and Training of Teachers Annual Conference, Dunchurch, October. Retrieved 22 February 2009 from www.actionresearch.net/evol/joanw_files/joanw.htm.

Whitty, G. (2005) 'Education(al) research and education policy making: is conflict inevitable?' Presidential Address to BERA 2005. Retrieved 13 August 2008 from http://bera.ac.uk/publications/documents/GWBERApresidentialaddress_000.pdf.

Wickham, J. (2009) 'How do I develop pedagogic practices to enhance the total learning experience for physiotherapy students?', paper presented at the symposium 'Academic Practioner–Researchers: Shifting the Epistemological Centre in Higher Education', British Educational Research Association annual meeting, Manchester, September.

Winter, R. (1989) *Learning from Experience*. London, Falmer.

Winter, R. and Munn-Giddings, C. (2001) *A Handbook for Action Research in Health and Social Care*. London, Routledge.

Zeni, J. (2001) *Ethical Issues in Practitioner Research*. New York, Teachers College Press.

Index